FORBIDDEN CREATURES

Inside the World of Animal Smuggling and Exotic Pets

PETER LAUFER, PhD

LYONS PRESS
Guilford, Connecticut

An imprint of Globe Pequot Press

Lyons Press is an imprint of Globe Pequot Press.

Project editor: David Legere
Text designer: Sheryl P. Kober
Layout artist: Melissa Evarts

The Library of Congress has cataloged the earlier hardcover edition as follows:
Library of Congress Cataloging-in-Publication Data
Laufer, Peter.
  Forbidden creatures : inside the world of animal smuggling and exotic pets / Peter Laufer.
    p. cm.
  Includes bibliographical references and index.
  ISBN 978-1-59921-926-4
  1. Wild animal trade. 2. Wildlife smuggling. 3. Exotic animals--Economic aspects. I. Title.
  SK591.L38 2010
  364.1'3367--dc22
                                        2010011817
  ISBN 978-0-7627-7180-6
  Printed in the United States of America
  10 9 8 7 6 5 4 3 2 1

With love to Sheila:
Thank you for introducing me to Amigo, Basher, and
Schrödinger

We do not belong to this material world that science constructs for us. We are not in it; we are outside. We are only spectators. The reason why we believe that we are in it, that we belong to the picture, is that our bodies are in the picture. Our bodies belong to it. Not only my own body, but those of my friends, also of my dog and cat and horse, and of all the other people and animals. And this is my only means of communicating with them.

—*Erwin Schrödinger, from* What is Life? and other scientific essays
(Doubleday, 1956)

CONTENTS

INTRODUCTION

From Butterflies to Big Cats, Great Apes, and Long Snakes

A late-summer evening, and I'm rowing my boat on the Bodega Bay, north of San Francisco. There is a slight breeze, and the air is as fresh as air gets. I'm taking a break from my work, the push and pull of the boat's oars providing an ideal counterpoint exercise for my tight shoulders hunched too many hours over a keyboard.

A friend gave me this rowboat over a dozen years ago. I love it, even though it's in ludicrous shape from deferred maintenance and the harsh winter weather. The starboard oarlock is about to fail any day. I'll be forced to paddle back to the dock if I don't repair it soon. The brass nameplate affixed on the inside of the stern is the shiniest thing on board. Designed by C. William Lapworth, it says, and built by Griffith Brothers. The sun slips toward the Pacific, silhouetting the pterodactyl-like pelicans. They soar high over the bay stalking prey and collapse into the water after the fish. Nearby sea lions bark. Gulls squawk in a feeding frenzy behind a fishing boat. Harbor seals follow me as I work the oars, the water lapping against the bow. They look like wet dogs when they surface, sticking their heads out of the water with their big brown eyes scanning the surface.

These are my exotic pets. Sometimes I wonder, wouldn't it be fun to bring a seal home and keep it in the bathtub? But I leave them alone, and they take care of themselves. I call out to them whenever they appear during a row, inviting them to approach. They keep their distance, however, and I refrain from bringing fish with me on the water, although the idea of luring them close with some rock cod perpetually appeals to me. But not only is it illegal to harass sea mammals, I also want them to like me for myself, not for the treats I bring to them.

Butterflies. That's what my last book was about. Symbols of beauty, innocence, rebirth, and, of course, metamorphosis. So distant, I thought when I started the research for that book, from my usual journalism beats of wars, pestilence, and other man-made and natural disasters. I learned quickly the reality: The butterfly story is much more than what flutters in front of the eye. Poaching and smuggling. Habitat desecration and species extinction. Species renewal and habitat restoration. Myths and magic. I met a cast of real-life characters to rival anything conjured by Hollywood, egoists engaged in conflict, survival, and some just interested in good, clean fun. The unexpected phenomena I found resulted in an invitation to talk about my adventures covering the butterfly beat with Jon Stewart on *The Daily Show*.

"There are butterfly poachers," Stewart told his audience with his trademark look of amazement, "people who catch them and sell them dead or alive for huge money." He said he learned about the criminals from the book and wondered who collects the hot insects: "It seems the only people who would do this are super villains." The audience laughed as he offered an example. "People that are saying, 'Hey, I live in a volcano and I'm building this laser that blows up planets. And you know what else I'd like to have? A room filled with exotic butterflies!' I mean," he asked me, "who are the people who are buying these?"

"I think that's not far from it," I agreed, and Stewart joined the audience laughing. "I conjure up somebody who buys stolen art," I explained to him. "Why are they buying stolen art? What kind of strange den do they have where behind a curtain there is the van Gogh, and there is the butterfly that is endangered and cost them thousands and thousands of dollars and they will go to jail if they buy it and they're caught?"

"Do they have a party," suggested Stewart, "and they say, 'I'd like you to see something, a blue morpho butterfly'?"

"I think so," I replied, "except not the blue morpho; it's not endangered and is legal to own."

It was great fun talking butterflies and laughing with Stewart, but his question is a haunting one: What type of people want to own exotic stuff that's dangerous or illegal, or both—especially animals? Is it because there's an element of the forbidden at work here?

——— ———

I encountered a host of questions about those who chase butterflies, questions that I soon realized relate not just to Lepidoptera.

Why do criminals poach and smuggle animals? Is it just for the profit, or are there other motives? How do traffickers obtain endangered species to sell? Who are the customers for the illicit trade in animals, and what do they do with specimens that are illegal to own?

These questions led to more.

What animals, besides butterflies, are being smuggled, and from where to where? Why is this trafficking illegal? What is being done to stop the trade? What are the prognoses for the future of threatened animals popular as targets for traffickers?

As I began research for what would become my next book, I learned that the trade in wild and protected animals is growing exponentially. According to Interpol, the International Criminal Police Organization, the trafficking in live wild animals is the third most lucrative illegal business in the world, trailing only drugs and weapons—and not trailing those scourges by much. Animal smuggling and trading are easy to accomplish, and the risks of capture are slim. Even if caught, the perpetrator often gets away with a nominal penalty, especially when compared with the stiff sentences and heavy fines meted out to those running heroin and AK-47s. Legal trade in endangered animals exists, along with trade that skirts the law. Legitimate businesses, too, can make their practitioners wealthy. Illegal wildlife trade, however, further threatens already endangered species. Estimates of its dollar value, made by international organizations such as Interpol, soar toward $25 billion a year. With such high stakes, wildlife law enforcement officials in the Third World who attempt to protect their charges are dying at the hands of smugglers, and their counterparts in the First World are well outnumbered by smugglers. Not all the smuggling is done by professional criminals. Amateurs seeking the animals for their own pleasure at home perform some of the more comedic cases.

For them, the embarrassment of capture (especially when the animals are secreted in embarrassing places) may be enough punishment to dissuade them from further attempts.

The butterfly story introduced me to U.S. Fish and Wildlife Service special agent Ed Newcomer. I was studying a case he made against the self-styled "World's Most Wanted Butterfly Smuggler," a criminal he stalked, arrested, and helped the U.S. attorney's office in Los Angeles send to federal prison for two years. I told Newcomer about my growing interest in forbidden creatures. He dug into his files and confirmed my guess that with this new project I was about to encounter characters who would be as weird and intriguing as the fanciers I met who were chasing butterflies. Authorities caught one fellow with a giant lizard secreted in an artificial leg. A woman was stopped at the U.S. border using a pregnancy prosthetic to secrete and smuggle a baby monkey home. Piranhas and stingrays are favorites of smugglers, as are threatened songbirds and colorful parrots. Just about every protected animal has been found at border crossings by inspectors.

Soon my own file was bulging, and I started testing factoids. The estimate that there are more captive tigers in Texas than wild tigers in India astounded friends and colleagues. Few knew that it's legal in many states to own chimpanzees and tigers as pets. That the Everglades teem with escaped pythons is a sure cocktail party icebreaker.

Vietnam is making an unfortunate name for itself as a wide-open source country for illegal live wildlife. In one case a bear was transported in a Vietnam ambulance, the poached animal dressed as a patient in need of urgent care.[1]

Pet Amnesty Day was coming up in the summer of 2009 at the Beardsley Zoo in Bridgeport, Connecticut, not far from where an infamous chimpanzee named Travis had lived and died. (Travis had recently attacked and tragically disfigured a friend of his owner.) I was intrigued to learn that there was a need for such a day. It seemed further proof that the story I was pursuing was not just a complex one; I was encountering a social phenomenon of consequence. A gray area of the law involves the trade in captive-bred endangered species, such as Travis. Why was this chimp living in suburban Stamford, Connecticut? What was his origin? Was the "pet" legal? How did local authorities handle complaints about the chimp's presence in the community? What motivated his owner, Sandra Herold, to cohabitate with Travis? And how is Stamford (and other communities where citizens harbor potentially dangerous animals) responding to the tragic cases of Sandra's critically injured friend and Travis, both of them victims?

The Internet continues to evolve as a sophisticated black market. With a few clicks of your mouse, you can find yourself a cute baby chimp or an entire exotic menagerie. The International Fund for Animal Welfare has documented thousands and thousands of wild animals for sale online—protected and endangered animals—including such rare oddities as a Siberian tiger offered for $70,000. Animal retreats proliferate, offering needed care and homes for creatures abandoned as pets, retired as performers, or rescued from the illegal trade. Other facilities masquerade as sanctuaries while operating as animal breeding grounds and tourist destinations. They use the animals' cute factor to make money, offering tours to paying customers and soliciting donations.

The illegal pet trade is devastating the Philippines forest turtle, an animal listed as critically endangered and once thought to be extinct. The little forest turtle was rediscovered because of the pet trade. Scientists found several for sale at a market and then discovered a population in the wild. That wild population was in jeopardy as soon as it was discovered because the rarity of the turtle added to its value for some collectors. Fifty dollars' worth of forest turtle in the Philippines can be flipped to a fast $2,500 when the reptile is smuggled into Europe, Japan, or the United States.[2] But turtle peddlers make handsome returns on investment without even leaving the States. Red-eared sliders, when they're young and still only about an inch and a half long, can be had wholesale in Florida and Louisiana for about fifty cents a turtle. Hustlers bring the reptiles to urban places far from their native habitat, like the streets of Baltimore. There they fetch $10 to $15 each in a thriving and illegal trade, illegal because a pet turtle in Maryland must measure at least four inches across its middle.[3] Federal regulators decided to ban the tiny turtles from the pet trade in the 1970s once researchers determined that the popular animals can transmit salmonella and that children are less apt to play with larger turtles.

Orangutans and gibbons in Indonesia are endangered in much the same way as the forest turtle in the Philippines: The apes' survival is threatened by habitat loss augmented by the pet trade. Compounding the tragedy are two unsettling facts. These apes are poached for pets as youngsters. That means their protective mothers usually are killed in the process.[4] Often pet owners tire of their responsibilities when great apes mature and become both strong and unpredictable. Many end their days in substandard sanctuaries or zoos.

Not unlike the illegal drug trade, not dissimilar to crimes involving the trading of firearms, animal smuggling exists because there is a market for it. People are willing to pay vast amounts of money for exotic animals. There's an allure to them that, before I began my research into this subculture, I failed to appreciate. Why would someone want to own a tiger, or a chimpanzee, or a python? Why would Paris Hilton, for example, have kept a kinkajou, a rare South American mammal with huge eyes for its tiny head, a monkey-looking tree climber with fleet feet that allow it to run with equal efficiency forward or backward? Late one night when Hilton was playing with her kinkajou, it bit her. She went to a hospital emergency room for a tetanus shot, but she and Baby Luv remained pals.[5] Kinkajous are also called honey bears and nightwalkers. Despite the bear nickname and the monkey look, they are part of the same group of animals as raccoons. The pet trade, along with habitat loss and hunting, is taking a heavy toll on the wild population of kinkajous, which—as was pointed out to Ms. Hilton when she showed up in Los Angeles with her animal— are illegal to keep as pets in California.[6] Michael Jackson performed with Bubbles, his chimpanzee, and he kept a zoo at his Neverland Ranch filled with elephants, tigers, giraffes, and assorted reptiles and birds. Bubbles grew strong and aggressive, and eventually he was shipped to the Center for Great Apes, a Florida sanctuary.[7] Teodoro Fino Restrepo was another private zookeeper, according to Mexican organized crime prosecutor Marisela Morales, who says the drug trafficker entertained his friends and colleagues with a collection that included lions, tigers, panthers, and a great ape—the animals were found living in urban Mexico City when cops raided his headquarters.[8] "It's a show of power and is incredibly common in the criminal underworld," was the response from Patricio Patron, Mexico's attorney general for environmental protection. "The worst of the worst have exotic animals."[9]

Boxer Mike Tyson secured a tiger for himself. During the divorce proceedings against his wife, Monica Turner, the fighter listed his tiger's care and feeding at $4,000 a month. Tyson's friend, the Chechen leader Ramzan Kadyrov, whom human rights activists call a murderer and torturer, showed off his pet tiger at a news conference. The Moscow newspaper *Komsomolskaya Pravda* printed a photograph of Kadyrov telling his tiger to eat the newspaper's reporter Alexander Gamov because he "writes incorrectly about me."[10] Actor Steve Sipek played Tarzan in a couple of Spanish-language jungle movies. At his Loxahatchee, Florida, spread in 2004, one of his big cats escaped its enclosure. Over twenty-four hours later an animal control officer shot and killed Bobo, saying the tiger lunged at him. The mourning Sipek called it murder, insisting the authorities should have stepped back and allowed him to retrieve the six-hundred-pound animal. "My beautiful Bobo that I loved all my life, gone. Gone, because heartless people would not give him a chance, would not give me a chance to walk him home or take him out of the area." In a bizarre sidebar to the Bobo story, police searching for Bobo cited Linda Meredith at the scene, charging her with animal cruelty when they found a piglet named Baby in the trunk of her Cadillac on a day with temperatures in the nineties. She suggested to the officers that they twist Baby's ears to make the pig squeal, a cry that she theorized would attract the tiger, which they could then recapture. "I can't believe they have the gall," she said about the authorities and her ticket, insisting her trunk was air-conditioned. "I was just trying to help the tiger find his way back home."[11] The pig was no pet; Meredith said she planned to eat Baby once it was grown.

Contemporary celebrities and dope dealers with their exotic pets follow a trend set by the rich and powerful throughout history. Graphic evidence in Egyptian tombs dating to 2,500 years before Christ show monkeys, hyenas, and other animals collected by royalty. Marco Polo was impressed when he watched Kublai Khan dominate a lion. "A great lion is led into the Great Khan's presence," he wrote, "and as soon as it sees him it flings itself down prostrate before him with every appearance of deep humility and seems to acknowledge him as lord. There it stays without a chain, and is indeed a thing to marvel at."[12] Change a few words, and it could be a visitor describing the bizarre scene of Sandra Herold in bed with the soon-to-be-vicious Travis, drinking wine with the ape. Or it could be Siegfried and Roy ordering around an unpredictable tiger on their Las Vegas show stage at the Mirage casino before the cat mauled Roy.

Myths tap into our atavistic longings throughout human history. It's understandable that attempts to cultivate relationships with wild animals transcend all cultures. The story of the runaway Roman slave Androcles dates to the first century B.C. He encounters a lion in a cave suffering from an infected foot. He pulls an offending thorn out of the lion's paw. He and the lion become pals, the lion acting tame with him. Androcles is later caught and condemned to death; the same lion is unleashed to kill him. Of course, it licks Androcles instead. He's pardoned, and freed man and healed animal spend their remaining days promenading around Rome, greeted by citizens saying, "This is the lion that was a man's friend; this is the man who was physician to a lion."[13] From Kublai Kahn to Mike Tyson, from Cleopatra to Paris Hilton, men and women keep seeking to make friends with wildlife.

Just as I began my study of the exotic pet trade and my effort to understand what motivates people to want to keep endangered and dangerous animals as "pets," a twelve-foot pet Burmese python escaped its vivarium in Oxford, Florida, and smothered a two-year-old girl before its owner could stop the snake. The snake was caught, and the little girl died.

Three highly publicized attacks—the incident involving the chimp Travis, the show tiger almost killing Roy Horn in front of a live audience, and the constrictor killing the little girl in a rural Florida trailer home—helped make contemporary society much more aware of the rampant levels of exotic pet ownership in its midst and of the potential dangers this subculture presents to neighbors, to the wild animals themselves, and to those who try to make them pets. The story I was researching jumped to the front pages, encouraging some of my sources to further rationalize their behavior, while others sought to hide from publicity.

At the same time, in my hometown, Bodega Bay, flyers were circulating advertising the annual appearance of Tippi Hedren. The actress starred in Alfred Hitchcock's *The Birds*—the movie was shot on location in Bodega Bay, and many of the famous scenes still are easy to identify in my neighborhood, essentially unchanged in the almost fifty years since the film was made. I was searching databases for exotic pet stories, developing contacts worldwide connected with the illicit trade in protected animals, and collecting reference books on endangered species for sale. But I had forgotten until I saw the notices that Hedren operates a reserve for big cats. Once a year, practically in my backyard, she holds court in the Tides restaurant, looking out on the bay where her character was struck bloody on the head—the first bird attack seen in the film. There she signs photographs of herself for a price, the money raised going to support her work providing a refuge for lions and tigers no longer of use to circuses and moviemakers, or of interest to pet owners.

Myself, I've been satisfied with dogs and cats, all of which arrived on their own, inviting themselves to join our family. Amigo was our lovely and loving Australian shepherd–husky mix, with his telltale freckles adding to the cherubic look of his face. An amigo he was for years and years. Our current cat—a pretty white Himalayan flame tip with firelike highlights—came to the door abused. Whiskers cut, he was bruised, abandoned, and afraid. Years later he's still skittish, and sometimes a crazed look crosses his face. His eyes seem to glass over, and he acts as if he does not recognize us. We learned from neighbors that his owners moved out of town and left him behind. They named him Toby, my wife Sheila calls him Sweetie, and my son Michael's choice is the official one on his tags: Schrödinger. Probably because I miss Amigo, I call him Puppy. That's as exotic as our pets at home stretch.

The word *pet* itself defines a questionable relationship. "Any animal that is domesticated or tamed and kept as a favorite or treated with indulgence and fondness," opines the *Oxford English Dictionary,* my pet dictionary. It's a broad-based definition, open to wide interpretation and in need of clarification. What constitutes a domesticated animal? Are any of us animals ever truly tamed? The *OED* adds "an indulged (and, usually, spoiled) child" to its definition and goes on to include "any person who is indulged, fondled, or treated with special kindness or favor; a darling." For many years I've published pieces of my journalism in *Penthouse.* Yes, the old joke is correct; some buyers of the magazine really do read the articles, and some of us who write them do on occasion glance at the pictures. So I'm aware of the *Penthouse* Pets. Is the term demeaning for the women? Or for the house cats and junkyard dogs so many of us enjoy? Is there a difference on the animal side of the equation if the pet is a traditional one like my dog Amigo or an exotic one like Mike Tyson's tiger?

"A pet is a diminished being," writes the philosopher Yi-Fu Tuan. "A pet is a personal belonging, an animal with charm that one can take delight in, play with, or set aside, as one wishes. Humans can become such pets, too."[14] Some slaves and servants are forced into the role of pets, as are, arguably, the well-compensated *Penthouse* Pets. Zoos in supposedly civilized countries have, in the not-too-distant past, displayed what they considered were savage humans alongside their captured apes and cats, individuals brought back from foreign lands. One of those so exhibited was Ota Benga, brought in 1904 from what was the Belgian Congo to America and eventually to the Bronx Zoo, where he was shown off as an oddity in the zoo's monkey house. Visitors thronged to see him, but protests soon convinced zookeepers to shut down the show.[15] The Ontario government took over custody of the Dionne quintuplets shortly after they were born and built a nursery for them equipped with one-way glass that allowed tourists to gawk. Quintland became the province's premier tourist attraction.[16] In more contemporary times zoos continue to experiment with human exhibits. In the summer of 2005, for example, the London Zoo placed five human volunteers wearing swimsuits in a "primate" enclosure. The zoo's communication manager, Simon Rayner, wanted to draw attention to the negative impact our species exerts on others. "We are saying, 'Look, here are humans stripped down and treated exactly the same way as other animals,'" Rayner said. "We are the same, and the way we treat all animals has consequences."[17]

"Control is an illusion," my wife tries to teach me, and I know in the long term she's correct. But when I called out, "Jump in the truck, Amigo," our dog leaped into the back of my pickup. I usually thought of it as an invitation, but Tuan notes, "Power over another being is demonstrably firm and perversely delicious when it is exercised for no particular purpose and when submission to it goes against the victim's own strong desires and nature."[18] I think I'm still okay. The purpose was clear: I wanted company in the truck on the run to the dump. And I'm quite convinced if Amigo didn't want to join me, he would have stayed home. But what about the captive animals serving as entertainers? Is that okay?

I became interested in the other dwelling places of exotic animals: roadside attractions, circuses, zoos, research laboratories, and sanctuaries—both the legitimate enterprises and the hustles. But ultimately I decided the more interesting story was in exotic pets and their keepers. I wanted to meet the people for whom Fido and Tabby weren't enough, the types who want big cats, great apes, and long snakes for pets.

The more I learn about the exotic pet trade, the more it is the pet "owners" who intrigue me. The poachers, smugglers, breeders, and legitimate merchants who litter the trade are important to note, but without demand from those who want to keep exotic pets, there need be no suppliers. Why is it that some people seem compelled to keep rare, dangerous, and weird animals? Are they motivated by a genuine love for the animal or a need to show off, or a desire to be in control of another being? Is it the thrill of commingling with a killer beast? What constitutes a pet as opposed to an animal that is a slave or being held hostage, especially one kidnapped from its wild home by poachers? Where does a captive-bred wild animal belong since it never knew the wilderness?

My attempts to answer these questions would take me to the esteemed museums of England and the swamps of Florida, to America's best universities, to the deserts of the Southwest, and beyond, as I journeyed from prosaic to exotic locales in my search for forbidden creatures.

CHAPTER ONE

Unexpected Mayhem

Travis Attacks Charla Nash

"THE CHIMP KILLED MY FRIEND!" AN UNDERSTANDABLY HYSTERICAL SANDRA Herold screams at the police operator as a primal screeching competes with her voice on the other end of the line.

The recording of the 911 call from chimpanzee owner Herold is haunting, and continual percussive screeching punctuates the call as the dispatcher responding at headquarters asks with appropriate cool, "What's going on there?"

Throughout the myriad, strange-but-true experiences I've had over the last year studying the relationships of my fellow humans and their so-called exotic pets, I remain haunted by that police recording. The plaintive, out-of-control human cry for help, combined with the even more primitive shriek of savage victory, stuck with me throughout my research for this book. It provided a constant reminder of a worst-case scenario for what can happen when we humans indulge a certain aspect of our nature. We want to tame the wild beasts. The sensational audio is in the public domain and was circulated by several newspapers, including the *New York Post,* which posted it on its Web site under a typical tabloid headline, "Why Chimp Went Bananas on Gal." I listened to the horrific, desperate call after first sitting through an online advertisement—bizarre because of its juxtaposition with the 911 message—for Pampers and the diaper company's Cruisers brand. The music is upbeat as the cutest little baby crawls determinedly across a shiny hardwood floor. "Cruisers flex to fit in high-motion areas, especially around the legs and waist," says the female announcer in a proud-sounding voice, and the picture changes to a mother figure bouncing said baby on her lap, flexing those legs and waist. "It's our best fit ever, to help stop leaks, no matter how much you move." An especially odd contrast considering that Travis, the chimpanzee screeching on the 911 recording, wore diapers.

"Send the police!" pleads Sandra Herold.

"What's the problem there?" asks the dispatcher at the police station in Stamford, Connecticut.

"The chimp killed my friend!" she yells.

"What's the problem with your friend?" he asks. For several seconds the only sound on the recording is the hideous screeching of the chimp, an aggressive cry that sounds crowlike.

"What's the problem with your friend?" the dispatcher repeats over and over.

"Oh, please," moans Herold.

"What's the problem with your friend? I need to know."

"Call the police!" she yells back. "With a gun, with a gun! He's killing my girlfriend!"

The dispatcher is heard on his radio sending a car to Herold's address.

"Hurry up!" she continues to yell.

"They're on their way," he tells her, "but I need more information. Who's doing this? Who has the gun?"

"No!" Her frustration is clear. "Bring the gun! You've got to kill this chimp."

"What's the problem there?"

"Hurry up!"

"I need you to talk to me. I need you to calm down. Why do you need somebody there?"

"He's killing my friend!"

"Who's killing your friend?"

"My chimpanzee!"

"Oh," says the dispatcher, and at this point his passive acceptance of a unique suburban crisis borders on the comedic. "Oh, your chimpanzee is killing your friend." As if chimp attacks in Stamford are routine.

"Hurry up, please!"

"There's someone on the way," he reassures her.

"Shoot him!"

"Tell me what the monkey's doing," asks the dispatcher, and Sandra Herold's immediate answer is unbelievable—and true.

"He ripped her face off."

"He ripped her face off?" The dispatcher sounds incredulous.

"He's tried. He tried. He's trying to attack me!"

Herold cries, pleading with the police to hurry. The dispatcher again tries to calm her and asks her to help her friend.

"I can't. He tried to attack me now."

"Okay. Then back off. Don't get any closer, okay?"

"He ripped her apart. Please hurry." She's sobbing. "Oh, my God. She's dead. She's dead. Oh, my God."

The police arrive after almost ten minutes of Herold's crying, "Please hurry," and the dispatcher urging her to breathe.

"Shoot him!" she yells.

Shoot him the police did. When the paramedics and cops arrived on the scene, Travis the chimpanzee ran off into the woods that surround Herold's home. Officers chased after him. He returned to the scene of his attack and assaulted cops who were guarding the medics as they treated the victim. Travis, who was intimately familiar with human tools—he was famous for drinking from stemmed glasses and operating a personal computer—opened the door of a squad car and went after the officer in the driver's seat. Police Captain Richard Conklin picks up the story by explaining that the cop in the cruiser felt forced to shoot to kill. "He's trapped in his car," the captain explains. "He has nowhere to go. So he pulls his sidearm and shoots the chimp several times in close proximity."[19] But the chase was not over. The wounded animal again ran into the woods, this time bleeding from what would become a mortal wound. Searchers followed the bloody trail back toward Herold's home, into the house, and to the chimp's cage. There he lay on his bed, dead.

Two days later Sandra Herold talked with NBC News correspondent Jeff Rossen, inviting the reporter into her home for an hour-long chat and a look at Travis' suburban environment. The accompanying cameraman shot video footage of Travis's primitive drawings decorating the refrigerator. "He couldn't be more my son than if I gave birth to him," Herold said about the late Travis. "Would I have done it again?" She rephrased the question when she was asked if she regretted creating a humanlike habitat for Travis, and she answered, "Yes! They're the closest thing to humans—to us. We can give them a blood transfusion, and they can give us one. How many people go crazy and kill other people? This is one incident, and I don't know what happened." She told Rossen that Travis used the toilet (apparently the diapers were a safety precaution), and he could brush his teeth and dress himself. "I used to buy everything for him—filet mignon, lobster tails, Lindt's chocolate," Herold recalled.

"He ate well," observed Rossen, in an awkward television moment during the wrenching report he presented on the network's *Today* show.

"I saw what was going on," Herold said, "and I hollered at him. He was just grabbing at her, and I went and got the shovel. I was trying to hit him with the shovel to stop it, and it wasn't working." So she grabbed a knife and stabbed him. As Herold recounts that awful moment, she cried. "He looked at me like, 'Mom! What did you do?'"

Herold also talked with Fox News just after the attack, saying that following the death of her husband and daughter, Travis was her family. "He didn't have anything but love until this freak accident," she said. "He was my life. Everybody knows it. I cooked for him, I shopped for him, I lived with him, I slept with him. He was just the only thing I had left. It's something I can't hardly live with because he went in his room and died, and I wasn't with him. I couldn't get back in the house." Not that Herold ignored the fate of her friend when she reacted in public. "I had to get a shovel, then a knife to get Travis off of Charlie," she told the *New York Post* just after her friend Charla Nash was mauled. "It was very difficult to do this, but I had to save my friend. I am so sorry for what happened to Charlie. She is my dear friend."[20]

Surrounded by photographs, toys, the drawings, and her memories, Sandra Herold told the *Today* show audience, "It's a horrible thing, but I'm not a horrible person, and he wasn't a horrible chimp. It was a freak thing."

Not such a freak "thing," according to Frans de Waal. He's the lead biologist at the Yerkes National Primate Research Center at Emory University in Atlanta. "They're very complex creatures," Waal says about all chimpanzees. And they're strong. The brute force of chimpanzees is measured at multiple times the strength of a human. Waal is both a psychologist and a biologist, and he says we humans can't know for sure what's going on in the mind of a chimpanzee. "People must not assume that with someone they already know there's not some underlying tension," he says of the manner in which apes relate to the humans with whom they interact. "It's often impossible to figure out what reason they have for attacking." With their potent muscles and massive canine teeth, chimpanzees are potential killing machines. "Having a chimp in your home is like having a tiger in your home," says Waal. "It's not really very different. They are both very dangerous."[21]

That NBC could feature the Travis tragedy on the *Today* show without a reference to J. Fred Muggs is a prime example of our popular culture's short attention span. The peacock network, and the *Today* show in particular, is responsible for presenting to a huge nationwide audience the image of the chimpanzee not as a wild animal but as a cute mascot masquerading as an almost-human.

In 1952 the network launched the *Today* show, with the erudite Dave Garroway as host. Ratings languished. In 1953, wearing diapers and a wardrobe that ranged from a T-shirt to a business suit, the chimpanzee called J. Fred Muggs joined Garroway on the set of the live broadcast. Eisenhower-era America became enthralled with the chimpanzee's antics—playing the piano, messing with his birthday cakes, "interviewing" celebrities—and ratings soared. Garroway and Muggs costarred until 1957, and by then the *Today* show had secured its permanent place as a morning television institution. Following a career that continued long after his *Today* show tenure, the chimpanzee, along with his owner and trainer, Carmine "Bud" Mennella, retired to Florida. In 1998 a Florida game warden fined Mennella $5 for possessing wildlife without a permit. "I was insulted," Mennella said, "that they could treat Fred like an animal and not a person."[22]

The morning Garroway–Muggs routine inculcated in the minds of its nationwide TV audience the idea that humans can coexist with wild animals, and that we can tame them and teach them to be like us. The role played by J. Fred Muggs was not that of a chimpanzee; he was anthropomorphized and so was a prime example of the popular media of the day teaching America—erroneously—that an uncontrollable and deadly strong species closely related to us would make a good house pet.

———⚬———

Charla Nash survived the attack from Travis, barely. Months later she was still hospitalized and in critical condition when one of her brothers summarized her condition for a public both curious and anxious to offer her support. "Charla is totally blind," he wrote. "Her last operation was to remove the eyes to prevent infections. Charla has lost her hands." He described in vivid detail her physical losses and the initial reconstructive work done by her doctors. "Most of Charla's face did not survive. From the bridge of the nose down to her bottom lip and between the cheekbones. A flap of muscle and skin has replaced this area to prevent any infection. A temporary pallet has been installed."[23]

Almost a year after the attack, Nash appeared on *The Oprah Winfrey Show* and publicly revealed the injuries her brother had described. "I'm the same person I've always been," she told the television audience. "I just look different. There are things that happen in life you can't change." She remained hospitalized, her bandages changed daily, and her food consumed through a straw fitted to where her mouth used to be. "I don't think about it," she told Winfrey of the mauling she received from Travis, a trauma she cannot remember. "There's no time for that because I need to heal, not look backwards." She said Travis scared her prior to the day he almost killed her. "He was big and scary. He was huge."

———⚬———

A horrific story, but rare. Other chimpanzees have mauled other humans, but such cases are few. Even dog bites don't kill in the numbers the worriers about vicious dogs may suggest. The Centers for Disease Control and Prevention figure about sixteen dog bite victims die in the United States every year. Close to five million Americans are bitten by dogs every year, and there are plenty of serious injuries.[24] Legal to own and supposedly domesticated, dogs bite, and dog bites man is not a news story precisely because it is so commonplace.

When supposedly domesticated dogs are responsible for so many attacks, when a chimpanzee who is considered a member of the family can literally tear a person's face off, one is forced to consider what the words actually mean, *wild* versus *domestic*. I contemplate the line separating those two types, wondering if there really is such a thing as a completely domesticated animal, wondering if there isn't forever a little wild in all of us.

"How many people go crazy and kill other people?" asked Sandra Herold.

For the next several months as I explored the complicated, morally ambiguous, and endlessly fascinating world of exotic pet ownership, Herold's question remained with me. It is nonsensical to compare humans violently interacting with each other and a wild animal attacking a defenseless woman. There is no parallel. Yet if we allow ourselves to keep dogs (which often are out of control and vicious), why not other animals like chimpanzees, even if they also might exhibit violent behavior? What's wild, and what's domesticated? We humans are, after all, animals, too, and at times a wild species. Does the value of exotic pet ownership outweigh the risks? Our pets often are extensions of ourselves, both psychologically and legally. When a dog attacks a person, its owner is liable for the damage. Was Sandra Herold alone responsible for the attack on Charla Nash? Perhaps we're collectively responsible since the law at the time allowed the chimp to live in the Connecticut suburbs. With those thoughts in mind, I headed to the Oakland airport and grabbed a Southwest flight to Spokane, hoping to convince a felon convicted of animal smuggling to open the gate at her isolated rural enclave and talk, the first stop on my journey toward some answers.

CHAPTER TWO

Monkey Smuggler

Survivalist Fran Ogren Conspires with Her Daughter

FRAN OGREN OBJECTS TO BEING CALLED A SMUGGLER, BUT THAT'S WHAT she is. She's a convicted felon facing a prison sentence for smuggling a monkey from Thailand through Los Angeles International Airport and up to Spokane. She conspired with her daughter, the jury at their trial decided, to bring Apoo, a two-month-old rhesus macaque, home from Bangkok by sedating the monkey and secreting it where it attracted no suspicion. Ogren's daughter, Gypsy Lawson, pretended she was pregnant. She walked through customs at LAX looking like what customs officers thought was just another expectant mother.

"The callousness and intent these people showed in carrying out their plan was egregious and placed at risk not only wildlife but potentially the health of other passengers on the plane and in their community," Paul Chang, the U.S. Fish and Wildlife Service special agent in charge of the investigation, said after the mother and daughter were convicted. "These animals are known carriers of viruses and parasites that can be transmitted to humans, although this particular animal tested negative."[25]

When I call Ogren from Spokane and explain why I want to meet with her, she is cordial but cautious. She feels the press mistreated her, that the coverage of her gambit was unfair. Nonetheless, after I explain my mission, she acquiesces to sit for an interview and gives me detailed directions to her remote wilderness farm. I head north on US 395 out of Spokane on a glorious late summer day. There's not much but two-lane blacktop between me and Canada except for sparkling deep blue lakes, broad valleys of rich pastureland, and dramatic rock outcroppings on mountainsides covered with thick stands of evergreens. The tableau reminds me of an old Hamm's beer commercial: From the land of sky blue waters, minus Shasha, the Hamm's bear. Later, Ogren and her husband will warn me to be careful on the twilight drive back to Spokane, because of deer on the highway and bears.

After about three hours on the road, I turn off 395, past placards that protest the National Animal Identification System, and—carefully calculating the mileage from a landmark Ogren cited—turn right on a dirt road marked with a sign advising PRIMITIVE ROAD, NO WARNING SIGNS. As it dead ends at her farm, I am greeted by a pair of snow white dogs that look to me like Newfoundlands. They don't seem particularly pleased to see me. I wait while Ogren's husband, Carl, comes out of their farmhouse to run interference with the dogs. The two are Polish Tatras, he tells me, and he confirms my suspicion that it was a good idea to stay put while they were busy barking and trying to get their big heads through the driver's side window.

Fran Ogren looks more like the grandmother she is than what Hollywood would tend to cast as a smuggler. We sit at her kitchen table, with me drinking a needed glass of water after the hot drive, while Ogren eyes me warily as I ask her general questions about exotic pets. Her unstyled reddish brown hair, parted in the middle, is accented with white tresses around her face. She's wearing a T-shirt printed with the farm's name and logo, pull-on pants, and flip-flops. Trumpkin Farm, she tells me, is named after a favorite pet deer. The scene reminds me of the basic, back-to-the-land kitchens where I've often visited friends. There's a wood cook stove, a couple of bowls filled with fresh fruit on the table, shelves stuffed with books, and an intriguing-looking contraption on a workbench that I learn later is an antique sock-knitting machine.

During a pause in the conversation, I take a sip of water and then ask, "So what constitutes an exotic animal?"

She points to a cage next to the front door and the slinky, elongated animal inside. "It's an open term," she says. "They call ferrets exotic, and yet they've been domesticated longer than cats. They're domesticated creatures, and they can't survive in the wild." What exotic means, she suggests, depends on the purpose of the definition. *Exotic* can mean "unusual" in lay terminology, even while biologists consider exotics to be anything nonnative.

After we've finished our small talk, I ask her what happened with the monkey.

"I'm politically active," is her explanation. "I fight for farm rights. There are groups that believe strongly that we should not have or control any animals, that we should all be vegetarian or vegan." She stops suddenly and looks across the table at me. "Where's your standpoint on that?"

This could be an awkward moment, I think. My answer could end the interview, but I pride myself on telling the truth and still getting the story.

"I don't eat any meat," I tell her, "but I don't have a problem with those who do. I carve the turkey at Thanksgiving dinner. I do a better job carving than anyone else in the family. I just don't want to eat the stuff. It doesn't matter to me that my wife enjoys cooking it and that the whole family likes to eat it."

"Okay," she says, and laughs with what sounds like cautious acceptance. I take her back to her version of the Apoo story. "I grew up around monkeys," she continues, "and they make wonderful pets. There is this fear factor going around about all the diseases we can get from them. It's totally absurd. They're incredibly great companions. They bring out the emotions that a newborn child does. They're just sweet and soft, and they cuddle and they like you. Most of the information that is out about monkeys is totally false. They were trying to claim," she says about the federal prosecutors, "that a little twelve-pound monkey could rip your face off and kill you." She laughs again, this time with disgust at the authorities who seized Apoo and were intent on sending her and her daughter to prison.

"I don't believe in laws to regulate," she explains. "I believe in education to regulate."

"And with Apoo," I say, "you guys were circumventing the existing regulations."

"That's what they claim."

"So, what happened?" I press further.

She tells me that the diaries she keeps, used as evidence against them at the trial, are a combination of fact and fantasy. "They now feel justified in putting a monkey that so loved his family and was loved—he ran around kissing everything—and he's so much better off," she finished the sentence with sarcasm, "in a rescue." Vivid descriptions written in her diaries of what she and her daughter did in Thailand were not necessarily true, she tells me. Rather, she insists, those diary entries may have been fiction.

—◆ ◆—

Apoo is living out his days at the private Oregon Primate Rescue sanctuary, where founder Polly Schultz says concern about his potential to spread disease to humans was valid, that he could have carried tuberculosis, herpes, or malaria. As it happens, however, examinations showed him free of diseases communicable to humans.[26] Schultz and her crew renamed him George and say their tests show that he suffered on the long plane ride from Thailand to the States. "Dangerous drugs that probably combined with improper type, strength, repeated use, and George's tender young age caused damage to his neurological system," is the Oregon Primate Rescue analysis. "We don't know if the tremors are permanent or if George may outgrow the condition in time."

After Apoo/George was seized by Fish and Wildlife Service agents, he spent three months in quarantine to determine he was disease free. "At this tender young age, George should have been cuddling in the security of his mother's arms, suckling and being groomed, learning skills to help him thrive as an adult, and chasing bullfrogs and butterflies with other babies from his troop," says Schultz. "But instead, following his cruel abduction, he spent three months frightened and alone in an unfamiliar cold steel cage, untouched, no mother to nurse or reassure him, not even a comforting bottle that he should have been on until at least one year of age."

Oregon Primate Rescue is now the monkey's permanent home, and as cute as she finds him, as much as she likes him, Polly Schultz considers his case tragic.

"He can never go 'home,'" she says. "He will have to remain in captivity, in a human's world, for the rest of his life. What happened to his mother, to his aunties, uncles, and cousins left behind? His mother, along with other troop members, was most likely killed during the abduction process. Troop members will fight to the death protecting their infants, as would you or I."[27]

Almost two years after Fran Ogren and Gypsy Lawson slipped Apoo/George through the Homeland Security phalanx at LAX, Schultz tells me the monkey "is doing really well. We're trying to find him a companion. Until then, I'm playing with him. He's going to be big before too long, and he's going to need a monkey buddy." Her voice has a pleasant, sing-song quality to it.

Schultz is confounded by the mother–daughter smuggling act since legal monkey breeding allows those who want a monkey in their midst to buy one without leaving the United States. "The frustrating part is, even if breeders have a U.S. Department of Agriculture license to breed and sell monkeys, they're not accountable about who they sell them to," she tells me. "They can sell them to people who have permits to keep them legally, and they can sell them to people who don't. The bottom line is, it's a business, and most of the time that's just what smugglers are looking for, the dollar." She favors outlawing the private ownership of monkeys as pets.

"Polly," I ask Apoo/George's new owner, "do you consider the breeding and trafficking in monkeys worse than puppy mills and humane societies overflowing with unwanted house cats?" I'm wondering if this caretaker of monkeys believes that the great apes require extra care and concern because of their genetic closeness to human beings.

"I've been around animals all my life," she says, "and monkeys are different. I love all animals, and I understand that monkeys are not human. I understand dogs and horses have feelings, too. But monkeys take it to a deeper level." She says that their behavior is humanlike and that she's convinced from interacting with them that they experience emotions similar to those of humans: "They have the same emotions we have; they just can't control theirs."

The margins can be healthy in the monkey business. Put a price tag on George's head, he could bring in $6,000 to $7,000 from the pet market. Cost perhaps was a motivator for smuggling Apoo/George; according to prosecutors, he sold for about $20 worth of baht, the Thai currency. The secondary market is another source of monkeys, with the Internet acting as a middleman and the prices as low as free. After four or five years, Schultz says, it's not atypical for a monkey owner to tire of an expensive and labor-intensive pet that no longer is as cute and cuddly as it was when it was a baby. Problem is, the new owner often tires of the pet soon after he joins the next household, "and the monkey gets bounced from one home to another and another and another. By the time they're all messed up really bad, they end up in sanctuaries or euthanized." Yahoo chat rooms, she says, are alive with monkey owners and monkey traders.

She is correct. After we talked I joined the first Yahoo chat room that came up when I searched with the key words *monkey, pet,* and *for sale.* Within moments I found a baby male marmoset posted for sale by one self-proclaimed Quincy Hottie in Illinois for $1,800. I scrolled down through the posts and stopped at another that caught my eye, titled "Capuchin scared," where I found this plea from Cindy: "Hello everyone, I am looking for anyone who has had this experience or knows the best way to handle my problem. I have a one-year-old capuchin, and he has never had any problems with diapering."

Capuchins are one to two feet tall with long tails. Their faces and chests are light; their body, arms, legs, and tails, dark. This is the species often used by organ grinders to solicit coins from passersby, and the intelligent capuchins are trained as service animals to work with disabled people.

Cindy continued:

About a week ago he all of a sudden went crazy when I tried to diaper him, not in an angry way but scared. It took three hours of trying and then backing off several times, 'til just as quick as it came on, his face changed and he came up, laid on my lap and let me change him. I thought perhaps he wasn't feeling well. Since then every so often he is doing this same thing. He screams, barks, and shakes in fear. I think it's fear. He has not been playing the past few days and just looks all over like he sees something and is shaking, then he goes right back to normal. I am trying hard to figure this out and do not want to do it in a way that makes it worse. If anyone has had this happen, please respond, I would appreciate any help or info. He is sweet and lovable, never mean, and this is only when he sees the diaper, it will wear off and then he is fine again. My heart is breaking as I don't know what has scared him, I don't know how I should try to fix this.

Three hours diapering a monkey? What type of person would want to keep a pet that requires such attention?

Polly Schultz understands Cindy's upset and attachment. "When they are infants, they are so humanlike!" she tells me. Now she sounds like a doting grandmother. "When you look at them, you see these little fingers that look just like little human baby fingers. You know what I mean?"

"Sure," I say. I've been enthralled watching monkeys, fascinated by the bridge they create, a connection like the one Jane Goodall describes about chimpanzees, a bridge from us to the rest of the animal kingdom.

"You give them a bottle, and when they're finished, you rub their little back, and they burp . . . just like a human kid burping. Their little belly buttons, their little toes, the expressions on their face," Polly Shultz lists the cute factors. "A lot of people dress them because it's so cute. You see this little monkey that is like a homely version of a prehistoric human, with this cute little frilly dress on. You know what I mean?"

I try to imagine a Cro-Magnon man in drag.

"Some of them wear earrings. You can hold them by the hand. They play with them," she says about many of the monkey owners she's encountered, "as a surrogate human child."

Is that wrong, I wonder, contemplating a jeweled monkey in a dress. Is this an example of philosopher Tuan's condemnation of pets as "diminished beings"? How could an owner ascertain if a monkey wanted to play dress up? Perhaps leave the frock and earrings around the house, and if the monkey chooses to dress itself . . . ?

"I don't think it's wrong that people don't understand," says Schultz. "I think that's what the problem is. I don't think that people are wicked and evil and want to do something that's going to harm this little monkey." She reminisces about dressing up her kitty in baby clothes when she herself was a little girl and pushing the cat around in a baby stroller. Were the trade in pet monkeys to end, she says, "it would save a lot of humans broken hearts, as well as messed-up monkeys that end up with no place to go."

Polly Schultz plays with Apoo/George and the other monkeys at her government-licensed refuge. Is there a double standard at work here? She runs a sanctuary and enjoys the company of the great apes she would like to forbid private citizens to keep as pets.

"This is the hardest thing I've ever done in my life," she tells me. She rejects my premise that hers is a double standard. "I love the monkeys. I care about the monkeys. If something could just miraculously happen overnight, and all of the monkeys that come to us could be rehabilitated and released into a more natural environment, oh God, I would do that in a flipping heartbeat." The sad truth is, however, there likely are more monkeys in need of a safe home than there is sanctuary space available.

"More than most people would realize," is how Fran Ogren characterizes the grief caused by her family's loss of Apoo. She calls him her grand-son, even though he lived with her daughter in Spokane, a three-hour drive from her farm, and only for a couple of months. "I was terrified of what they would do to him. I was terrified of what he would go through because they ripped him away from everything familiar. Monkeys don't readjust well. They're no different than human babies that way. He had a good life. He was loved and cared for. He slept in bed with my daughter, whom he considered his mom. He had a dog whom he ran to when he felt uncomfortable, for security, and a house full of animals of several species. He would smear up the fish tank kissing it. To see that life for him ripped away . . ." She pauses and adds, "I know what some rescues are like."

Oregon Primate Rescue does not allow Ogren or her daughter to visit Apoo. They haven't seen him since January 2008, when the police came knocking on her farmhouse door and her daughter's home in Spokane, where Apoo lived.

"The feelings that Apoo brought out were much closer to how I would feel about a grandchild. There's a different bonding, and it's almost immediate. The emotions are the same. We're hardwired for it. If you hold this little baby—"

"Monkey," I interrupt.

"Monkey," she agrees, "or human, they will bring out very similar emotions. When he's treated as a baby and held by a mother, whether it's his species or not, he feels the same."

"Maybe so, but why did you need this particular monkey at this particular time?"

"He needed to be in a stable situation," she says quietly and credits her daughter and herself with being the true rescuers. "If he were in Thailand in captivity," she says, still speaking softly and trying to choose her words with care since her conviction was in the middle of the appeals process when we talked, "his mother was already killed and eaten, and he would have been on the menu soon."

Nonsense, insists Polly Schultz. "There were no statements that the abductors 'rescued' George from being eaten by residents of Thailand," she says in response to Ogren's claim. "Those who eat monkey would have no interest in an infant weighing only ounces. It would take years for a baby monkey to gain any substantial size for that unthinkable purpose and simply not worth the time or money with so many adults readily available. As long as selfish individuals are willing to pay, poachers will continue to kill adult parent monkeys to abduct and sell the infants."

I ask Fran Ogren why she didn't seek a legal route and try to adopt or buy Apoo with official approval. She waves off my question for the same reason she gives when I next ask her to explain how she and Gypsy obtained the monkey. She worries about prejudicing the appeal of her conviction.

"I'm not saying he came from Thailand. We went to Thailand to work with elephants. And then we rode horses. We did a little bit of traveling, and we came home. The crimes that they're pinning on us are political, they're not based in fact." Daughter Gypsy Lawson told a different story to the TV show *Inside Edition*. She confirmed to reporter Jim Moret that the two bought Apoo for $20 and that she breezed through airport security even though inspectors subjected her to a pat-down search. "I guess Homeland Security is not what it's cracked up to be," she said. "It was extremely easy."[28] Perhaps because crossing four international borders presented no problem, Lawson felt comfortable parading the monkey around Spokane. She took it with her to a shopping mall near her home on the north side of the city and showed him off at Fashion Bug, a women's clothing store that shares the mall with PetSmart (where monkeys are not among the animals for sale). A suspicious clerk called game wardens.

Fran Ogren says she was targeted because of the lobbying work she did in the Washington State legislature, "and that's where I made my enemies." She opposes the National Animal Identification System (NAIS). Anti-NAIS signs pepper the Washington landscape. The U.S. Department of Agriculture wants farmers to register their livestock so that when diseases strike, inspectors quickly can locate infected and exposed animals. The USDA says participation in NAIS helps limit the spread of disease; hence fewer animals are lost to illness. Opponents see NAIS as government intrusion on family farms and worry that Washington wants to identify and track all the animals in the country, including pets—a policy they fear carries nefarious potential. They worry about government control over their animals and their lifestyle.

Fran and her husband, Carl, are survivalists. Carl traps. They grow and raise their own food, and Fran shears her sheep and spins the wool to make yarn for her sock-knitting machine. They slaughter lambs for chops and tan the hides. "They know they have a good life," she says about the sheep, then provides details that offer a glimpse into her primal world. "They don't get upset when we butcher babies. They say good-bye. There's no trauma. They're very calm. We don't like sending anything off to be butchered because the trip, the slaughterhouse, the strangers, are scary. And you're not going to explain that away to them. But doing it here, calmly and routinely, I think they know they're a food animal, whether it's for us or for a cougar or a bobcat. I know they're not traumatized. I watch it. It takes life to support life, and I think they accept that better than most of us. We're just part of nature, we're not apart from it."

In addition to the sheep, they raise llamas, turkeys, ducks, and geese. Their farm is also home to a horse and a couple of dairy cows. "We're totally self-sufficient," she says, "and I'm fighting for this lifestyle politi-cally because I know that the corporations want to eliminate it."

Fran and her daughter were convicted of two felonies each, smug-gling and conspiracy to smuggle, and have been sentenced to two months in prison. They were facing as much as twenty-five years behind bars, but Ogren considers the penalty unreasonable. "Two felonies in a three-strikes state?" Three felonies can be interpreted by the courts as habitual crimi-nality worthy of a lifetime behind bars. She worries about travel restric-tions and the loss of her right to vote, along with damage to her credibility as a lobbyist.

"No one has the right to abuse anything," she says, "whether it's an animal or a human. I'm very much an anarchist. Your rights end when you're stepping on someone else's. I believe if the animal is happy and benefiting, and it's a symbiotic relationship, nobody is being hurt."

"How do you know if an animal is being hurt, or happy for that mat-ter?" I ask.

"Anybody who is an animal person and spends time around them will just know. You get the feelings from them."

"And is it right for humans to own other animals?"

"If you could ask most of the animals that are owned and cared for decently if they would want to go off and fend for themselves, they'd laugh at you. They have us trained. I'm not opposed to ownership. I'm opposed to little cages."

There's no question that monkeys fascinate us humans. We celebrate them and their antics from storybooks (*Curious George*) to axioms ("Monkey see, monkey do") to Maria Muldaur's whimsical song lyrics ("Just let me lay around and grin like a monkey"). We seem to be intrigued with any other animal that exhibits anthropomorphic features. We like to see our-selves mirrored. Perhaps it's an example of our arrogance as a species— we want other animals to seem to mimic us. Perhaps it makes them appear more accessible than those with vast differences. My family and I visited the wild monkeys living on Gibraltar. At first glance I thought they looked cute, but as we got closer, they acted aggressively, knowing we—like the throngs who preceded us—probably carried food. We gave them some biscuits, as I recall, or maybe nuts. They were spoiled and spurned our offerings. Taking one of them home never occurred to me; I was pleased to leave them on their rock to scratch and chatter among themselves.

Lopburi, in Thailand, is equally famous for its monkeys. A couple of thousand macaques roam the city streets, begging and stealing food from tourists and mating with each other, making more macaques. The Thai government responded to Lopburi's increasing monkey population in 2009 by rounding up males and sterilizing them.[29] While there, Fran Ogren and her daughter responded as many tourists do. "We were playing with pigtailed macaques in Lopburi," she says, enthused with the memory, "and they bit. They were wild monkeys! We'd grab 'em or grab a baby off a mom, and the whole troop would land on us. They'd be pulling our hair, and they'd be fighting. We hardly even got bruises. They would all calm down. They stole one of Gypsy's earrings. They were fascinated with her earring, and all was well." She giggles.

The day is waning. I thank Fran Ogren for her time and pack up my camera and audio recorder. As I head past the ferret to the door, she asks me to consider one more thing: "Did primitive man restrict himself to dogs and cats? I think it's in a lot of people to have a deeper relationship with more varieties of animals. When someone says, 'Why do you need an exotic?' that's really narrowing the field. There's so much more we can interact with, and we benefit." She tells me about her pet deer, Trumpkin. She fed the orphaned fawn milk from her goat. "She knew our names. She loved ice cream. She slept in our bed. Anytime you live with something different, your world expands. One of our grandkids has a skunk."

I point the car I rented back toward Spokane and contemplate the idea of a deer sleeping in my bed. Deer are not strangers in our neighborhood. They range freely in our yard, eating the low-hanging apples from our tree, and in dry weather my wife leaves buckets of water for them. But that's the extent of our interaction. They're wild and free, and I, for one, would not want their tick-infested hides under my covers.

As I drive into the twilight, I glance back at Ogren's homestead in the rearview mirror. It's bucolic; her valley is a paradise. But it's impossible for me to muster sympathy for the predicament she has created for herself. I embrace good old-fashioned, rugged American individualism; however, her convoluted rationale for the mess she made of her (and her daughter's) life lacks credibility. What the visit did reinforce was my own growing intrigue with learning more about the types of people who keep exotic pets and why they choose their unusual hobby. My visit to Trumpkin Farm left no question in my mind that I was encountering a world far from Main Street, U.S.A.

CHAPTER THREE

Federal Case

The Prosecutor and Gypsy Lawson's Pet

IT'S SAFE TO SAY AFTER TALKING WITH ASSISTANT ATTORNEY GENERAL
Stephanie van Marter that the prosecutor thinks that Fran Ogren and
Gypsy Lawson are skunks. From Ogren's rustic homestead I go, on a
sunny summer day, to Van Marter's conference room in the elegant and
sleek Thomas S. Foley Federal Building in downtown Spokane. She's
a cheery blonde wearing a summer dress to match the toasty weather
outside. She offers a wide smile that alternates from a fixed professional
look to a natural expression of delight, depending on the content of our
conversation.

"Gypsy decided she wanted a pet," is how Van Marter sums up her
theory for Ogren's motive. "I honestly don't know why they decided
that this was something that they were going to do. There's no rhyme
or reason to it other than Gypsy wanted a pet, and her mom helped her
get it."

Laws specific to pet monkeys differ across America. There is no federal ban on pet primate ownership, but the practice is illegal in some
states. In others, some cities and counties have decided to control private
primate ownership. Breeders where the pet monkey trade is legal offer
captive-bred macaques like Apoo/George for sale. Wild Animal World is
an example. The Louisiana-based company, when I checked, was selling
baby male bonnet macaques for $5,500, females for $200 more, and a
one-year-old rhesus macaque for just shy of $3,000. "No refunds will be
given because of state laws," warns Wild Animal World in its literature.[30]
"Do your research before purchasing." The disclaimer is followed by ten
exclamation points. The company's home state now forbids monkey pets.
The ban against importing monkeys into the United States as pets has

been in effect since 1975, when the Centers for Disease Control listed the primates as dangerous disease carriers, and taking a monkey across state lines without proper documents violates the Lacey Act.

"If Gypsy just wanted a pet, why make a federal case out of one monkey?" I ask.

Stephanie van Marter says she considers the crime serious, and not just because monkeys (albeit not this one) carry diseases that can infect humans. "The idea behind somebody on their own smuggling any type of dangerous animal into the United States while avoiding all customs, that kind of conduct, I don't care who you are, should be addressed." That's why she wanted the pair locked up for six months. "The actions that they committed were incredibly selfish," says the prosecutor, citing the possibility of the monkey spreading diseases. "These are two women who selfishly exposed thousands of people because they wanted a pet." Van Marter sounds piqued and judgmental as she adds, "That shows no social awareness to me."

Although Apoo/George did test free of disease, there is legitimate concern about diseases crossing species lines from exotic pets to their human handlers and beyond. Hollywood made the threat into a thriller starring an infected imported monkey smuggled out of a lab animal warehouse in California in the movie *Outbreak*. Rene Russo plays a CDC doctor trying to trace the source of the disease before it spreads across the country. "Jimbo!" she frantically asks a dying victim. "Were you in contact with any animals?" (Jimbo was, but he dies before he can help investigators.)

To bolster their prosecution, authorities acted as if they were working from a Hollywood treatment for a police search when they turned Fran Ogren's house inside out, seizing photographs, diary entries, and e-mail files. These documented the monkey's trip from Thailand to LAX (via Korea) and on to Portland, Oregon. "We found e-mails from Fran Ogren soliciting the purchase of the monkey. She described trying to lure monkeys into their hotel room and keep them," Van Marter tells me. The hotel room gambit was memorialized with photographs of the mother and daughter interacting with Thai monkeys.

This was not a case of a sophisticated crime ring. It was an amateur mother–daughter act. Why throw the book at them, send them to a federal prison, and leave them marked as felons for life?

⎯ ⎯

That the Ogrens were bumbling country bumpkins is another argument Van Marter rejects, based on the evidence. "They knew the consequences. They made several statements in e-mails and journals: 'Oh, geez, I hope we don't get stuck in a Thai prison.' They're lucky they didn't. A Thai prison is not where you would want to be.

"They're very lucky because they would have stayed there," she continues. "It was not only a violation of our laws, it was a violation of Thailand's laws. The penalties that they received in this country are far less than they would have been potentially exposed to when they took this monkey." Van Marter cites damage to the monkey's health as another factor weighing against the smugglers. "They tortured this monkey. They repeatedly injected this infant monkey with sedatives because they wanted a pet. There's nothing to suggest that they should be treated any differently than anybody else who purposely and intentionally violated a number of laws."

The crime took place a few years after police raided a diploma mill in the Spokane Valley where another monkey was living as a pet. That animal threw its own feces at arresting officers, adding to the Spokane monkey folklore.[31] "It's the Spokane Vortex at work," former Spokane *Spokesman-Review* reporter Bill Morlin told me over coffee, local journalists' shorthand for weird stories with Spokane connections. Morlin knocked on Gypsy Lawson's door shortly after she was arrested and the monkey taken from her. "He was my baby," she complained to Morlin, "and completely nonaggressive." She told him the monkey liked to cuddle and sleep with her Jack Russell–poodle mix. "They bonded immediately," she said about the monkey and the dog.

"I'm innocent," she declared to Morlin. "I never got the monkey in Thailand. There's no way they can prove I smuggled a monkey."[32]

Wrong.

The Spokane Vortex was at work deep in the grand jury indictment that began the legal process against Gypsy Lawson and her mother. "On or about November 26, 2007," it reads, the legal language about to tangle with the Vortex, "Fran Ogren sent an e-mail to NE_Washington_Witches_and_Pagans@yahoogroups.com and asked for last minute energy to help them safely smuggle the monkey into the United States. The Witches group replied by e-mail, 'consider it done.'" Prosecutors used the e-mail, along with other similar intercepted messages, to show planning and intent. After we met, I exchanged e-mail messages with Ogren and asked her about the witch connections.

"It was just another way to twist things and try to get public sentiment against us," she wrote, "or more, me. I belong to a pagan online list, where we talk about such radical things as how our gardens are doing, and exchange seeds, herbal treatments for various things, and so on. Pagan, meaning of the earth, but it was used to make me sound like a 'Satanist,' whatever one makes that out to be! When they got my e-mails, as Google gave them all up even before they had a warrant, they tried to use a lot of that, which had absolutely no bearing on anything, and most of it the judge refused to have admitted. Of course it came out anyway!"

———

"I know that there were arguments that he was going to get eaten," Stephanie van Marter says about the monkey's future in Thailand, but she says there's no proof he was in jeopardy of becoming bush meat. She's convinced that living in Gypsy Lawson's Spokane home was not a better environment for him than his Thai home. "They hurt this monkey. They had no knowledge whatsoever about primates." While she calls them ignorant about the monkey's needs and his potential danger to public health, she finds them quite knowledgeable about monkey smuggling. "They knew exactly what they were doing with respect to violating the law. They knew it wasn't okay. They intentionally and purposefully set out to violate the law." She gives me the professional smile and adds, "I mean, you don't hide something under your shirt," and she dismisses the absurdity of it, "and be, like, this is fine."

"Ruins their lives, two felony convictions . . . " I start.

"I think that would be an overcharacterization as to what is going to happen to these two ladies," is the assistant attorney general's response. "There are hundreds and hundreds of people who survive in every community who have criminal histories and who have moved forward and have led very successful and socially responsible lives. We aren't monsters behind a desk looking to ruin people's lives."

"Maybe they've learned a lesson."

"That's the whole point. The point is not to devastate them. Sometimes federal convictions are the impetus for all kinds of life changes. People get clean and sober. People end associations that were getting them in trouble and move forward with a productive, happy life."

"Or hunker down and hate the government."

"Or hunker down and hate the government," she agrees, "and that's too bad. I hope that's not a choice that they make. No government entity caused them to make this decision. They made this decision all on their own."

"Do you have a pet?" I ask Van Marter, and my question elicits her natural smile.

"I have two dogs."

"What kind of dogs?"

"Very lovely dogs. I have a solid brown German shorthair and a very old black Lab." Her voice drops. "He's fifteen. I love my dogs, and my kids love my dogs. I am a pet lover."

So are we, was the message from Fran Ogren and Gypsy Lawson. Smuggling the monkey was "legally wrong," Lawson acknowledged after the trial, but not "morally wrong."[33]

Of course, there's a world of difference between Van Marter's dogs and a smuggled pet monkey. The German shorthair and the black Labrador joined the assistant attorney general's household with shots and a license; they weren't smuggled through LAX. And dogs in general have enjoyed a long, successful history of cohabiting with people in Spokane homes. As my quest into the netherworld of exotic pets soon would teach me, the same cannot be said for great apes—in Spokane or elsewhere.

Stories of pet monkeys attacking their owners are common, as are attacks on friends (as was the case with Travis), neighbors, and passersby. But not all exotics are illegal, and not all attacks are lethal for human exotic pet owners and other people who come in contact with unusual beasts. In fact, common are stories from bloodied owners excusing monkeys' behavior. Their postattack defenses remind me somehow of political wives who stand next to their rogue, apologetic husbands as they try to save their careers from scandal.

Cathy Huscher let her Great Java macaque, Zip, out of its parrot cage for the first time in two months while her husband was down the street grabbing Chinese takeout for dinner. The monkey "sat there for a second before letting out this blood-curdling scream. He then attacked me in the head, arms, and legs," biting her until she bled. The husband returned to their Lansing, Michigan, home to find his wife on the floor, bleeding from multiple wounds. "I thought I was going to die," she said. But stabilized at the hospital, she missed her Zip. "Don't make him out to be a monster. He was my baby."[34] Seven-year-old, twenty-five-pound Zip was euthanized so his brain tissue could be tested for rabies. Mrs. Huscher was distressed about her loss and about her husband's response to Zip's death. "He said he wants to use the head as a paperweight."[35]

Phyllis Booth called for help from the Hillsborough, Florida, sheriff's office when her pet monkey, Angel, inexplicably started biting her, literally biting the hand that fed it. "I can't understand her going so crazy," said Booth. "I don't understand it. She likes me so well. Why would she turn on me for no reason?"[36] Her son-in-law, Lee Skowronski, agreed, saying, "She's generally a good monkey." He had a theory for her sudden mood swing: "She came into season for the first time, so I guess it's PMS or something."[37]

Chicago construction worker Peter Bukowski bought a monkey he called Oliver for his wife, Monika. As a girl she read about Pippi Longstocking's monkey and wanted one of her own. Over time the cute factor was augmented with aggression. "The older he got, the less he listened when I commanded him to drop things," Bukowski said about the mess Oliver made of his household. "Once he jumped on my daughter's neck with a knife and was waving it about her face." But the Bukowskis forgave him. "A monkey is something special. They look in your eyes with such intelligence, and they reach out and stroke your face with the palms of their beautiful little hands. We were so nuts about Oliver, we put up with the bad stuff." Put up with it until Oliver attacked Bukowski, biting his stomach and drawing blood.[38]

One after another I found stories in newspaper files that mimicked these three: attacked monkey owners excusing their pets. But as my research continued, I found the same phenomenon close to home.

— ～

"He was affectionate and nice with the family."

A few weeks after my encounter with smuggler Ogren, I'm eating lunch in San Francisco with my high school chum Chris Slattery, and he's remembering growing up in suburban Orinda, where a neighbor friend's little sister owned a chimpanzee. I'm finding that almost invariably when I mention to people that I'm researching a book about pet wild animals, they've got their own story to tell. The daughter had been desperately ill as a child, and before a critical operation, her parents asked her what she would like for a present after the surgery. "A chimpanzee," was her answer.

"But I never really felt comfortable around him," Slattery says of the chimp. "If you looked at him, if you made eye contact with him, he would run over to you, flip, and grab you around your calf, then bite onto your Achilles tendon." This was an experience Slattery did not like at all. "It was weirdly immobilizing. You just had to freeze." Freeze until a family member would peel Junior off the outsider. The family took a laissez-faire attitude toward Junior's ankle-biting antics, considering it cute.

Junior had the run of the household, Slattery remembers. He wasn't caged. He had his own room, but he spent plenty of time roaming around the house. Junior grew older, and the cute factor disappeared in a hurry. The neighbors called Slattery's doctor father. The chimp had attacked the little girl's mother "and just tore her up. A million stitches, a real savage attack." That was the end of the relationship; the chimpanzee was donated to a zoo.

The Slatterys also harbored an exotic pet—a kinkajou named Pardito, kinkajous undoubtedly being the only common denominator my friend shares with Paris Hilton. In the wild, kinkajous live in groups, spending most of their time in the forest canopy. At Slattery's house, theirs lived in an enclosure his father built in the backyard.

"A patient of my father's had been stationed in Venezuela and brought this animal home. Pretty quickly realized he couldn't keep it, so he gave it to my father. I don't know why my father thought he could keep it," he reflects on the childhood memories, "but he did." Slattery remembers that prehensile tail and "little gripping hands" that served Pardito well in the treetops. "On the ground he was kind of awkward." *Cute* is the word that first comes to his mind when I ask what the animal looked like. "Very sweet little face, very teddy bear looking, dense brown fur. Really, really, really cute. Really cute." So far, so good.

The enclosure offered Pardito a couple of trees to climb on and sleep in, along with some pipes for swinging. "We'd bring him in the house in the evening, although he was really destructive. He climbed everything. He would climb a shelf of glasses, and everything would end up on the floor. But he was sort of sweet and affectionate and got along with the dogs okay." He lived with the family for several years and interacted with them. "He'd climb all over you. He didn't really like being on the ground, so if you had him out of his enclosure, he was always in motion. He would climb you. He'd eat from our hands. We'd buy cases and cases of Birds Eye canned vegetables." He smiles at the memory. "And figs. He liked figs a lot." In the wild, kinkajous like honey and termites, along with fruit and mammals—small mammals that they can grab with the sharp claws on their front paws.[39]

The kinkajou and the Slatterys lived happily together until "one day he just started getting mean. Biting. And you couldn't unpeel him from you. He went into this attack mode, and you couldn't get him off you. Whenever you unwrapped—he had four really strong-gripping legs and then this tail—he wrapped you again. So if he was on you, he was *on* you. It was scary." The meanness came on suddenly, and the Slatterys gave

Pardito to a zoo. The zoo gave them a couple of tame raccoons to take home in exchange.

The raccoons lived in Pardito's old enclosure but were allowed to roam the yard. Slattery's father periodically enjoyed sleeping in the garden, and the raccoons would cuddle up next to him in his sleeping bag. One night when he was sleeping outside, he heard banging in the garbage cans, and he called out to them using their collective nickname. "Come here, honey. Come here," he encouraged the raccoons. But the banging persisted, and they didn't come to him, so he called out louder, "Come here, honey," again and again, lifting his sleeping bag for them to join him. Still the raccoons didn't come. Curious, he sat up and looked around for them. There were no raccoons at the cans; all he saw was the garbage man looking at him. It's a story they're probably still telling down at the garage.

Another friend of mine sent along a snapshot of a placard she saw while taking her usual morning walk. Affixed to a power pole and scrawled with a black marker, it read, "Lost monkey. Need your help to find it. Last seen at Gita's Gourmet. Be careful; the monkey knows kung fu!"

CHAPTER FOUR

Attempted Amnesty

Connecticut's Animal Control Czar Susan Frechette Tries to Corral Unwanted Pets

THE FIRST EXOTIC PET AMNESTY DAY AT THE BEARDSLEY ZOO TOOK SOME fauna exotic to Connecticut off the streets, but it was not the grand success organizers hoped to experience. The zoo, along with Connecticut's Department of Environmental Protection (DEP), urged fanciers of unusual pets to drop off their beasts—legal or illegal—for a no-questions-asked good-bye. Beardsley, the only public zoo in Connecticut, decided to follow the amnesty lead of Miami's MetroZoo after Travis, the chimpanzee who lived for years in a rambling Stamford home not far from Beardsley, attacked Charla Nash.

Frustrated owners, such as Jeff Seeps, hauled well over a hundred exotics to the zoo. Seeps drove a few hours to the zoo from New York City, his over three-foot-long alligator in the car with him for a one-way trip. He bought the alligator when it was a cute baby conversation piece, but he waved good-bye to it because "it was getting too big for home."[40] He called his gator Petey and described Petey as "pretty tame and nonaggressive." Petey bit Seeps a few times, but he dismissed the bites as just "nips." The predator liked to swim with Seeps, who proclaimed himself "a little sad" as he left his pool partner. "I knew he would grow," he said about the reptile that was already three times the size it was when Seeps first brought him home. "I just didn't realize how fast he would grow in captivity."[41]

As expected by the zookeepers participating that day, most of the animals that were given away were reptiles: boa constrictors, pythons, alligators, a rattlesnake, and an anaconda. A monkey was left behind, as was a pair of tortoises. They had hoped for some dangerous mammals: big cats, and maybe a chimpanzee.

The two tortoises were dropped off by Andrew Bowie, who came to the zoo from Norwich. Although they had grown as big as hubcaps since his wife brought them home, it wasn't their size that bothered Bowie. He wanted more attention from the otherwise occupied Spike and Spot. "I liked them a lot," he complained as he off-loaded them, "but they don't give you any love. They just want food."

Landlord Mark Bernier evicted a tenant from a property of his in Milford, and he was left with the tenant's alligator, a burden named Allen. As they tried to find a new home for him, he and his family fed Allen frozen mice, hot dogs, and goldfish. The Beardsley Zoo offer to take him was just what they needed. Whenever they walked into the room Allen called home, Bernier complained, "he would hiss."[42]

Susan Frechette, as deputy commissioner of the DEP, was in charge of that amnesty day. Her portfolio includes work for the state Environmental Conservation Police, the unit of government responsible for enforcing laws pertaining to wildlife. After just starting to delve into the world of exotic pets, it seems to me that the failures of owners to keep pets are as revealing as what the owners consider successes. As I talk with Frechette about her amnesty offer, she tells me that calls come frequently to her office from citizens wondering what to do with exotic and unwieldy animals they want to get rid of. These calls continue to surprise her. "I can't see why anybody would want a five-foot-long crocodile as a pet," she says, mystified. About alligators and caimans and long snakes, she tells me, "Sometimes we find them out in the wild. We wanted to provide a proactive setting for people to turn in their unwanted exotic pets rather than release them in the environment or keep them and have a dangerous situation in the home front."

Not that pythons and other potentially dangerous cold-blooded animals pose the same long-term threat in New England as they do in Florida. Most of those let loose won't survive the nasty Northeast winters. But short term, Frechette worries. "The alligators that we have found could certainly cause some harm to a pet or a child or the native wildlife in the course of looking for a meal every day."

Attempted Amnesty

The Beardsley Zoo planned to start processing the discarded animals at ten in the morning. Almost an hour before opening time, the menagerie started lining up. There was a steady march of surrendered animals throughout the day. As the animals were separated from their owners, Frechette watched human emotions run the gamut. "Some people were sad and tearful; this had been their pet and their companion, and they had made the choice to say good-bye. For others it was just pure relief; they didn't know what else to do with the animals. They needed a way to get rid of their pets, and this was the way."

Mixed in with the alligators and other reptiles was a capuchin monkey. Capuchin monkeys are little guys, weighing in at just three to nine pounds, and cute as your favorite child. In the wild they live in large groups, hanging out in trees. These monkeys can jump as much as nine feet, a feat they use to travel from tree to tree. They rarely come down to the ground except to find drinking water. And they coexist with human colonies, some of which hunt them for their own mealtimes. They do have a rather base method of marking their territory: They soak their little hands and feet in urine and wipe them on their turf. Native to Brazil and other South American countries, they are not just cute but also smart. Since they are trained as pets, entertainers, and service animals for the disabled, finding a home for such cute fellows usually is an easier task than for reptiles, but the zoo promised to do everything possible to find good homes for all the giveaways.

The diminutive monkey, eight parrots, and loads of reptiles were turned into the zoo, but no great apes and no big cats. "We were a little disappointed," is Frechette's day-after-amnesty reaction, "because there is definitely the sense that this is the tip of the iceberg, that there are a lot more exotic pets out there, and perhaps some that are potentially more dangerous than some of the ones that came in." Not that she dismisses the danger presented by a five-foot-long caiman, "a pretty large animal with a lot of sharp teeth that can really do some damage." Missing were animals she says she's been told "anecdotally" prowl Connecticut: "No large cats, none of the larger primate species. Nothing really venomous, other than a rattlesnake."

In Connecticut it is illegal to keep big cats: tigers, lions, leopards, cheetahs, jaguars, lynxes, and bobcats. Wolves and bears are also verboten. After Travis attacked Charla Nash, chimpanzees, gorillas, and orangutans were added to the no-pet list. Yet the state law remains vague regarding some animals. For example, alligators and caimans are not expressly forbidden, but the Connecticut DEP does not issue permits for them because it considers them dangerous wild animals. The fact that the alligator owners can't get a permit from the state doesn't necessarily mean keeping them in your Connecticut bathtub is illegal. In order for the department to demand that you get a permit, as I understand it (and I'm not sure after talking with Frechette that she or anyone else understands the law better), DEP officials would need to make a case that your animal presents a danger to you and your community. Across America, the laws on keeping wildlife as pets are a confusing patchwork.

Susan Frechette and her deputies lobbied for a much more extensive list. They presented the legislature with almost two dozen animals they wanted to keep out of private hands. The initial list of those "pets" they proposed to ban makes impressive reading, but such a comprehensive ban was rejected by lawmakers. Thanks to that rejection, if you live in Connecticut, it presumably is still legal, for instance, to own tigers, servals, and caracals; you can still keep gorillas, chimpanzees, and orangutans; you can raise kangaroos, wallabies, and wolverines, hyenas, elephants, hippos, warthogs, cobras, pythons, crocodiles, Gila monsters, and Komodo dragons.

＿＞ ＿＞

American laws regarding the keeping of exotic animals are mixed. Federal authorities regulate imports and protect migratory birds and animals covered by the Endangered Species Act. The act also addresses the keeping of exotic animals for exhibition, entertainment, and breeding. State and local laws oversee pet exotic animals not considered endangered and vary from zero restrictions to the opposite extreme. The nuances are complex. A tiger born in the wilds of Asia is endangered and protected, for example, while one captive bred in Texas for a pet can be bought and resold in the

Lone Star State as if it were a common house cat. Some local communities have drafted precise, restrictive laws that limit and control the types of animals their citizens can keep. In other locales, it's a Wild West mentality, and you can unload Noah's ark on your private property. For some exotic animals—tigers, for example—a simple-to-obtain permit from the U.S. Department of Agriculture, in the absence of more restrictive local regulations, makes legal ownership a cinch. But those permits are required only of exhibitors, entertainers, traders, and breeders. The USDA does not regulate owning exotics as pets, and the federal Animal Welfare Act mandates that as long as an animal can stand and turn, a cage is legal for its home.[43] Often, unless there are complaints from neighbors or passersby, a live-and-let-live mentality prevails, and collectors keep unusual pets in our midst, undiscovered by overworked and understaffed animal control authorities. Until something goes amiss.

My reading of the statutes shows that West Virginia stands out as the only state with no rules regarding exotic species kept as pets. Wisconsin is just slightly less wild. The only restriction on exotics is that if they are brought in from out of state to be sold in pet shops, they must be certified as healthy. In Missouri you can keep a lion, tiger, leopard, ocelot, jaguar, cheetah, margay, mountain lion, Canada lynx, bobcat, jaguarundi, hyena, wolf, coyote, or any deadly, dangerous, or poisonous reptile as long as you register the animal with your local sheriff's office. In contrast, the ban in Hawaii is all-inclusive: It is unlawful to introduce exotic animals for private use into Hawaii, period. The atmosphere is changing nationwide. The trend is that lawmakers are writing restrictive regulations, especially as sensational encounters with exotic pets such as the Travis tragedy make headlines. But many jurisdictions that ban wild animals allow owners who already had their animals when the law was passed to keep them as long as the exotics live.[44]

It's hard for me to believe there is no accurate, national accounting of the cats, apes, snakes, and other exotics in private hands. Sanctuaries fill up with unwanted exotic pets. Removing a potentially dangerous pet to a sanctuary is no guarantee it won't cause problems. In 2005 two chimpanzees escaped their enclosure at Animal Haven Ranch east of

Bakersfield, California. They attacked St. James Davis, who was visiting another ape, a chimp that formerly was his pet. Davis barely escaped with his life, but he lost much of his face, along with a foot and his testicles, to the marauding animals.[45]

Breeding exotic animals is controlled under another set of laws, and breeding, too, differs radically from state to state. Breeders must obtain a federal license, but where they operate affects how they operate. In Alaska, for example, there are no restrictions on breeding. Colorado, Iowa, and South Carolina are among the other wide-open states. Texas regulates only the breeding of white-tailed deer (a host animal for the Lyme disease–transmitting tick); it's open season for anything else. There are so many captive-bred tigers in Texas that TRAFFIC and other worldwide animal welfare organizations estimate that there may be more tigers in Texas than there are wild tigers; some five thousand tigers is the figure TRAFFIC cites for the worldwide captive-bred population, more than twice the number thought to be wild.[46] There is no official captive-bred tiger census. No government paperwork records captive-bred tiger births and deaths. Arkansas regulates only wolf breeders. Vermont lawmakers expect citizens to simply do what's right. Laws there state that a person may obtain a license to propagate fish and wild animals if the application appears to be made in good faith. A quaint caveat: good faith. Good faith and a $50 annual fee.[47]

Activists concerned about animal welfare and public safety lobby for more restrictive laws. The independent Animal Protection Institute, for example, investigated private ownership of exotics in North Carolina, Ohio, and Washington. Study authors reported:

> *We uncovered the shocking conditions in which exotic animals are kept, the suffering they endure, and the inadequate and inappropriate care and treatment they receive, as well as the real threats that exotic animals pose to public safety. Especially troubling is the fact that the majority of instances of inadequate care and treatment did not violate any current Federal law or respective state law.* [48]

After the 2005 study was made public, some controls over exotics were established in Washington State. But no matter how restrictive the laws are in one state, it is easy enough to buy an animal elsewhere in the United States and move it to a state where breeding and possessing that species is prohibited, even if doing so runs a risk of federal intervention.

The Lacey Act, named for Representative John Lacey of Iowa, an early conservationist, dates from 1900. To quote directly from the law, it "makes it unlawful to import, export, transport, sell, receive, acquire, or purchase in interstate or foreign commerce any fish, wildlife, or plant, with some limited exceptions, taken or traded in violation of the laws of the United States, a U.S. State or a foreign country."[49] One of Lacey's campaigns was against the turn-of-the-twentieth-century fashion to adorn women's hats with bird feathers. In a passionate 1905 Waterloo speech to an audience composed of members of women's clubs from across his state, Lacey pleaded, "We have a wireless telegraph, a crownless queen, a thornless cactus, a seedless orange, and a coreless apple. Let us now have a birdless hat!"[50]

The Lacey Act is an all-encompassing piece of legislation, extensively used by law enforcement, and most recently amended in 2009. The law covers wild animals, dead or alive, even if born in captivity. Penalties are severe. Read the Lacey Act, and you may hesitate to picnic on the California side of Lake Tahoe if your hotel is on the Nevada side, on the chance an endangered field mouse hides in your picnic basket. It allows federal authorities to press charges against an ape lover who buys a baby chimpanzee in Missouri, for example, and takes it home to Connecticut. Keeping the chimpanzee, post-Travis, is now illegal in Connecticut even though breeding and selling it are legal in Missouri, where Travis was born.

If a potential owner of an exotic pet wants to stay on the safe side of the law, it is prudent to check with federal, state, and local authorities. Since counties and municipalities can restrict pet ownership in jurisdictions without statewide controls (even where ownership of animals is wide open, as in West Virginia), a myriad of laws can affect exotic pet ownership. Government agencies can exert their authority if an animal is dangerous or mistreated. But the real loophole in restricting exotic pet ownership is the freewheeling attitude in many jurisdictions to the captive breeding of wild animals. Why risk smuggling when you can breed exotics without violating the law?

"I don't think anyone should have them," Morrison County Sheriff Michel Wetzel said about big cats after a ten-year-old boy was mauled near Minneapolis by both a tiger and a lion. A Minnesota businessman had been showing them off to the boy and his father. Wetzel took a common sense approach to the law: "Just because you're legal doesn't mean you're safe."[51]

— ~ —

Finding exotic pets for sale is as close as your nearest computer with Internet access. Google *exotic pets,* and you can find almost any animal for a price. Along with the Internet offerings of exotic pets for sale are the pleadings from animal rights organizations, zoos, and—perhaps the most passionate example—former exotic pet owners: detailed lists of why big cats, great apes, and long snakes make poor pets.

For one-stop shopping, check out *Animal Finders' Guide,* a shopping periodical that promises to inform readers how "to humanely and profitably" raise captive wildlife.[52] The bulk of its twenty-four newsprint pages are filled with want ads, animals for sale. For the uninitiated, reading the advertisements is a window into the exotics world.

Here are some sample listings:

Bottle-fed female dromedary camel, great personality
Tame sloths, $1,500
Female kinkajou, hand raised, nine months old, $1,200
Grant's zebra bottle babies ready now, $2,000–$4,500
Group of spider monkeys: nice friendly monkeys, $24,000 for all
Common marmosets—potential breeders, $3,000 per pair
Wanted—Egyptian fruit bats
Slightly older bottle baby male serval still in house, sold then buyer
    flaked, special price $1,200, 3 months old
Red kangaroo, healthy, six months old, bottle baby male, $2,500

Animal Finders' Guide editor Pat Hoctor offers stream-of-consciousness advice in his "Message from the Editor" column, from reports on his personal health to etiquette advice for those attending animal auctions. "This is a brotherhood (and yes, sisterhood) of animal lovers—not animal rightists," he writes in the September 2009 issue.

We work hard to care for and protect our animals so they might have the best quality lives possible. Why? We wouldn't be in this business if we didn't love being around animals. We are smart enough to know that if we don't give our stock good care they will be sickly, be poor producers, any offspring of weakened animals will be sickly, the animals can't give us good quality enjoyment when they feel bad, and it is just plain bad and evil to make anything suffer when we have the ability to make it feel better.

It's hard for me to imagine anyone walking down a Stamford street with a leashed kangaroo or a rhinoceros—both still legal in Connecticut—but then the image of Travis in bed with his owner sipping wine out of stemmed glassware is a stretch as well. One thing we do learn fast in the journalism game is that for pretty much anything we can imagine, some-one, somewhere has done it or wants to do it. Nor are journalists neces-sarily exempt. Indeed, I'm guilty of the lure of the animal weird myself. On assignment years ago in Florida, I had a half day free and meandered east from Miami out on Alligator Alley to the Miccosukee Indian Vil-lage and its roadside attraction: alligator wrestling. I stood with a sparse audience watching what was not so much a fight as it was a process of the "wrestler" manipulating the long, mean-looking alligators. It was impressive, and I sure had no desire to try it. Despite their courage and expertise, the showmen (and women) do get bitten. I confess to buying my youngest son a key chain adorned with a severed baby alligator foot, a trinket that he made good use of by showing it off to his grammar school classmates. Later I read a neat analysis of the qualifications for alligator wrestling. "You have to have your heart in it. You have to be very patient," said Jimmy Riffle, a wrestler at the Miccosukee tourist trap since he was twelve years old. But that's not all, he deadpanned. "It also helps to have a low IQ."[53] Alligator and crocodile lore is pervasive (alligators show off a U-shaped snout; for crocs, it's a more pointed V shape—both employ sharp teeth), with perhaps the most common myth being the toilet tale. The usual scenario has it that alligator babies brought back to New York from Florida vacations are flushed down the toilet when their owners become disenchanted with them. In the New York sewers, they thrive, grow, and multiply. The horror stories conclude with the gators resurfacing in Manhattan bathrooms, threatening to bite New Yorkers when and where their bare anatomy is vulnerable on the toilet seat.

Not to worry. There's no truth to the urban legends, according to Barbara and David Mikkelson, who run snopes.com and are the leading popular debunkers of urban legends, at least now that the University of Utah–based folklore expert Jan Harold Brunvand is retired. Professor Brunvand, author of the seminal work *The Vanishing Hitchhiker: American Urban Legends and Their Meanings,* directed me to snopes.com when I asked him about New York's rumored rogue alligators. The Mikkelsons quote a chief of design at New York's Bureau of Sewers. "I could cite you many cogent, logical reasons why the sewer system is not a fit habitat for an alligator," is the assessment from sewerman John T. Flaherty. "Suffice it that, in the twenty-eight years I have been in the sewer game, neither I nor any of the thousands of men who have worked to build, maintain, or repair the sewer system [have] ever seen one."[54]

Crocs and gators do show up in unexpected places, however. On an EgyptAir flight from Abu Dhabi to Cairo in the summer of 2009, for example, a baby alligator about a foot long slipped out of someone's carry-on (how did it get past security?) and took a stroll around the cabin, scaring screaming passengers. Crew members caught it, and no one claimed it. EgyptAir gave it to the Cairo zoo.[55] Life imitates art: The flight brings to mind the 2006 Hollywood thriller *Snakes on a Plane.* One of actor Samuel L. Jackson's lines in the movie (he played the FBI agent Neville Flynn) could have been swiped from federal biologists working to keep

Burmese pythons out of the Florida Keys: "Everybody, listen up! We have to put a barrier between us and the snakes!"

— —

"Where is the line?" I ask Susan Frechette. "How do you distinguish between an animal that we would consider domesticated and an animal that we would consider wild? Where is the line separating animals we would consider safe for neighborhoods and families from animals that are potentially dangerous?"

"I'll be interested in reading your book," was Frechette's initial response to my query before adding, "because those certainly are lines people interpret differently. It's a tough one."

It's fascinating to watch as different people observe the same animal, some embracing it as a lovely pet, others wanting to make it illegal and a dangerous threat. Reminds me of the gun ownership debate—except that many animals somehow do make decisions; firearms don't.

"Some people feel as long as they're responsible, they have the right to have anything they want as a pet," Frechette says, but she is of the better-safe-than-sorry school of government regulation. "There are a lot of responsible pet owners out there, but all it takes is one incident. I understand a child was killed by a python recently." (She was referring to the now infamous Florida case.) "All it takes is one incident like that, and it gives people pause." Now I'm thinking about all the idiots with driver's licenses. Do we outlaw private car ownership in an attempt to save the fifty-thousand-plus lives lost on our highways each year? But Frechette is contemplating her amnesty day clients. "There were clearly a number of people who had gotten in over their heads in terms of 'Oh, he was so cute when I got him, and now he's so big,' or 'Now he's more aggressive.'"

Perhaps a compromise is to hold regular amnesties. Not necessarily a good idea, Frechette explains, as she again laments that no one turned in illegal big cats or long snakes beyond the lonesome rattler. "If you create a situation where it becomes easy for people to dump a python, they'll go out and get one without really considering the consequences. That's one aspect of this we're still trying to wrestle with. We're very cautious about aiding and abetting people who want to go out and buy a caiman because they can always dump it if it gets to be too much." It's a delicate balance. If regulations become more stringent, there's always a chance the black market trade will become stronger and harder to control.

At home, Susan Frechette is not burdened by such concerns. She shares her place with a dog, three cats, and the occasional garter snake that sneaks into her pre–Revolutionary War house from her garden.

CHAPTER FIVE

Stop Cat Sales

Tippi Hedren's Second Career

IT's A FOGGY FOURTH OF JULY IN BODEGA BAY, A THICK, WET FOG, THE KIND that leaves the deck damp. The night before we watched our local fireworks display. The pyrotechnics were set off from across the bay, many of them disappearing up in the fog clouds, exploding to make the translucent fog glow red and blue and a stark white—the booms, as always, scaring Schrödinger the cat. Later this morning I'll walk down to the Tides and stand in line with the tourists seeking autographs of the actress Tippi Hedren; I want to talk with her about her sanctuary for wild cats.

Tippi Hedren starred in Alfred Hitchcock's *The Birds*—the iconic horror movie shot on location in my hometown, Bodega Bay. Many of the famous scenes still are easy to identify in my neighborhood, essentially unchanged in the almost fifty years since the film was made. Hedren now operates a reserve for big cats. Once a year, practically in my backyard, she holds court in the Tides restaurant, looking out on the bay where her character was struck bloody on the head—the first bird attack seen in the film. There she signs photographs of herself for a price, the money raised going to support her work providing a refuge for lions and tigers no longer of use to circuses and moviemakers, or of interest to pet owners. Her Shambala Preserve, home to as many as seventy big cats, is also meant to "educate the public about the dangers of private ownership of exotic animals."

Hedren has married her celebrity status to her animal rights activism. She embraces her acting career and the notoriety it continues to bring to her, reveling in the adoration she receives as a former Hollywood star. And she works that attention to her animals' advantage at events like the Tides appearance, raising money along with Shambala's public profile.

Shambala was founded in the early 1970s by Hedren, and the preserve is spotlighted by celebrity and supported by donations. Loni Anderson, Bo Derek, Ken Howard, and Lilly Tomlin are among the long list of notables on the advisory board. Some funding Hedren solicits at grassroots events such as the one at the Tides. Patrons with deeper pockets are invited to "adopt" a specific cat and send a monthly stipend to help defray the cost of its upkeep. High rollers can donate $3,000 and in exchange relax with Hedren at the preserve while eating a gourmet dinner, then sleep in a safari tent at the preserve, serenaded through the night by the roars of big cats (all safely contained behind secure fencing, of course). Consulting veterinarians provide Shambala the expertise and guidance needed to maintain the cats' health.

Fourth of July 2009 I find a half dozen Hedren fans lined up at the Tides in anticipation of her ten o'clock arrival, anxious for her to sign an eight-by-ten glossy publicity photograph from the film. Their $25 fees will serve as a donation to Shambala. This is not the ramshackle Tides made famous in the movie. In the 1990s it was rebuilt into a glitzy tourist mecca that looks more like an airport departure lounge than a fisherman's hangout.

CNN is droning in the lobby as I take my place in line. I glance over at the TV screen, and the story is about the toddler strangled a few days before in Florida by a Burmese python. The latest developments: The snake's owner is expected to be charged in the death, and neighbors are telling reporters that, prior to the attack, they were worried about the dangers posed by the python. Another chilling 911 audio recording offers instant insight into the terror of the moment. "The baby's dead!" The caller is both sobbing and screaming. "Our stupid snake got out in the middle of the night and strangled the baby! She got out of the cage last night and got into the baby's crib and strangled her to death." Pictures flash on the screen of the eight-and-a-half-foot-long snake being removed from the house—nothing compared with the really long Burmese pythons on the loose in Florida. Burmese pythons are not native to Florida. They've come to the Sunshine State as exotic pets. Many escape or are let loose by owners who can't deal with them as they grow, and they thrive in the Florida wilds, really thrive. Who can blame the errant owners for not wanting the adults around? These snakes can reach over twenty-four feet in length and weigh in at over two hundred pounds.

Another television is set up in the lobby playing *The Birds*. As I wait in line, I look over at the Tides Fish Market and see lobsters, their claws banded, crawl along the floor of their tank/cage. By now another half dozen fans are in line behind me. One of Hedren's handlers looks at her watch, and another comes over to our line, where conversations are politely hushed.

"She'll be here in a few minutes," the handler announces. "Could I ask you when she walks in the door to scream and holler? She loves it! We do it every year."

Moments later Tippi Hedren walks into the ordered applause and a few whoops. She looks great at seventy-nine, just an older version of Melanie Daniels (the San Francisco socialite she played in *The Birds*), in designer jeans and a brilliant red sweater with a stars-and-stripes Louis Vuitton scarf around her neck. A gold brooch is pinned to her sweater: three soaring birds. She sits down in front of posters from the movie and begins her workday, happily signing one picture after another. She signs with care, checking the spelling of fans' names. The guy in front of me asks her to sign his "To Roberto with all my love." She looks at him and she signs, "To Roberto with (almost) all my love," and they smile. She adds a squiggle after her signature, the sign of a bird in flight. Throughout the weekend, the line of fans buying photographs and autographs in support of Tippi's sanctuary is nonstop. I say hello, show her my butterfly book, tell her I'm now writing about the abuse of exotic pets, and request that we get together after her day of work to talk. She suggests a glass of wine at five that afternoon.

We meet in the Tides bar, she sipping a glass of something white, I a Pinot Noir. After seven hours of signing publicity pictures and smiling for photographs with her fans, Ms. Hedren—as I now feel compelled to call her—shows no sign of flailing energy. On the contrary, she is anxious to talk about her cause. I suggest it is understandable that fanciers are lured by the idea of owning a big cat. She agrees.

"They are lured by many reasons," she says. "One is that they are magnificent animals. Another is that it is so easy to buy a lion or a tiger in the United States."

Despite my earlier investigations, I still find myself surprised by her statement. It's only logical to assume that something as fierce as a lion or tiger would be well regulated. But of course we can buy just about anything we want in this country—legal or illegal. The real surprise is that so much of the big cat trade is legal. Although there are some restrictions in some places regarding cohabitating with an exotic pet, there are no laws unilaterally across the United States that prohibit the selling and buying of lions and tigers. Yet by definition, since these cats are apex predators, they do not seem an ideal choice for a pet.

Too often, no matter the animal, humans don't think about the future when they choose cute baby animals as pets. "They don't investigate," Hedren says, taking a sip of her wine. "They don't do any research. Very often you hear," she says about frustrated owners, "'Oh, I got this little dog at the pound, but I didn't realize it was going to be so big, and I don't want it anymore.' When you get into lions and tigers, there's hardly anything cuter. They are cute."

But it's not just cute that fuels the big cat pet trade.

"They might feel that they want to master the beast. They may not even realize that this is going to be a four-hundred- to five-hundred-pound animal, with very sharp claws, very big teeth, an appetite, and instincts that never can be removed," she says. Hedren is petite. As she speaks about the enormity of the cats she cares for, her size makes them seem even larger in my imagination. I think of her sitting, recently, with two of them—albeit with the cats caged.

Michael Jackson died just days before she and I talked. When he shut down his private zoo at Neverland Ranch, Hedren brought his two tigers to live out their captive lives at Shambala. When he died, she broke the news to Thriller and Sabu. "I went up and sat with them for a while and let them know that Michael was gone," she told reporters. "You don't know what mental telepathy exists from the human to the animal. But I hope they understood."[56] While she held the attention of a news media anxious for Michael Jackson sidebars, she lobbied for her pending pet legislation: a federal ban on the private captive breeding of big cats.

Federal protection of species other than humans exists, of course, depending on the animal. We're looking out on the pristine Bodega Bay, and it's a picture postcard day. The seals and the sea lions frolic just outside the Tides bar windows, protected by the federal Marine Mammal Protection Act.

"What is that animal going to need?" Hedren is musing again about irresponsible pet owners making impulsive decisions to buy big cats. "What is it going to cost? You have to have a very secure area for these animals to be safe—for the human and for the animal. They eat an enormous amount of food." She smiles quite sweetly and says to me, "You know, it's like putting a loaded pistol on your coffee table. Maybe nobody will pick it up. But who would take the chance?"

Owning a big cat is legal in many states. In those states, she says with disgust (and a dose of Hollywood hyperbole), "it's probably more difficult to get a license for your dog than to have a lion or a tiger living in your backyard. This is craziness because these animals have injured and killed so many people." Her eyes grab mine as she continues to preach. "This is insanity. This is something you can prevent. This is something that can be stopped." Tippi Hedren knows about the dangers firsthand. Working with big cats on the set of her movie *Roar* motivated her to create Shambala.

There is a toll on humans who keep big cats as "pets," but it's the animals that appear the real victims, spending their long lives confined to relatively small spaces. "It isn't fair," she tells me. "There is not one thing that we can give a wild animal in captivity that they need." Hedren's voice rises as she exclaims, "Nothing! Whether it's a squirrel in your backyard or a Siberian tiger, there is nothing we can give them that they need." Her point: By definition, wild animals ought to be finding their own place to live and arranging for their own dinners.

The big cats traded as pets are bred in captivity, but the wild is not bred out of them. "There is nothing you can do to take that wildness out," insists Hedren. Nonetheless, you can buy one today. Just look on the Internet, she tells me.

"How much will I need to spend?"

"Whatever you're foolish enough to pay. I've seen them for $300 or $400 at the swap meets to $24,000 on the Internet. Whatever you're foolish enough to pay," she says again.

—— ～——

I did as Tippi Hedren suggested and punched in a simple "tiger for sale" Google search. She was correct; in an instant I was confronted not only with solicitations, but also with conflict.

The first hit offered a "young tiger for sale." The cub was listed as one year old, "female, housebroken, and gentle." The sticker price was a cool $28,000. I clicked on the site for more details and learned only that it was a Bengal tiger. A close-up picture was posted showing a decidedly sad-looking magnificent cat peering at the camera through cyclone fencing. For more details there was a form for me to fill out that required my e-mail address. I was advised that I must be over eighteen years old to inquire.

The second listing was headlined "Siberian tiger for sale," but it was a ruse. When I clicked the hit, I was offered photographs of cats with this warning: "Do not seek a Siberian tiger for sale as they need conservation; their pictures can be taken either in the wild or in zoos." The admonition was illustrated with the photograph of a tiger, its jaws wide open, showing off its mouthful of serious teeth—especially the long and sharp canines.

I found a story from the McAllen, Texas, newspaper, *The Monitor.* Reporter Ryan Holeywell joined police as they stopped the sale of six Bengal tiger cubs in a Wal-Mart parking lot near Jackson Avenue and Expressway 83—some costing over $5,000 each. There, Holeywell wrote, "a group from Spring Hill Wildlife Ranch in Bryan was selling the cubs—four white ones and two orange ones." These cuddly babies would grow to some nine feet and over five hundred pounds. Owning them in Texas can be quite legal. The Wal-Mart bust occurred because authorities were convinced the buyer was a Mexican national who intended to transport them across the international border. Even though the cubs were captive bred, they are an endangered species, and carrying them into Mexico required special permits that neither the buyer nor the seller was able to show police.

The next tiger I found for sale was announced in a story reported by the Spokane television station KREM. This was no baby. The Bengal tiger in question was nine years old and carried a $20,000 price tag. Weighing in at 350 pounds, Lilly goes through five to ten pounds of meat daily, the price of her care and feeding substantively adding to the amount of the investment.

Curious about Lilly, and a few weeks after my drink with Tippi Hedren, I make the trip to Oldtown, Idaho, to her current place of residence, the Newport Feed and Pet Company. I find a no-fooling country feed and pet store—bales of hay piled up outside the front door and cages of rabbits stacked on the sidewalk.

On the front door is a sign reading ATTENTION! THOSE WHO WISH TO DONATE FOOD FOR LILLY: WE ASK THAT YOU PLEASE ONLY DONATE THE FOLLOWING MEAT PRODUCTS SUCH AS BEEF/CHICKEN/PORK/VEAL/ELK/ETC. PLEASE DO NOT GIVE US: FISH/PRODUCE/LARD/SEAFOOD/BREADS. PLEASE LIMIT YOUR DONATIONS TO MEAT ONLY! WE DISPOSE OF ALL OTHERS IMMEDIATELY. LILLY HAS NO INTEREST IN THOSE ITEMS OR CANNOT HAVE THEM. THANK YOU FOR YOUR CONSIDERATION. In the front window a T-shirt is displayed for sale emblazoned with the store's name and address and Lilly's picture. T-SHIRT SALES WILL HELP BUILD AN OUTSIDE PEN AND KEEP LILLY HEALTHY, reads another hand-lettered sign.

Produce is for sale in boxes out near the rabbits. Big red, ripe tomatoes, $1 a pound; $3 a pound for the bell peppers; 50 cents a pound for the apples. Inside, the store shelves are filled with feed and pet supplies. A steady flow of customers keeps the shopkeepers busy hauling hefty bags of feed. Another sign reads PLEASE DON'T TOUCH THE ANIMALS. Kittens are labeled $8.99. Cages are $2.99, or "free with the purchase of a small animal," for example, gerbils at $10 and "common mice" for $2.50 each. A steely-looking mountain horn lizard is $30. I continue to wander through the store. My host, owner David Vanderholm, is busy with customers and so invites me to tour the place while I wait for him.

A sun conure, its feathers bright and golden, is eating in its cage and available for $300. It's labeled as being male, very friendly, hand-raised. Sun conures and other parrots are big business. After dogs and cats, parrots are the most popular pets in America. They live long, they're smart, and they talk. Poaching and smuggling for the pet trade are pushing some parrots to extinction, while captive breeding is flooding the marketplace with others. In her book *Of Parrots and People,* Mira Tweti tells of her own love affair with the birds while chronicling one ghastly story after another of abuses in the parrot trade. In Baja California, for example, she stops at a store in Rosarito and reports, "It's a horrible sight. Parrots of all kinds in filthy, rusted cages with feces-filled drinking bowls and no food or little seed scattered along the bottom, resting in feces. The birds, all without shade, sit in the blazing sun."[57] What she saw makes the conditions at Vanderholm's store look idyllic.

Lovebirds are for sale for $75 for blue and $60 for green.

They look passive in their cage, and their label advises VERY FRIENDLY. The sign on the cage promises HAND RAISED. They sing and look soft and lovely, their feathers showing off a variegated blue or green. A fellow walks by and tells me he raises his own lovebirds and hand feeds the babies. "They only stay friendly if you keep handling them," he tells me. "They go wild pretty quick." As do we all, I'm beginning to think, as I continue to wrestle with a litany of terms and how they interrelate: wild, domesticated, tamed, feral.

In a tub is a three-month-old potbelly pig, wagging its tail, its nose sawdust covered from the padding on the floor of the tub. It's available for $75. I turn away from the pig and see Lilly. She looks back at me with a gentler look than I often get from my house cat, Schrödinger. Lilly, sedate and stately in maybe a ten-by-thirty-foot cage, is labeled FEMALE BENGAL TIGER. 9 YEARS OLD. $20,000. Another hand-lettered sign says that Lilly was taken from the wilds of northern China by poachers when she was a cub and that she was smuggled into the United States and declawed before the poachers were caught. The announcement informs the curious that the storeowners rescued Lilly through the offices of the U.S. Department of Agriculture to prevent her from being euthanized.

A little girl standing near me looks at Lilly through the cage wires and says to her father, "I wish I could pet her."

"We don't pet wild animals," he teaches.

"I wish we could buy her," the little girl says dreamily.

"She's not a toy," instructs her father.

"She has pretty eyes," she says.

"Yes, she does," he agrees.

Lilly is huge; 350 pounds is a lot of tiger. Among the gerbils and the mice, the lizard and the lovebirds, her sheer bulk is an awesome contrast made more prominent by the relatively small cage and her close proximity to us onlookers. She is confined behind two arrays of wire mesh separated by three feet. The second fence is to keep the curious from touching Lilly; no one's arm is longer than three feet. Nonetheless, attempts are made.

I watch as a teenage boy sticks his hand through the first line of defense, waves it, and taunts Lilly with a call of, "Bite me!"

Lilly, who moments before was sitting quietly looking at the admiring little girl, roars back at him and starts pacing in her cage. Lilly's owner, David Vanderholm, was with us now, freed up for a while from his workload.

"Is she mean?" asks the boy, as Lilly continues to roar.

"Only to you," says Vanderholm without indicating if he's joking or disgusted with the boy's antics. But Lilly does have her likes and dislikes.

"She doesn't like men with baseball caps, long hair, and facial hair." I'm somewhat in need of a haircut this day, never wear baseball caps, but haven't shaved since high school. He looks me over. "If you were to put on his baseball cap," he points to the boy taunting Lilly, "and let your hair grow a little longer, yeah, she'd be growling at you."

Why, he doesn't know. He and his family have kept Lilly since she was about six months old, he says. She's about ten years old as we talk. Perhaps the poachers who traumatized her exhibited the caps and hair. Vanderholm takes me over to a back corner of the store, pulls a couple of bags of livestock feed off a shelf for chairs, and we talk tiger. It's not just Lilly who is for sale. Vanderholm is joining the Border Patrol (Canada is a couple of hours drive north), and he's selling the store.

"You'll be keeping the Canadians out," I congratulate him on his choice of public service.

"That's right," he acknowledges the attempted joke, one he'll probably hear often once he puts on his uniform. "I was raised in here," he points to the feed and animals, and says the family business no longer challenges him. "A farmer comes in and tells me a problem, I can give him exactly what he needs almost every single time." Vanderholm graduated from college and went off to Ireland and South Africa to do missionary work for his church; he's Mormon. He speaks slowly and precisely, telling me how a family friend rescued Lilly, was going to use her in an act, but decided the training would be too arduous. He asked the Vanderholms to help out, and Lilly has been their charge since. She splits her time, he tells me, between the back of the store pen and a fenced acre in the countryside.

During his time in South Africa, David Vanderholm was a zoo volunteer. One of his jobs was to feed the tiger cubs, an experience that led, he says, to the U.S. Department of Agriculture licensing him to keep Lilly. I was skeptical. USDA exotic animal exhibitor licenses are notorious for being simple to get. Many pet owners circumvent local pet restrictions by obtaining a USDA exhibitor's permit.[58] "She's here because she was going to be euthanized," he explains, and not as a watch cat as some news reports suggested. The $20,000 price tag was slapped on the cage, he tells me, in response to the continuing complaints he was hearing from critics who claimed he was abusing Lilly by keeping her in the back of the store. "No one is buying her, and no one should be buying her. If someone were to come in and say, 'Hey, I want to buy her,' they would have to go and get a USDA license, and it would take them about six months to a year to do so." Not according to People for the Ethical Treatment of Animals (PETA). The animal rights organization insists licenses to keep and display wild animals are easy to procure. In fact, such licenses *are* easy to obtain. Aside from a pile of paperwork, the USDA requirements are minimal.

The FOR SALE sign, Vanderholm tells me, is a first response to those who think they can care for Lilly better than he does and who believe that keeping her in a small pen is abuse. The critics may be well meaning, he says, but they don't take the time to understand the care he provides. "By putting that sign up, I gave all those people an option. I say, 'Here you go. If you really want to do something about it, then do it. But if not, leave us alone, please.' We haven't had any problems since I put that sign up."

David Vanderholm's smile is warm, and his eyes bright blue. He's wearing a T-shirt exploding with tigers. He's a clean-cut guy with short dark brown hair and, of course, no beard. Lilly would not like that.

He did get a couple of what seemed like serious offers, one from a local neighbor and another from a collector in Wisconsin. But he doesn't expect a sale. PETA hopes there isn't one. Lisa Wathne, PETA's captive exotic animal specialist, sent a letter to him after she spotted news reports about Lilly. "Although you clearly care for this tiger," she wrote, "life on display in a cramped cage can never provide her with the space and privacy that tigers need." Wathne suggested a sanctuary life for Lilly, "with grass, trees, and fresh air as well as opportunities to swim and roam," a move PETA would help arrange. "The chances you'll be successful in finding a buyer for Lilly are exceedingly slim. At any given time, dozens of tigers—including cubs as young as twelve weeks of age—are available for little to no cost to anyone who will take them."

⁓ ⁓

When I contact PETA's Wathne, I tell her I'm fascinated by the complex controversies I'm finding as I probe the exotic pet trade. "It's a real can of worms," she says. I like the animal metaphor; it's appropriate coming from PETA. Wathne works from Seattle, and her concern for the treatment of animals dates to the days during her early twenties when she worked as a volunteer at the Seattle Zoo. "Zoos," she decided after two years on the job, "are nothing but misery for animals." She traded her zoo job for one with the local animal shelter and was again appalled by conditions she described as "abysmal." She calls her work with PETA—heading the group's activism regarding captive wildlife—a dream job, and she prosely-tizes with ease. "Anyone who thinks a wild animal enjoys being kept as a pet is delusional, and they're not looking at the situation from the point of view of the animal. It's ludicrous to assume that a private person, unless they are fabulously wealthy, can provide adequately for these wild animals." The cage in the back of the feed store looks small compared with the massive beast, but Vanderholm says Wathne is wrong; Lilly is happy in the quarters he provides for her, and the intimacy of the space gives her a sense of security. "People think tigers are wild animals that are constantly running, which is true in the wild. But if you look at the tigers, the only time they are running is when they have to eat. Lilly doesn't have to kill. If we turned her loose, she'd probably go up to the first human and lick his face. He'd probably freak out and shoot her. And all she was doing was saying, 'Hi.'"

"I could not disagree with Mr. Vanderholm more," Wathne tells me when I check in with her after meeting Lilly. Not only does she consider the cage cruel, she does not believe the story of Lilly's provenance—that she was poached from the wild in China and smuggled into the United States. The story doesn't make sense to her for two reasons. There is an active market for tiger parts in China, so she questions what would motivate a poacher to risk smuggling one. And captive tiger breeding in the United States is so prolific that tiger cubs are easy to procure. In fact, when I asked Vanderholm if he would introduce me to the family friend who gave him Lilly, he shrugged off the question, saying, "Brian" (he was not forthcoming about a surname) was difficult to contact.

"The idea that her being in a small cage makes her feel more secure is simply ridiculous," is Lisa Wathne's analysis. She cites a 2003 Oxford University study as proof that wide-ranging carnivores fare poorly in any type of captivity—especially tigers, which roam hundreds of miles in their natural habitat. She rejects Vanderholm's claim that Lilly is happy to sit in her cage-apartment since she doesn't need to chase prey. "Go back to their basic inherent instincts," advises Wathne, and appreciate that "tigers need to roam. When they're kept in captivity, they suffer miserably. That's why, when you go to zoos, you see tigers pacing. They develop neurotic behavior and pace constantly."

Brian, in fact, was not difficult to contact. A public records request to the Idaho Department of Agriculture resulted in a copy of a Deleterious Exotic Animal Declaration Form filled out for David Vanderholm's father on March 29, 2003. It lists Lilly's age as three and a half years and Brian Staples as the source of the tiger.

I find Staples in North Carolina, where he is preparing a lecture for the International Wild Waterfowl Association's 2009 convention. He returned my telephone call after I left a voice mail message for him. Staples operates a company he calls the Staples Safari Animal Reserve and Rescue. He tours the country with animal shows and exotic animal petting zoos, provides exotic animals for movies and TV shows, and conducts programs with his animals for schoolchildren. While we talk on the phone, I hear a primate chattering in the background. It's Wilson, Staples tells me, a capuchin monkey.

"Lilly the cat did live with me for a very short while," he tells me.

"You owned the cat first, and then you turned it over to Vander-holm?" I ask.

"No," he says. "In this situation I was only the transporter." He says he acted as an intermediary for someone in Austin or San Diego—he can't remember which—who had arranged for the Vanderholms to obtain Lilly, and that he spent about a week with her en route to the feed store. "I thought I was doing a pretty ethical favor in taking the cat to another location. She was delivered to me, and I continued on up to Washington to deliver her up there." He hesitates, and says, "You turn an animal over, and you expect they have the staff and the education and the resources to take care of animals." He hesitates again before adding, "I've kind of fallen out of the loop, but I have suspicions that this facility up in Washington has got issues." He tells me he's not seen the feed store cage where Lilly lives. I describe it. "To have my name attached to something even questionable really puts me in jeopardy," he tells me. He hesitates yet again before saying what I initially thought was a joke, but he doesn't laugh. "I'd hate to be known as the guy who takes an animal into the lion's den."

"Vanderholm says the cat is declawed," I tell Staples. "Do you know when that operation was performed?"

"I sure don't," he says. "It's not legal to declaw a large cat, and it's sure not kind or ethical. They're too heavy. You put a cat that weighs four hundred pounds on tendons that have been severed, and you're going to cause premature arthritis or some other problems."

I tell Brian Staples about the signs at the feed store explaining that Lilly was poached and smuggled into the United States from China. I ask him if the story is credible. Wilson the monkey chatters again in the background.

"Goodness sakes," says Staples. "Who is going to catch a wild tiger and smuggle it into this country? I cannot imagine that was the case. Any animals I would ever come in contact with would have a trail of paperwork that would show their absolute origins. To consider taking a baby tiger cub away from a carnivorous mother, I would be absolutely amazed if that could ever be the case. If I had known that any story like this could have arisen, I would have chosen a much different place for that cat to go."

After we hang up, I search Staples's Web site. On the "Celebrities & Animals" page, he is shown leaning over a couch, bottle-feeding a tiger cub. Lounging on the couch with her arm cradling the cub is a publicity-posed blonde in a leopard-print swimsuit. The caption doesn't jibe well with the interview I conducted, even if the name is spelled differently—Lilly in the feed store, Lili on the Web site.

"Lili lounges around," says the headline, followed by this brief story: "WB's Angel star Julie Benz poses with Brian and Lili, a three-month-old Bengal Tiger Cub. Lili cannot be reintroduced to her natural habitat or even left among other tigers in captivity at this age as she was de-clawed before being rescued and cannot defend herself."[59]

I find it odd that Vanderholm and Staples both seem to stray from the truth. Why would they choose to deceive me? Perhaps there is further nefarious activity that they wish to keep from my prying eyes and ears. Or maybe they are so accustomed to being vilified by critics that they've adopted personas based on obfuscation. No matter their motives, I find their inconsistencies or lies make it impossible for me to embrace the rationales they offer for keeping their exotic pets.

U.S. Department of Agriculture records add questions to the Lilly story and are an example of how government officials attempt to keep track of the exotic pet populations. Their efforts often are in vain because owners do not comply with their requests, the authorities are understaffed, the law does not require owners to provide details about their animals, or a combination of those three factors. The USDA documents for a July 18, 2001, inspection in Clayton, Washington, where Staples was then head-quartered, found records that show

> . . . *an exchange or transfer of a 25# male declawed Bengal tiger from Mr. Staples to a person in N. Hollywood, Ca. on 12/1/00. There is still a young tiger at the facility in Clayton, Wa. and it is unclear at this point if the tiger from Texas is the tiger in Washington or if there were two tigers and one was 'exchanged or transferred' in California, in which case there needs to be an acquisition record for the second animal. There also needs to be a clear and unambiguous record of where the tiger now residing in Clayton, Wa. came from.*

If Lilly is that tiger that was in Clayton, a Washington State locale close to the Idaho–Washington border city of Oldtown, then the record—at least the public record—of where she came from is anything but clear and unambiguous.

Lilly draws the curious to the feed store, a phenomenon David Vanderholm has been witnessing all his adult life, and not just with Lilly. Throughout the store's history exotic animals have been on display: Monkeys, a caiman, and a zebra were in periodic tenancy. "I think part of it has to do with just the beauty of the animal," he says in an attempt to explain the draw. Using the animal to achieve social status is another part of his equation, or as an experience compensatory for being the victim of schoolyard bullying or to feel potency by controlling a killer animal—two more factors he believes lure some people to exotic pets. But those reasons don't define the appeal for him. "She's my little kitty cat," he tells me. "She's extremely friendly. I could open those doors and take you back in there; she'll jump on your shoulder and lick your face. It might scare you for a second. It scared me the first time," he says. "I go in there, and as long as I'm sitting there, she's as happy as can be. I can leave those gates open" (he points to the double doors of the cage) "the entire day, and she will not come out of that cage." His soft, slow voice belies the thrill he feels spending time with his tiger. "To be with an animal that is so powerful and yet so calm and loving and nurturing . . . " His reverie stops for an example. "We had a little, tiny puppy, and I have absolutely no idea how the puppy got into Lilly's cage. We didn't notice. It was on a Saturday. We're not open on Sunday. We were back here come Monday, and she had that little puppy cuddled up right next to her just like it was her own baby. Oh my goodness, the fit that she threw when we had to take that puppy away from her!"

The question emerges in my mind once again: What is the difference between wild and captive bred? "I don't think," Vanderholm says about his kittycat, "that you can ever tame a tiger."

"Even captive-bred tigers?" His Lilly supposedly was born wild, so there was no possibility the wild was bred out of her.

"Even captive-bred tigers. I've been around a lot of tigers, and there is a difference between wild ones and captive bred." Lilly was taken from the wild at such a young age, he says, she never learned to hunt. She never did the things a wild tiger does. Nonetheless, when Vanderholm enters Lilly's cage, he takes precautions. "I always have a short stick in my back pocket, maybe a little over a foot long. Ever since she was a baby, when she started becoming a little bit more aggressive, I'd just tap her nose with it and say, 'No teeth! No teeth!'" Even at 350 pounds, he's convinced she will always respond to the stick and the command. When Lilly is in heat, he finds her unpredictable. "Just like every other woman in the world, things change a little bit," he says with a quiet laugh. "She becomes more aggressive." Only her front paws are declawed, but she can grab. Still, Vanderholm says, at the sight of the stick, she backs off. He no longer needs to tap her now big nose, a nose situated right above her razor-sharp teeth. But in almost a decade, she's never broken his skin. She's bruised him up a bit when they've boxed, but that's because—he's convinced—she doesn't know her own strength, not because she wanted to hurt him. "She can do all kinds of damage if she really wanted to," he tells me. It's that possibility that keeps him cautious. "I never turn my back toward her when I'm in the cage. I never fall down when she jumps up on me. I'm always bigger than her, always taller than her. I'm her alpha male."

Being an alpha male doesn't mean swaggering into the cage as if you're in a Wild West saloon. "You don't just think, 'I'm Mr. Cool, Mr. Big Shot, and I'm going to get that tiger to do whatever I want.' That tiger will rip your head off if you try to do that." Showing respect results in gaining respect, he says. "She'd jump in front of a bullet for me. I could start screaming in the middle of this room, and she would go ballistic. If I had those doors open, and you hit me, and I started screaming, that would be it for you. Tigers are extremely protective of the people who respect them."

Vanderholm seems right that the wildness is ever-present, even in captive-bred cats. The 2003 attack on performer Roy Horn during a Siegfried and Roy Las Vegas show by one of the tigers Horn raised from infancy is an example. Even if the show's official explanation of the events that evening is accurate (that the tiger was trying to protect Horn by taking him back to its offstage cage), it still shows the tiger's wildness. "The first voice they hear is mine, the first touch they feel is mine, the first human face they see is mine," Horn says about his charges, tigers the show captive breeds and takes from the mothers soon after birth. "They just think I'm a strange tiger who walks on two legs."[60] Perhaps they do think he is just another tiger, but tigers kill each other.

Think of your house cat, suggests Vanderholm. "If you tell it to sit, and if it doesn't want to sit, it's not going to sit." That's certainly true in my household. Schrödinger won't sit, or do anything else, unless he chooses to do it. He can be purring and rubbing up against me one minute, and clawing at my bare foot the next. What sets him off? Who knows? Vanderholm's grandfather was killed by a charging bull while he was mending a fence. Why? He was not molesting the bull, but something made the bull respond to his grandfather's presence by attacking. There is wild potential in all animals, he and I agree, including humans. Perhaps maturity and civility among us humans can best be defined by our control of latent wildness.

But random attacks are not the rule with animals, Vanderholm insists, tigers included, as our chat leaves Lilly behind, and we grapple with philosophy and religion. "I believe animals were created to help men as a gift from God so we could use them to help us by plowing our lands, hauling stuff around, by eating." He pauses.

"Us eating them?" I want to clarify.

"Us eating them," he repeats, "not them eating us." The tiger sits quietly in its cage while we talk, more than capable, I think, of eating us were those doors open, no matter how confident Vanderholm is of her passive nature.

"You think animals were created for our use?"

"Some kind of a god or being created animals to assist us in our living," he says. Animals assist his family by living in the pet and feed business. But we're not without responsibilities in his scenario. "I believe God entrusts us to take care of them properly," he says.

From the Garden of Eden to Oldtown, Vanderholm's God is invoked to rationalize man's attempts to dominate other animals. Were I to preach to him and others who argue that animals exist for man's pleasure, I'd invoke lines from the Judeo-Christian literature, such as "Do unto others . . ." and "Thou shalt not kill. . . ." Give me a Hindu sacred cow over a hamburger any day.

Before we say good-bye, I suggest that David Vanderholm take Lilly with him when he signs up with the Border Patrol. No one will get past him. "I never thought of that!" he says, grinning at the image of Lilly on patrol. "I can say, 'Go get 'em, Lilly!'" It's quite an image, a tiger patrolling the Canadian border.

CHAPTER SIX

Who Belongs to Whom?

Philosophers Mark Rowlands and Peter Singer Weigh In

BACK FROM THE NORTHWEST, I'M EATING A BOWL OF OATMEAL AND DRINKING green tea, looking at the headline of the newspaper I just fetched from the driveway: "Palin quitting; next step unclear." As was the case when I delved into the dangerous world of butterflies and encountered them in the least expected places, so it is with forbidden creatures and humans who abuse them. One of the footnotes of Sarah Palin's failed flailing at the vice president's office was her hearty endorsement of hunters who take to the Alaskan skies in airplanes for the purpose of shooting wolves dead— supposedly to cull the wolf packs so that human hunters face less competition when they go after elk, caribou, and moose. Not only did Palin endorse existing Alaskan policies that allowed such aerial stalking and killing, under her administration's rules hunters who brought in proof of a kill—in the form of a left foreleg—were awarded a $150 bounty. Critics of the bounty went to court and stopped the payments based on a technicality: The governor's office did not enjoy the authority to make cash awards for dead wolves.[61] Her policy was another example of how wild animals are often exploited for human entertainment, in this case, blood sport.

Philosopher Mark Rowlands lived with a wolf for several years, an animal he bought after seeing wolf cubs advertised for sale in a local newspaper while he was teaching at the University of Alabama. The experience provided him insights into the relationships between humans and other animals. "If I wanted a one-sentence definition of human beings," he writes, "this would do: humans are animals that believe the stories they tell about themselves. Humans are credulous animals."[62]

His cohabitation with a wolf and his lifelong study of how we humans interact with other animals made me choose to add him to my itinerary when I headed across the country to Florida. I caught up with Rowlands at the University of Miami, where he ponders the moral status of animals. I wanted to ask him two questions targeting his experiences and specialties: How do we determine the line that separates wild and domesticated—does it really exist? And is it possible, as so many exotic pet owners insist, to know what is going on in the minds of other species?

"Right," Professor Rowlands says, then sits for a moment in silence, both his British accent and reserve on display. He repeats my questions, good academic that he is, to make sure he is clear about what I seek to learn from him. He's wearing shorts and a T-shirt, the shirt emblazoned with the legend SO GOOD SO RAD SoCal, as in Southern California. He's wide, built like a football player, with hair short-cropped on the sides and surfer-blond strands on top. His smile is wide and open, and it comes fast and with ease. Rowlands is convinced mental states can be attributed to other creatures: thoughts, feelings, emotions—not that we humans necessarily know what those thoughts, feelings, and emotions are. "Certainly it's possible, if you spend enough time with a creature, to work out what it's going to do, but then extrapolating from that to what's going on in its mind is a bit more risky," he says.

"But if we're crossing species lines," I ask him, "how can we even know that we're knowing what the creature is thinking?" Rowlands combines the intellectualism of an academic philosopher with the practical hands-on knowledge gained from years of living with and working with a wild animal. From the moment I join him in his sparse office in the Ashe Building on the sprawling campus south of downtown Miami, I feel as if I am in a graduate seminar.

The same problem exists human to human, he says, and we tend to rely on the behavior of others to judge what they're thinking. With humans, we can add speech as a tool to understand the thoughts of others. "But they can be lying," he pragmatically points out. "They could be deluding themselves." And there are things going on in our minds that are not necessarily reflected in what we're doing. "It's an instance of the same problem."

"Right," I agree. "You don't know what I'm thinking right now, and I don't know what you're thinking right now. You could be thinking, 'Ah, let's get this over with, I need to pick up my kids.' I could be thinking, 'I just need one good quote, and then I can get out of here.'"

"Exactly!" he says. He's smiling, but I don't think he wants to rush out of the meeting; he seems to enjoy the queries and the banter. I've been immersed in these questions from coast to coast and border to border; to jaw about them with a philosopher who specializes in them is a treat.

"It depends on how much time you spend with an animal," is the professor's take, "and even more importantly, the sort of time you spend with it." He uses a wolf, of course, as an example. If a wolf is confined by an owner in a backyard run, and interaction with the animal is limited to feeding it, it is unlikely that owner will know what it's thinking. "The more the animal becomes enmeshed in the rest of your life, that's when there is a possibility of mutual understanding."

The order of an animal is a factor in achieving some sort of cross-species understanding. Professor Rowlands with his wolf, even Sandra Herold with Travis the chimpanzee before he ran amok, are more likely to establish consequential communication with their animals than the guys parading a few miles from us along South Beach with Burmese pythons slung over their shoulders.

"Pythons," he considers them for a split second and concludes, "it's difficult to know if anything is going on there, if the lights are on at all." Dismissing the snakes, he cites a recent study suggesting that smarter dogs like collies and German shepherds show an intelligence about equal to a two-and-a-half-year-old human in terms of vocabulary and ability to follow instructions, a level about equal to great apes. "We have this idea that we're obviously the best" (his smile suggests he doesn't necessarily buy the argument), "and therefore the things that are closest to us have got to be the next best." But because dogs and humans have coexisted for so long, he thinks their intelligence may have developed in a manner that facilitates communication between us and them. "Whenever a dog comes across a problem it can't solve itself, the first thing it does is look at its owner's face. We've become dogs' problem-solving mechanisms, part of the dog's extended mind."

But there is no biological aspect to this dog–human relationship that allows for some understanding back and forth; it's an environmental connection. "There's more to the mind than biology," is Professor Rowlands's conclusion. "I think culture is just as important a part of the mind as is our biological nature." If that collie or shepherd looking for answers from its owner is abandoned on the streets of Tijuana, it becomes wild. I admire the view out the office window, the graceful, grass-covered quad, adorned with majestic cypress and palm. The landscaping is a direct result of Hurricane Andrew. Rowlands tells me it cut a swath of destruction across the campus, and government relief money procured replacement trees "to hide the ugly buildings." The same Hurricane Andrew is blamed by some theorists for the python plague in Florida: The storm damaged pet shops, zoos, and research facilities, allowing snakes to escape into the wild.

It does not surprise Rowlands that animals can seem content in habitat far from their natural homes, habitat like Lilly's pen in the back of the Newport feed store. "A lot of us have this idea that animals can only be happy and fulfilled in their natural environment. That's well meaning, but it's a subtle form of human arrogance. It denies that other animals can have the kind of flexibility in the way they live that humans have." He tells the story of a fox he witnessed begging for table scraps at an outdoor restaurant in England. Why should that fox be chasing rodents when easy pickings are available? "For the past few thousand years, England has not been the environment the fox evolved in. Animals, like the rest of us, are dealt a certain hand in life. They can play it well or badly. I think that fox was playing his hand quite well."

His is an intriguing argument, and I must admit, except when the arrogant teenager was yelling, "Bite me!" at her, Lilly the tiger acted content, nestled there in her cage. Not that Rowlands advocates capturing animals and exhibiting them in austere conditions. Referring to a wolf held captive in a concrete enclosure in a Spanish zoo, he says, "You can be pretty sure that wolf is not happy."

I tell him the story of my visit to the Heidelberg zoo, an experience that ended my ability to enjoy zoos. My wife pointed out the elephant in a tiny concrete cell, putting its foot on the spiked concrete that created a line between its quarters and the moat that separated the beast from us.

The poor, trapped elephant kept placing its foot on the spikes, testing the confinement, testing and testing, endlessly testing.

"I hate zoos," Rowlands agrees. "I think generally animals are not going to be as happy there . . . " He stops himself to adjust the word for an animal's feelings. "I think they're not going to be as *fulfilled* there as in the wild. Flexibility is limited. I wouldn't be happy sitting in a cage."

I ask him why he avoids the word *happy* when speaking of animals' emotional states and instead chooses *fulfilled*. "I'm not sure what happiness is," is his response. "We have this idea that happiness is a warm, fuzzy feeling. If that's what happiness is, I'm not quite sure happiness is particularly important in life. Whether an animal's life is going well or not presumably is not a matter of the number and intensity of warm, fuzzy feelings it has." What the fox was doing did bear some sort of relationship to its natural life. Therein, the philosopher figures, lies fulfillment. And whether it is a wolf or a dog or a wife, he says, if we wish to help them feel fulfilled, we can study them and then make a best guess of what to do.

"But your wife," I protest, "unlike your wolf and your dog, can speak to you and tell you exactly what she wants."

"Yes," he agrees with a smile and a dramatic pause, "but she could be lying."

Higher-order mammals, especially apes and humans, practice deception for individual gain, and in order to deceive, one must understand what is going on in the minds of others. Psychologists call such behavior the Machiavellian intelligence hypothesis. For example, you might look elsewhere when something interests you that you do not want a companion to notice because you know if you're obvious, this companion will become aware of the objects of your desires and may make a play for them at your expense.

Because great apes engage in deceptive behavior, Mark Rowlands is convinced they're a bad choice for a pet. "You can't trust them. They're manipulative, they're deceptive, and they're obsessed with power. They're too like us to make suitable pets." But deceptive personality is not the only reason Rowlands opposes human ownership of other apes. He considers them "persons." The rollicking exchange we're experiencing in the philosopher's sparsely appointed office is moving into intriguing new territory: chimpanzees and monkeys as persons. Persons he defines in a philosophical sense as "subjects who have things like hopes and fears and thoughts and expectations and beliefs and emotions."

"A lion sees a zebra running in the savanna, desires it, and chases it. Is that the work of a person?" I ask.

"I think all higher mammals are persons. Probably birds, too."

"Birds?"

"Yeah, I think so." A person, he says, further refining his definition, is a thing with mental states complex enough to believe and desire and feel. And it understands that there is a past and a future. His definition is compatible with the opinion I heard from fellow philosopher and animal rights advocate Peter Singer, that rationality, autonomy, and self-consciousness are the types of characteristics that make up a person. "When we elevate companion animals to the status of persons," writes James Serpell, director of the University of Pennsylvania Center for the Interaction of Animals and Society, "when we empathize with them and acknowledge their resemblance to ourselves, it becomes obvious that the notion of human moral superiority is a phantom: a dangerous, egotistical myth that currently threatens our survival."[63]

"Do you have pets?" I ask Professor Rowlands. I'm finding it a revealing query for the sources I'm questioning about exotic pets. I want to know why and where those with pets draw a line between their animal companions and the exotic pets that they consider inappropriate for others to obtain.

"I have a dog, yeah."

"And the dog is one of those higher mammals."

"Yeah."

"And you own this dog, and the dog does what you tell it to do."

"Yes," says the professor, patiently enduring my interrogation.

"But if I think you're kind of an interesting guy, and I decide I want to take you home to my wife and kids and keep you around the house to amuse us, that would be against your will, illegal, and hence difficult to accomplish."

"Yeah, yeah."

"So is there something inappropriate about your owning this dog?"

"It's a very good question," he responds. "I think about it in terms of guardianship. I own the dog in the sense that I paid money for it, but I don't think that's the fundamental relationship. It's like if I had a two-and-a-half-year-old brother and had to attend to him as best as I could. I think a two-and-a-half-year-old is a person, but it doesn't follow from that that I can let my two-and-a-half-year-old brother simply do whatever he wants, because I'm his guardian."

"If you say, 'Sit,' does the dog sit?"

"I do that because the type of dog that he is, he enjoys it." (The dog's a German shepherd.) "He loves doing things like sit, and then I give him a treat."

"Isn't that sit-and-I'll-give-you-a-treat relationship a reflection of your desire to exert power over an animal that could rip out your jugular if it wished? He sits just because you're going to give him a biscuit." I'm wondering how much difference there is between the professor telling his dog to sit and a drug trafficker keeping "pet" lions or Sandra Herold sipping wine with Travis the chimpanzee. Aren't these all examples of humans trying to dominate other species?

Professor Rowlands sits up in his chair, smiling and animated. His usual sotto voce delivery disappears, and he explodes with an enthusiastic "This is good! I like this!" He sits back, points out that treats for his dog are pieces of turkey, not mere biscuits, and explains, "When I had the wolf, I taught him to obey me because I needed to make sure he wouldn't hurt anyone, and he wouldn't get hurt. I taught him 'stay,' and 'don't move.' 'Out' was the most important; leave." But he's experimenting with his German shepherd when he trains him with treats offered for complying with commands. He's trying to determine if the dog is self-conscious, if he has thoughts about himself. Immanuel Kant wrote that self-consciousness comes first, and the ability to resist impulses comes second, and Rowlands the philosopher wants to determine if his German shepherd, a dog he already regards as a "person," might also exhibit the characteristics of a self-conscious moral being. He believes Kant made an error. "The ability to resist impulses comes first, and that is what gives you self-consciousness." If animals resist impulses, he theorizes, they can become moral creatures. "I think when someone says, 'That is a good dog,' it can literally be true, and it can't be true unless there is a primitive form of self-consciousness and an associated ability to resist impulses."

If these higher mammals can be conscious of themselves, that self-consciousness would seem to support my developing opinions about wild versus domesticated animals. The more time I spend with exotic pets and their owners, the more I question taming and domestication as nothing more than subjugation, when instigated by humans. Some evolutionists question our claim that we can domesticate other animals. Since domesticated animals are successful from an evolutionary perspective, perhaps animals that choose to be cared for by humans should get some credit for the roles they assume. Cats in Egypt, for example, found easy pickings in piles of stored grain that attracted rodents. The result was a symbiotic relationship: You keep the rats out of my grain, and I'll let you stay in my safe and comfortable house.

All of us animals, people and sheep included, no matter how well trained or how long in the service of humans, can turn wild. There is latent wildness in us all. Hence keeping big cats and great apes and long snakes will always be problematic. I personalize the issue for the professor. "One day you could wake up and decide the heck with the wife, the heck with the kid, the heck with the university, and just start walking west."

"Yeah. With that criterion, many humans are not domesticated," he says and cites his experiences with sheep in Wales. "Sheep become wild very quickly when they are not herded by humans."

What makes an animal break into wildness? Why does an individual change from being compliant and controlled to wild? Self-preservation is one reason. An abandoned dog or cat may well become self-sufficient in order to survive. The complacent Burmese pythons, happy to eat dead rodents while in captivity, wildly attack potential meals (even combative alligators) once they're on their own in the Everglades. Mark Rowlands offers dogs again as an example. If a dog decides it is the pack leader within a household, and its human companions object, the dog tends to exhibit wild reactions to the human challenges. Rowlands is quiet for a moment.

"Maybe this wild-versus-domesticated issue isn't as interesting to you as it is to me," I say, offering to wrap up our seminar.

"No, I think it's very interesting," he objects. "I wish I'd thought about it before, actually."

There is the distinct expectation that animals can be classified as either wild or domesticated, and I'm coming to believe, and Rowlands's comments only augment my stance, that the division is an error.

"We're not domesticated," he says, suggesting we're self-sufficient. He takes a swig from a plastic water bottle.

I disagree. "Perhaps we're self-domesticated," I suggest. "We're not self-sufficient. Where did you get that water? You have no ability to get your own water."

"Right," he says. "So we fall on the side of the cows."

"Yeah, we're docile and completely at the mercy of the Publix supermarket down the street, the paycheck, or the welfare office."

"Then domestication," he says, "applies at the level of individual animals, not species."

"Perhaps. Maybe every animal is wild. Within a species some individuals are called domesticated because they are, for the moment, subjugated. Each has the potential to become wild. And that," I say to my new philosophy tutor, who is being so patient with me, "is my working thesis regarding these issues I'm just beginning to grapple with."

"Hmmm," he murmurs, either being polite or considering it. "I'll be thinking about this domestication issue now. I probably won't be able to sleep." We agree to keep in touch and continue the seminar.

***

What is ethical for a human being to do with and to another animal? I posed this question to bioethics professor Peter Singer when I sat down with him in his quiet corner office overlooking the bucolic greenery of the Princeton University campus. Controversy follows Singer, and his appointment at Princeton resulted in demonstrations against him and the university. He was first noticed outside his Australian base in the early 1970s, when, as a young philosopher, he argued that those of us who live in affluent societies ought to reduce our standards of living to the point of subsistence and contribute the rest of our wealth to those in need, no matter where the needy live.

A few years later he became a spokesman for extreme animal rights when he published *Animal Liberation,* a book that promoted vegetarianism and argued that other species ought to be considered equal to humans. That book helped create the animal rights movement.

Singer grew up in Australia (his parents emigrated from Austria following Hitler's Anschluss), where he majored in law and then philosophy at the University of Melbourne; he continued his studies at Oxford. It was at Oxford in the early 1970s that he first thought through the philosophical implications of eating meat, choosing instead a life of vegetarianism. He decided it is wrong for humans to consider that other creatures should enjoy no basic rights, and that it is wrong for humans to believe that they are a species superior to others. He coined the awkward word *speciesism* for those who think other animals exist for humans to use as they wish, a practice he considers "species racism," and a practice he sees as unethical as believing one human race is inferior to another.

We talk about the hierarchy in the animal kingdom, and he makes it clear to me that he believes killing a human being is a greater moral wrong than killing a chicken—because of human potential. "I believe that it is worse to kill a normal, self-aware human being than a chicken," he says. "But I think that because of the capacity that the normal human has, not because one being is a member of the species *Homo sapiens,* and the other is not." In fact, Singer tells me, he believes that the continuing societal taboo against humans engaging in sexual relations with animals may be based on a human desire to separate ourselves from animals. "Condemning as criminal sex with animals is one way of preserving that separation. We want to elevate ourselves above others," he explains. "We want to be the pinnacle of creation."

But, I point out, from our perspective we are the pinnacle of creation. He accepts the argument.

"There's a case for saying that as far as we're aware, no other species has the intellectual capacity we have. That's probably true."

"Doesn't that make us superior?"

"On some level, yeah, that's true," Singer agrees. "We can look at things about the future of the planet that other animals can't." But he rejects a superiority that rationalizes our using animals for our own ends against their will. "That's not a reason for saying we have rights over them, that we can use them for our means, that their interests don't count, that simply being a member of our species makes us automatically more important than being a member of some other species."

Which brings us back to his position on bestiality, and I ask Professor Singer if gaining consent is the only device adequate for ascertaining if such interspecies acts do not constitute abuse.

"Clearly animals can't consent in the full sense that you would get humans to consent." He contemplates the issue. "But I suppose you can give them the opportunity to move away, to walk away. Then I would say if it continues to do it, it's consenting."

"So if you want to do it, and the animal wants to do it, there's nothing morally inappropriate about the act continuing?"

"Yeah. It's not to my taste, but I don't think it ought to be made a crime."

Consider the idea of consent in the context of animals captured, transported, sold and bought, locked in cages, declawed, devenomized, and kept far from their natural habitats for the gratification of their so-called owners. Hard to imagine—given the opportunity—that most exotic pets would give their consent.

CHAPTER SEVEN

Crimes for Pets

Roller Pigeons Attract the Fish and Wildlife Service

IT'S PROBABLY EASIER TO COME UP WITH A LIST OF ANIMALS NOT KEPT AS PETS than to compile a record of all the different exotic pets that are kept by fanciers. In fact, there may be nothing on a list of animals that hasn't been kept by private owners. While I crisscross America finding pet stories, I search for examples of ultra-exotic pets. It fascinates me when I discover something previously unknown to me, and it turns out to be a component of a vibrant pet subculture.

How about a white rhinoceros? South African National Parks put one hundred of them up for sale in 2007 to raise money for conservation projects. Full grown, these rhinos can weigh as much as a car, 4,000 pounds. That means they need to eat plenty, over a hundred pounds of feed a day, and that food generates a consequential cleanup task. Nonetheless, they would make for an unusual, if high-maintenance, pet, and certainly would make a conversation starter. "Rhinos actually become—I wouldn't say affectionate—but they certainly become very accustomed to being around humans," says Randy Reaches, who managed a herd of them at the San Diego Zoo. He calls them "trainable, quite intelligent" and says they "figure out things quickly."[64]

Prefer a kangaroo? Bobbie and Charles Kennedy had two, Sheila and Sydney. Until the animals were found dead in the Kennedy's Kingman, Arizona, yard in 2008—apparently killed by stray dogs—they were ersatz children. "If you ever sat down and fed a baby kangaroo, it's almost like feeding a fuzzy child," Bobbie Kennedy said about her companions. While they were babies, she carried them around Kingman in fabric pouches, to try to provide them with the type of comfort their mother would have offered. As a result of her pseudo-mothering, she became known as the Kangaroo Lady.[65]

Maybe a piranha? Practice caution during the care and feeding of these exotic pets, no matter how tempting it may be to show off animals like piranhas to easily impressed friends. Mark Rizzo was moving his almost foot-long diamond rhombeus piranha named Markov from one tank to another in 2006. Far from its native South American habitat, in East Lansing, Michigan, the fish tried to leap out of the transfer net. He put out his hand to stop it from jumping, and the fish used its razor-sharp teeth to bite off a piece of Rizzo's right index finger. "He got a hold of my finger damn well," Rizzo said after a trip to the emergency room for three stitches. "At first it was extremely painful. I think that a lot of it was due to the initial shock as well as seeing the skin and flesh dangling off and seeing blood literally spurting out as my heart beat, and just forming a large pool on the floor." Rizzo provided further graphic details: "He bit all the way down into my knuckle and broke the capsule my knuckle is in and chipped a piece of bone off it. The bite also went through the nerves and other stuff in my finger." Rizzo kept Markov after the incident, and he kept most of his finger.[66]

In the summer of 2009, U.S. Fish and Wildlife Service special agent Ed Newcomer arrested a husband-and-wife team, Isaac and Catalina Zimmerman, for illegally importing piranha into California, advertising them on the Internet for sale, and transporting them to customers outside California. When the cuffs clicked on the wrists of Isaac Zimmerman at his Southern California business, River Wonders, he complained to Newcomer, "I don't understand. What's the big deal? It's just a bunch of fish." Eight hundred twenty-seven piranha to be precise, according to the indictment. A bunch of fish becomes a big deal when federal law is violated. The Zimmermans faced multiple charges: smuggling, falsifying documents, and lying to federal law officers. But wildlife cops face a battle for credibility even with their peers. When Agent Newcomer booked Isaac Zimmerman, the Bureau of Prisons intake officer tried to joke. "What did he do," he asked Newcomer, "molest a turtle?"

A counterpoint to the stimulating deskbound philosophizing with Mark Rowlands came to me one evening in Los Angeles when Agent Newcomer invited me to join him on the stakeout and arrest of another animal trader he had targeted as an outlaw, offering me an opportunity to witness first-hand a predatory wildlife criminal. His exotic pets were birds known as roller pigeons.

The seedy Los Angeles parking lot of the McDonald's at Sunset and Western, an intersection strewn with trash, the restaurant grounds protected by a high fence from the street scene, was a locale crowded with a collection of characters actively engaged in what a friend of mine calls "skulking with intent to lurk." Newcomer was going to show me the type of surveillance work he does to build cases against violators of fish and game laws.

"Wear boots and grubby clothes," he warned.

For a year Newcomer had been working undercover, infiltrating Birmingham roller pigeon racing clubs. Roller pigeons get their name from the odd behavior they exhibit of falling and rolling in flight. Aficionados breed the pigeons to roll and fall as much as possible without crashing into the ground. During races, trainers get points for their pigeons based on the number and style of rolls they make while flying in circles with other birds. The trouble is, hawks eat pigeons, and when pigeons are rolling and falling, they look as if they are in distress and hence easy prey. There are some 250 roller pigeon racers in L.A., and during his investigation, Newcomer found only one who said he refused to kill the pursuing hawks.

Urban Los Angeles is home to a vibrant community of hawks. As Newcomer became one of the guys at the three pigeon clubs he joined, pigeon trainers freely explained the hawk problem to him. And they freely told him that they trapped hawks, shot hawks, poisoned hawks, and clubbed hawks. Newcomer set up surveillance cameras pointed at club members' homes and secured footage of his new colleagues baiting traps and catching hawks. They then shot or beat the hawks to death. He had pictures of them dumping the dead birds—with gunshot wounds or blunt force trauma—into their garbage cans, birds Newcomer and his crew gathered from the garbage for evidence.

I follow Newcomer's undercover car up into the Hollywood Hills, a short hop from the squalor of Sunset and Western to the multimillion-dollar homes with sweeping views of the L.A. basin. We park at a quiet corner, and Ed pulls on his bulletproof vest. It has a badge over the heart and FEDERAL AGENT in big, bright letters on the back. His semiautomatic pistol and handcuffs are on his belt. He stashes night vision binoculars in his backpack and briefs me on what to expect. We are going to hike a few hundred yards up a culvert that runs between the swank homes and then on up the hill until we're looking into the backyard of the national president of the dominant roller pigeon club.

"Since I've got the vest, if there's any trouble, just stay behind me," Newcomer suggests. His biggest concern is that we will stumble over a homeless person living in the culvert who will consider us to be trespassing on his property. But he mentions that if the homeowner sees us spying on him, it could turn ugly. We walk a half block down the sidewalk. During a break in traffic, Newcomer motions for me to follow him. He had already alerted the LAPD that we were in the neighborhood. If a citizen spotted the two of us prowling around the city, cops would know why. We scale a cyclone fence and head toward our prey.

It's a warm night with a cloud cover that reflects the city lights. "Keep down," Newcomer warns as we hike. We can see in the windows of the homes, and presumably the occupants can see us. "Try to be quiet," he says as I snap branches and stomp on discarded Styrofoam containers behind him. When we arrive at the backyard in question, Newcomer retrieves the night scopes. He eases up to the fence and looks over. No trap is where he had last observed one. He pans the yard and finds it, moved behind a tree. He motions me over, and I look through the binoculars. The night turns bright as day, and where he had pointed I see a wire mesh trap, waiting to snag a hawk. I give Newcomer a thumbs up, and we head down to the street. Each day he can witness a baited hawk trap, it's another criminal count against his club's president.

When we arrive back at the car, Newcomer pulls off his vest. "Was that fun?" he asks. This is a man who clearly loves his work, but it's not just the thrill of the chase; he loves the animals he protects. While he is packing up the binoculars, he glances across the street and points. His voice is excited. "Look! A coyote!" And sure enough, a scrawny coyote is ambling down the sidewalk, another example of the megalopolis–wildlife interface that is Los Angeles.

A couple of days later, Agent Newcomer and I meet again at Sunset and Western, this time just after dawn and accompanied by backup: other Fish and Wildlife agents, California Fish and Game wardens, and LAPD officers. Newcomer has his warrants, and we're poised to arrest the president of the National Birmingham Roller Club, Juan Navarro, for killing hawks. His easy smile is gone as he gathers his troops for a preraid briefing, filling them in first on the crime and then on his strategy for the arrest. Fish and Game specialists estimate about 1,500 hawks are killed each year by pigeon racers in Los Angeles alone. "Look for talons," Newcomer instructs, regarding evidence. Pigeon-racing hawk killers cut off talons as trophies and give them away as gifts; some hang them from their car rearview mirrors instead of fuzzy dice. Possessing any part of a falcon or hawk is a violation of the Migratory Bird Treaty. Navarro had bragged to Newcomer that he kills forty to fifty hawks a year, saying, "I don't shoot 'em, I hit 'em with a stick." He was concerned that gunfire would disturb his upscale neighbors.

The plan is to get up to the Nottingham Avenue house before Navarro leaves for the day. Our seven-car motorcade races up Western, past the Griffith Park entrance, and blocks traffic as we turn left onto Nottingham and up two blocks to Navarro's neo-Tudor house and its perfectly manicured lawn and garden. The LAPD officers jump out and secure the perimeter. Newcomer knocks on the front door, warrant in hand. "Police!" he barks out. "Open the door!" It opens a crack, and the surprised and scared maid says a soft, "*¿Qué?*" While agents flood the backyard and search, a Spanish-speaking agent convinces the maid to call Navarro. He says he'll be back in ten minutes. During the wait, Newcomer and his team locate the trap baited with a live pigeon and find a dead hawk in a garbage can.

"Here comes the Navigator," one of the LAPD officers calls out as Navarro's car turns onto Nottingham and comes up the hill. It pulls into the driveway, and a female agent, her badge and gun backing up the FEDERAL AGENT scrawled across her bulletproof vest, approaches the driver. "Are you Juan Navarro?" As soon as he says yes, she tells him, "You're under arrest." Handcuffed, Navarro—in an elegant sports jacket and slacks, looking bewildered—is led over to an unmarked Fish and Wildlife Tahoe and belted into the back seat. He appears shocked as she reads him his Miranda rights, complaining that he doesn't know why he is being arrested. "Migratory Bird Treaty violations," she tells him. Another female agent joins her at the squad car, and the two of them begin questioning him. Here we are just above Hollywood, and the scene is cinematic: two women agents giving the third degree to a confused and trapped villain, a villain accustomed to being in charge and instead cowering in fear.

I watch and listen as he meekly squawks excuses and denials to their queries about the trap and the hawks he caught. "I'm the president of the Birmingham Roller Club," he keeps saying. "Look at the Web site." But while he is insisting over and over again that any hawks caught in the trap he took out to the desert and released far from his pigeons, other agents had already dug into his garbage cans, where they found the freshly killed hawk. He was lying to federal agents; that's a violation of 18 U.S.C. Section 1001, a felony.

"Happy?" I ask Newcomer as the Tahoe pulled away, hauling the still shocked and pale-looking Navarro downtown for booking.

"Oh, yeah," he smiles. "We found a hawk in the garbage, and that's the quintessential body in law enforcement." He said he was sure his crime lab would prove the hawk was killed by blunt force trauma, as he preened again, "We have the body!"

Navarro pleaded guilty to sixteen counts of violating the Migratory Bird Treaty Act. His exotic pet roller pigeons were perfectly fair game to keep and train. But his decision to violate the law in order to try to protect them from predators was his downfall, an example of the lengths some enthusiasts go to pursue their pet passions.

Unfortunately, Newcomer's efficient experience securing a conviction for the raptor killings is more the exception than the rule. Law enforcement with regard to exotic animals is frustrating and difficult, handicapped by a number of obstacles. While drug smuggling attracts an enormous amount of well-funded judicial attention, the dollars and expertise devoted to wildlife crime are minimal by comparison. Only some two hundred special agents are on duty for the Fish and Wildlife Service, and the agency's annual operational budget is some $60 million. Compare that with over five thousand agents at the Drug Enforcement Administration and their $2.5 billion budget.

Evolutionary biologist George Amato is intent on helping to rectify the inequities.

— ~

The hallways behind the scenes at the American Museum of Natural History in New York City are perfumed with formaldehyde and lined with cases full of specimens. My guide opens a door to an office with a majestic view of Central Park. This is where evolutionary biologist George Amato is working on what he calls a DNA bar code—a tool that will help agents like Ed Newcomer and international border inspectors in their fight against illegal wildlife trafficking.

The idea is to create a data bank that can identify the specific DNA of protected species. Law enforcement officers out in the field cannot be expected to recognize all illegal animals and their parts. But if a sample of the DNA inspectors suspect may be from a protected animal can be compared with a sample known to be from that species, the guessing is over.

Dr. Amato's bright blue shirt, wide white smile, and Versace glasses add glamour to his enthusiasm for the project. Amato is a conservationist who envisions a near future when an inspector anywhere in the world can take a tissue sample from an animal and know in seconds if it is on the endangered species list. The DNA bar code technology already has been successful in identifying some illegal shipments of dead animals: whale, dolphin, and smoked monkey meats destined for someone's dinner table. The DNA bar code takes its name from the bar codes used by retailers because just as those refer to only one unique product, these are the markers of a unique species.

"Even with these methods of identification," Amato tells me, "this will never solve all the problems associated with smuggling." Of course, but the portability of the technology is a game changer. "The idea is to make this technology available at the point of origin, and you won't have to be a molecular biologist to manage it."

Amato is working toward his initial goal of a data bank identifying the DNA bar codes (nice that bar codes are also known as zebra stripes) for some five thousand endangered species, all available via the Internet and accessible from the field with a handheld DNA reader. "In a marketplace or a port, you could use a single hair or a scale or a feather—you don't need a blood sample—and be able to generate the DNA sequence. That information would go to the Internet, and you'd get your match."

He and his colleagues essentially designed an iPhone application for international wildlife cops, men and women often frustrated because they simply do not have the expertise to differentiate that which is legal from that which isn't, especially when the two look similar and are mixed together in a shipment. "We would be asking an awful lot of our agents to be the taxonomic experts on every group of organisms that might be part of the trade, including butterflies and fishes. We really needed a new way of doing this," Amato tells me. He smiles about the potential, calls it transformational, and says that while the science involved is exciting in its own right, he's thrilled that his work may result in the continued existence of various species. "We can make this, in theory, accessible to the whole world." And not just for police and scientists. He hopes hobbyists will take advantage of the data for amateur identification of backyard fauna and flora, and animal traders intent on obeying the law could use it to verify their purchases.

George Amato expects publicity about the accessibility of the DNA data bank will serve to dissuade some wildlife smugglers, but while the field devices are still in the research and development mode, law enforcement officers wishing to use his DNA library must bring samples to Amato's lab—or a handful of others involved in the project—for comparison against the DNA that he and his colleagues have already assembled in their growing collection. Within a few years he hopes to equip field inspectors with the revolutionary technology.

Before we say good-bye, I take a last look at the magnificent view of the park and notice a bumper sticker on Dr. Amato's wall. It shows the fish outline that is used as a religious symbol, except this one has legs and the legend WE HAVE THE FOSSILS. WE WIN.

CHAPTER EIGHT

Chimps as Children

Roberta and Her Apes

A 1996 DOCUMENTARY FILM BY FLAVIA FONTES, *LIVING WITH CHIMPANZEES*, followed Phil and Roberta (no last names are offered in the film), a husband and wife who live with two chimpanzees. The chimpanzees enjoy the run of the living room and the dining room, they wear little girls' clothing, and they are locked in cages at night, supposedly for their own safety. But Roberta admits early in the film that chimpanzees—theirs included—are potentially a threat to human life. "They are considered to be wild animals," she says about her captive-bred housemates. So why do she and Phil keep them? Solely for their own amusement. "We get so much joy from living with these creatures," Roberta says as she diapers one of them.

The couple cuddle the chimps, feed them at the dining table, give them colored markers to draw with and skates to roll around on in the living room—a room devoid of furniture and equipped instead with a trapeze and climbing ropes. "We had absolutely no idea what we were getting into," says Phil about their decision to cohabitate with chimpanzees. Insisting that the chimpanzees are not replacements for children (the couple has no human babies), they exhibit a strange element of control mixed with displays of adoration. "Want to go play in the trees today?" Roberta asks as she feeds one of the animals, then immediately adds, "Are you going to be a good chimp today?" The animal kisses her on demand and heads from the table. "Then stay right here," she tells her, chiding her with a control line so familiar to chastised children, "You're not listening." This is followed immediately by the demanding, if loving, "Hold my hand."

Roberta and Phil indulge the chimpanzees, but they also enforce their dominance of the two animals, constantly telling them what to do, usually for the amusement of the human primates. No question it is fascinating to see chimpanzees painting pictures and roller-skating with finesse. The two furry animals are indeed cute, with their big, round eyes and long lips, in part because of their humanlike qualities. They help each other take off their roller skates and socks with the same sweet clumsiness of a child. Perhaps the lure is that they act humanlike while they connect us with the wild that is missing from our own lives and remind us that we once were something else besides stuck in rush hour traffic on the freeway en route to eight hours in a cubicle pushing paper with the promise of a martini at the end of the day. "It's very risky to have them," Roberta muses while the film depicts the chimpanzees asleep in their cages. "I think they know how powerful they really are, and they know they could kill you. They are unpredictable. Even though we're very vigilant in terms of watching this behavior that could appear at any time, there's another element that I definitely sense, a certain love and affection that they have. They would never cross a certain line. I doubt that they would ever, ever attack me. I'm basically their substitute mom." Her soliloquy is followed by the candid admission, "I really believe this," and then, "I don't really know if it's true." But she ends her speech with renewed confidence. "I can sense that, with the love and affection they have, they would never hurt us."

"There's always the possibility of either chimp getting angry enough to fight with me or attack me," is Phil's analysis. "I don't think they would necessarily plan to do me real harm, but just because they're so much stronger." The scenes of dominant teasing and the talk of danger suggest Phil and Roberta don't just thrive on controlling the chimpanzees; there is a thrill for them as they ponder the danger lurking within their charges.

"They are something more complicated than an animal," says Phil, comparing chimpanzees with dogs and cats, "but not as complicated as a human. I do not want people to think that chimpanzees are pets, because they're not pets."

Phil is wrong. His chimps are his pets, pets he dominates and pets that dominate his life.

———

I contact filmmaker Flavia Fontes to learn from her more about her experiences with Roberta and Phil, and I let her know that I want to be in touch with the couple. Their chimpanzees must be grown. What is the endgame in their bispecies version of suburbia? Days later, my phone rings, and I'm surprised to hear at the other end of the line Roberta introducing herself. Fontes gave her my number and told her about my interest in her "family."

She informs me that she and Phil continue to cohabitate with chimpanzees, but that she is looking for a sanctuary where they can be moved. I ask her why she wants them out of the nest. "I really don't, but they are way too strong," she says. The animals no longer enjoy the run of the household. They live day and night in a cage, and mesh separates the cage, keeping the two apes from physically interacting with each other "because we don't want them to reproduce, and we don't want them to hurt each other." One of their original chimps died, and the couple felt compelled to replace her with another—a male—to keep the other company. Roberta's dream had been to create an outdoor paradise for the chimpanzees, so that they could exercise, maybe a place big enough so that she and Phil could create their own sanctuary. But the land they proposed to use was in New Jersey, and authorities there rejected their application for the special use permit that was required to keep great apes on the property.

Just rooming with two chimpanzees—never mind inviting more to join the clan—became more problematic after Travis ran amok in Connecticut. Neighbors and local government officials started asking more questions than before the catastrophic attack, worried about the neighborhood's safety. Behind the closed cage doors, Roberta and Phil try to keep life as normal as it ever was for the chimpanzees. The day before we talk, one of the chimps celebrated a birthday and blew out a candle to mark the day. The human apes and the other two apes were separated by the cage bars during the party, as they always are since the chimps have grown big and strong, for some ten years. Ten years in a cage seems cruel to me, but Roberta insists there is no other option.

She tells me her life is totally consumed by the care and feeding of the chimps, as is Phil's. "We're constantly playing with them and grooming them and cleaning them and making sure their TV is on the right channel and that they're comfortable with their blankets. Basically, we're offering them room service. We talk chimpanzee," she explains, "and they understand English." She offers an example of her side of a chimp chat. "What would you like now? Would you like a drink? Would you like this, would you want that?" Room service behind bars. "We have to do that. If we don't do that, we're not being responsible because these chimps are very strong." A radical change from the frolicking shown in the film.

The Travis incident "devastated" Roberta, who says she knew his owner, Sandra Herold. "She started early on to treat this chimp like it was her son," she tells me. "I offered her some advice. I said, 'They're not people. They're chimps. Don't get mixed up here. He's going to get stronger, and you have to have a proper environment for him to contain him if necessary.' She scoffed. I was worried that this was an accident waiting to happen." Suddenly and abruptly she changes the subject, using a gruff and authoritative voice: "This is a very informal interview that I'm giving you, and I don't expect you to use my name and write this whole story."

What the heck does she expect? She calls a journalist, spills her guts, and figures it's just between the two of us? But I honor her request to excise her surname from the text; it is superfluous to the story. I call her only Roberta, as she was identified in the *Living with Chimpanzees* documentary.

⌐ ⌐

I ask her if she can explain the appeal of keeping exotic pets like chimpanzees. "I'm not one of those people who want exotic pets," she says, this from a woman who's lived with chimpanzees for about twenty years. "I don't have other exotic pets, and I never wanted chimps." She says she was "roped" into the experience because she tried to save chimpanzees no one else wanted to help, and there was no place for them to live other than her home. Years later, does she regret accepting the guardian role?

"That's a hard question to answer. We were trying to do what was best for them, and nobody helped us," she answers. She says she's going to become what she calls "an animal activist" as soon as she can place her chimps in a suitable sanctuary. She advocates laws to prevent private captive breeding and commercial trafficking of exotics: "It needs to be stopped; it should have been stopped a long time ago." But she understands she lacks credibility, making that argument even as two chimps live with her: "We're saying you shouldn't have these in your home, yet we have them in our home." Roberta sees her relationship with the chimps in her house as both "incredible and stifling, stifling because no one else can take care of them but us."

"You must resent the imposition at times."

"Never," is her immediate response. "I never resent them. See, you're writing your own story now." She's irritated with the messenger again.

"No," I explain patiently. "I'm just curious."

"This is what I don't like about journalists," she says with greater irritation. "Why would you say I resent them?"

"No," I say again, "I asked you." I feel like I'm trapped in radio talk show land. "I'm curious because you think private ownership of exotic pets is wrong and that the experience co-opted your life."

She transcends her dislike of journalists and answers the question. "On one hand, it's been amazing to live with them, a privilege and an incredible experience. On the other hand, we've been totally stifled in terms of our own lives. But I don't resent them for that. Why would I resent them? That was my choice."

"Even if laws are passed against private ownership of exotic pets," I venture, "there always will be people who think a chimpanzee is a compelling pet."

She answers with a speech. "Let me liken it to the drug problem. Yes, everybody who does have an appetite for drugs gets illegal drugs any way they can because they have an appetite for them. You make it against the law, but if you don't enforce that law, it's just going to keep on going on. You have to enforce the laws. This is what's wrong with our country. It's too freaking liberal. They make laws, and then they don't enforce them. They only enforce the ones that they think they should, or they feel like."

I steer her back to her chimpanzees and ask why it's been so difficult for her to find a new home for them.

"Because there are not enough sanctuaries, and they don't have enough money, and they don't have enough space. There are just too many chimps and not enough places."

"And the private commercial breeding continues," I remind her, reflecting on the over two hundred chimpanzees estimated to be in individual private hands in the United States alone. Hundreds more are distributed around the country in overloaded sanctuaries.

"And the breeding freaking continues," she concurs. "Right now I could breed my two chimps and make baby chimps and sell them for $75,000 each. I'm perfectly free to do that according to all the laws. The hell with that! That's why I'm so careful about not letting them get across the bars or do anything with each other. I've been responsible as far as I can go with these guys. I've been as loving as I can. I've been concerned that they go to the right place, because if they go to the wrong place, they could get ripped apart."

"Ripped apart?"

"Yes, by other chimps." Her voice is distraught. "I have a huge dilemma here to do the correct thing for these guys." I cite the Travis attack, remind her she told me that her own chimpanzees pose such a potential danger that they must be caged, and ask her again if she believes keeping exotic pets like chimps should be outlawed. First time around, she did not answer my question but deflected it by insisting such a law would be violated. Other chimpanzees have attacked people, Roberta knows, "but there's always a reason," she says, in defense of the animals. "It's always because of the people, not the chimps."

"Yet they are dangerous," I point out. "That's why you keep yours in cages."

"I have to. They're much stronger than we are." Now they are caged; when they were younger, however, Roberta and Phil not only allowed them out of their cage, they took the youngest around their local main street, to meet and greet the townsfolk. The chimps starred in commercials, work that brought some money into the household to defray some of the extraordinary costs of keeping such animals in a private home.

Hiring out pet chimpanzees is not uncommon, according to Steve Ross, a specialist in great apes at the Lincoln Park Zoo in Chicago. He lobbies against the use of chimps in advertising and says that animals often suffer abusive training and poor living conditions once they are forced into early retirement, after they grow too strong for advertising agencies to control them. (Travis himself starred in Old Navy and Coca-Cola ads.)[67]

Studies at Ross's zoo have convinced him that much of the public is unaware that wild chimpanzees are an endangered species because chimps frequently appear as entertainers on TV, in the movies, and as advertising hucksters. "Do we value that brief chuckle over the welfare of these highly sentient animals and the sustainability of the species?" Ross asks. "Weighing the moral costs and benefits of common practices is something that a progressive society does on a regular basis."[68]

Ross opposes breeding chimpanzees for the pet trade for obvious reasons: They are separated from their own kind, they're dangerous when they grow strong and unpredictable, and they suffer when frustrated owners tire of them and dump them in less-than-desirable new homes. "I'm not sure they understand what they are," he says about chimps raised with humans. But "put the chimp in a tutu and a top hat, and it's still a chimp." That's why no one ought to be surprised that chimpanzees act aggressively when they become adolescents. They fight among each other, establishing hierarchies in the wild, and they'll tend to exhibit similar behavior in captivity.[69]

— ⁓

"They never should have been taken from the wild," Roberta now concludes about her and all pet chimpanzees. "But the wild is disappearing, and some of them in the wild are in even worse shape. They're being eaten."

Indeed they are. They're prized as bush meat. I've read the reports. Ape meat is illegal to trade and hence commands a premium price. It's sought after as a delicacy for traditional reasons by some people and as a novelty by others.

"It's a horrible thing, to live with chimps for twenty years, know how incredible they are, how close to people they are, how they understand everything, how they feel everything, and to know there are cousins of theirs in Africa that are chopped up!" Her voice cracking with emotion, Roberta cries for a moment and sniffles.

Once she finally finds a new home for her two chimpanzees, the changes will be traumatic for the chimpanzees and for Phil and her, she forecasts. "It's going to be super hard separating us from them, and them separating from us. I'm just hoping it will make up for it when they get to play with other chimps and run around more. But no matter how painful it's going to be, I have to do it because they need better. They're going to outlive us. Cheetah is still alive at seventy-five. Did you know that? Cheetah, from the movies, from *Tarzan,* used to wheel his owner around in his wheelchair." Quite the image: chimp pushing infirm Hollywood producer, although the story may be apocryphal, as may be the age she cited. Apparently more than one chimp played Cheetah, and well-documented details of which did what and who is where seem to be lost to Hollywood history.

"Why is it that we're so fascinated by their anthropomorphic behavior?" I ask her, and she speaks slower, as she thinks through her answer.

"That's a good question. They're just so close to being like us. I just love my two, and I love chimps because I know how they are as chimps. Not because they're people. You understand what I'm saying? They're just so close to being like us. And yet, they're not. Like Jane Goodall says, the chimps are a bridge between people and the animal world. It's true. They're like the link because they're not animals, and they're not people. They're in between."

Goodall does indeed call chimpanzees a link. "The chimpanzees, and the other great apes, form a living bridge between 'us' and 'them,'" she writes about nonhuman animals, "and this knowledge forces us to re-evaluate our relationship with the rest of the animal kingdom, particularly with the great apes." They should be treated with consideration and kindness, she insists.[70]

"When you look at those links in the cage, do you feel that you're wronging them?" I ask Roberta.

"I am stressed every day when I see them in those cages," she says, "because if I were in their place, I would feel as if I were in jail. They tense up in the cage; you or I would as well." It's a burden and a responsibility to care for them, she says, a physical and psychological burden. It's a burden, she tells me in late 2009, that she hopes to be relieved of soon, but not one she regrets. "A lot of people, when they can't deal with big chimps anymore, they sell them to a lab, or they end up on a roadside show somewhere or who knows where, who knows what? That's horrible. If you cared about this creature, how could you say, 'Let's just get rid of him?' How could you do that?" Her voice fills with emotion as she repeats, "How the hell could you do that?"

People are more dangerous than chimpanzees, Roberta says, and presents Travis's owner, Sandra Herold, as a prime example. "She was a total nut, and she made it bad for other people who have chimps, like me." The Stamford attack jeopardized other exotic pet owners; their compounds were scrutinized with fear that they harbored another Travis. "I'm not a nut and irresponsible like that idiot woman. I feel sorry for her, but she never listened to reason. From when he was two years old, she was saying, 'He's my son.' She was mentally ill."

"Sitting in bed drinking wine from stemmed glasses with a chimpanzee sounds a little weird," I agree.

"How about a lot weird?" she says.

Roberta laments the loss of native chimpanzee habitat and blames humans for the declining wild chimpanzee population. "People are ignorant and arrogant and violent. They're so much worse than chimps. Where did we go wrong? Seven million years ago we made a wrong turn, I think." She laughs, a laugh of despair. "A lot of people who hear me would say, 'Oh, she's a nut. She thinks people are worse than chimps.' But read the freaking news," she cries out, apparently forgetting for a second that it's written by "freaking" journalists.

— ⁓

"They're so much like us." Filmmaker Fontes is talking with me about her experiences living with Roberta and Phil's chimpanzees when she shot the documentary. "One forgets that these are animals that belong somewhere that is not the human world." She and the animals interacted directly; bars or glass did not separate them. "But I was always sad because they were so outside of their world. I would always come back from shooting with this existential question: How can we repair the fact that we took these animals from their habitat?"

After the myriad of interviews I've conducted for this book, the research I've studied, and the captive animals I've observed in their lock-ups, I'm inclined to think we can't repair the damage. The best we can do is try to mitigate the messy results of the meddling we've done with Mother Nature. The chimps exist in limbo, not able to integrate fully into the human world, but removed from the wild chimpanzee world. Humans propagated them in an artificial environment, and there they must remain.

"Absolutely," Fontes agrees. "I always felt sad. I felt sad for them." The film ends with the chimpanzees and their human caretakers looking at a children's book about chimpanzees. "It was this nuclear family, this interspecies family, looking at what should have been, because they're looking at chimps in the wild," she remembers thinking as she shot the scene. "I see these huge hands turning the page," she says, "and then Charlie—one of Roberta's chimpanzees—kisses the book. It was so beautiful and sad. Will she ever understand what she's doing, that she's kissing this picture of a place where she should have stayed?"

Just as humans find watching and interacting with their chimpanzee relatives captivating, after interacting intimately with the characters in her film, Flavia Fontes decided the feeling was mutual. "I always felt the chimpanzees were fascinated with us," she tells me. She fantasized as she observed them that perhaps they felt sorry for us hairless beach apes, as the comic strip shark Sherman calls human beings. "These are chimps that are uglier than us," she figured they were thinking, "but they know where the food is."

Writer Charles Siebert came to similar conclusions after spending several days watching and being watched by a retired circus chimpanzee named Roger. "It is a beguiling mix of amazement and apprehension," Siebert noted about Roger's stare, "the look of a being stranded between his former self and the one we humans have long been suggesting to him. A sort of hybrid of a chimp and a person."[71]

CHAPTER NINE

Trapped Together

Connie Casey and Chimpanzee Factory

I WANTED TO FIND OUT MORE ABOUT WHERE ROBERTA AND PHIL'S CHIMPANZEES were born. Turns out, it was in Missouri, on a breeder's farm south of St. Louis. As I continue to research chimpanzees as exotic pets or ersatz children, it is striking to me how relatively commonplace such a relationship is, and with commercial captive-breeding facilities such as Chimparty busy generating supply, at least some of the demand is satisfied.

Chimparty is the brand name Connie Casey and her husband, Mike, conjured for their Festus, Missouri, compound, acreage literally crawling with animals, including a posse of chimpanzees. Connie Casey is regularly mentioned in news items regarding chimpanzees, and she continues to celebrate the private ownership of great apes. (She and Mike Casey are no longer a couple; the word around Missouri is that he lit out for Hollywood with their best money-making chimp.) Travis was born at the Festus compound, and Travis's mother, Suzy, was shot dead in a Festus neighbor's driveway when Suzy and two other chimpanzees escaped their confinement and went for a walkabout. The shooter, a self-described "country boy" named Jason Coates, claims he feared for his life when he encountered the free-ranging Suzy, yet he went to jail for the killing. After Travis attacked Charla Nash, Coates petitioned the governor for a pardon.

A colleague working at a St. Louis television newsroom told me that Casey no longer talked to journalists. Stories about her and her chimps had made for sensational headlines; my colleague thought gaining an audience with her would be a tough sell. I decided against just showing up at her front gate and pressing the buzzer, and I figured that the usual strategy of calling on the phone and suggesting an appointment would not be a good approach, either. I ruled out subterfuge: falsely presenting myself as in the market for a pet chimp in order to get inside the perimeter.

The Fox News show *Inside Edition* already went that route when one of the show's reporters, Paul Boyd, toured Chimparty posing as a prospective buyer. Instead I sent an old-fashioned letter to Casey and enclosed a copy of my butterfly book in the parcel.

"I know that there have been considerable controversies surrounding Chimparty, and, of course, that is one of the reasons I wish to speak with you," I wrote. "I am committed, as a journalist, to doing all I can to understand an issue, and that means talking with primary sources." I drew attention to the fact that nobody I interviewed for the butterfly book complained about his or her portrayal in its pages. "If you look through *The Dangerous World of Butterflies,* I think you will agree with reviewers and with those I interviewed for the book that I reported accurately and treated all fairly. From what I've heard, you have important and fascinating stories to share, stories that I know will help me properly explain to the uninitiated the world of exotic pets."

I waited a week and started calling Connie Casey. Each time I called, the voice mail answered, and each time I left a detailed message and my phone number. I arrived in St. Louis and left yet another message, this time announcing that I was in her neighborhood. Casey finally returned my call, apologized for ignoring me, expressed worry that she might be making an error by opening Chimparty to my prying eyes and ears, and then invited me to Festus.

At this point I'm several months into my investigation of exotic pets and their owners. I'm finding it hard to accept the arguments offered by most aficionados of exotics to rationalize their hobby. As I worked to gain access to Connie Casey and her compound, I expected the experience to reinforce my growing prejudices, but I'm prepared for them to be debunked. Perhaps once I'm inside the perimeter fence, I'll find a happy interspecies homestead and a rationale for populating the heartland with captive-bred wild animals that belong in the jungles of Africa.

The weather is gray, and it's drizzling as I drive through the verdant hills on a Jefferson County road, keeping track of the passing miles and watching for landmarks. I come around a curve, and there it is, impossible to miss: Chimparty. A few of what initially look like farm silos sit in clear view of the road, but these are silos with their tops cut off and with wire mesh instead of walls. Even from the roadside the animals inside are easy to spot. Monkeys, monkeys, and more monkeys. Casey is waiting for me and opens the chain-link fence gate. She's wearing jeans and a blue T-shirt emblazoned with an American flag fluttering in the wind. Her hair is short and brown, her blue eyes look wary, but her hospitality is warm and generous. She escorts me to her house, and we settle into chairs on the front porch, looking out at enclosures filled with a variety of primates. A capuchin monkey directly across the drive from us rattles a loose piece of corrugated metal, its clattering impossible to ignore. "He's just trying to attract attention," Casey explains away the noise. Dogs join us. "He's got allergies, and he stinks," she says about her old white boxer, as he comes to nuzzle me, "but I still love him." To gain the few steps up the porch, Casey, who limps slightly, uses a hanging rope to hoist herself. Similar ropes are spotted around the house and the cages as exercise equipment for the apes. We exchange pleasantries and waste no time. I ask her why people are captivated by apes.

"They're so smart, and they're so fast, and they're so inquisitive, and their social group is so amazing. They have hands; they can manipulate. They're lucky because they have tails, so they have a fifth hand. I think people see reflections of themselves in primates."

"But why own a pet ape?" I ask. "And is *pet* the correct word for an animal that is so much like us?"

"Most people who have a primate as a pet, so to speak—they're not pets. They call them family members. They come into your home, and they come into your heart. The primate becomes part of the family."

"But they're not just like us."

"No, I'm not trying to say that. They're definitely not." She searches for the words to explain why she surrounds herself with apes. "I can't explain it. It's just in your heart; it's either there, or it's not." Casey tells me that she believes most animal lovers, given the chance to interact one-on-one with a monkey or a chimp, would want one of their own. "People will probably think I'm awful, but I have to say, I probably love them as much as I love my children." In the same breath she adds quickly, "And

I love my children. My daughters grew up with these chimps." They're off and married now, but they come to visit. "They still look at these chimps as their brothers and sisters, because they grew up with them." From where we're sitting, we can't see those chimp brothers and sisters, only the silo-cages across the driveway filled with various monkeys, and the capuchin and a lion-tailed macaque living in side-by-side cages next to us on the porch.

"It takes a lot of work," Casey says about ape keeping. A duck or a goose squawks from the pond next to the house. "I don't ever go on vacation."

"I can't imagine you could," I say, looking out at what I can see of her collection. She takes care of the animals with the help of one employee and a part-time volunteer.

"Truthfully, I don't want to go on vacation. I want to be here with these guys. People say, 'Don't you ever get tired of staying at home?' I do, sometimes. But I love my guys."

It's easy to see their appeal, even as she talks. The capuchin in the cage is playing with a napkin, acting as if it is a kerchief, making itself look like a babushka. It is cute, humanlike, and intriguing to watch.

"Why do we want to be with something that is so much like us but isn't us?" I ask.

She's been living with and breeding chimpanzees and other primates for forty years when we talk. The movie *Toby Tyler* introduced her to chimpanzees. Toby runs away from home in the 1960 Walt Disney production and joins the circus. From wide-eyed Bambi to Toby Tyler and movie houses full of other animal-filled titles, Disney—like NBC with J. Fred Muggs—has perpetuated the romantic notion that humans and wild creatures can live in Technicolor harmony. At the circus Toby Tyler meets Mr. Stubbs, the chimpanzee. "Toby's best friend of all is a frisky chimpanzee, Mr. Stubbs, who is nearly killed in a hunting accident—the film's closest brush with drama," wrote Howard Thompson in the *New York Times*.[72] The preteenaged Connie Casey was hooked and a few years later bought her first chimpanzee, Coco. Coco was bred in captivity; in those days trafficking in wild chimpanzees was still legal. Coco was one of the chimps off the Casey property when Jason Coates shot Suzy. He survived that day and died a few years later of an aneurysm, a loss that's still difficult for Casey to talk about. She tears up as she tells me, "You know, there's nothing like your first one. There's not a day goes by that I don't think about him."

What lures people to want to own apes is a question Casey ought to be able to answer. But she reiterates her inability to explain that lure. She sighs and says, "I'm at a loss for words. I love 'em." Hints of an Ozark accent slip into Casey's speech, along with dropped *G*'s and contractions.

Most baby animals exhibit appealing characteristics that attract our nurturing instincts. But prospective pet owners need to be educated about what happens to these sweet-looking fur balls once they mature. What's not to love when they're babies, but at adolescence ape cute turns to unpredictable and incredible strength.

Casey rewrites my sentence and says, "Cute turns into amazing and beautiful, incredible strength; the love's still there." She smiles at the thought. Then she makes what strikes me as an odd comparison. "Do you love your ninety- or eighty-year-old-grandparents even though they're not young and going places and doing things? That's the only way I know to explain it. People say, 'Oh, my God, they're so big. Aren't you scared?' I love 'em," she says, and she doesn't stop loving them when they grow too old to play with and cuddle, too old for them to run around her house and yard. When I visit her, of all the chimpanzees under her control, only one is still young enough to clamber out of its cage (they range in age from fifteen months to fifty-two years). The others, and there are many ("They all have their own personality!" she says), are permanently sequestered, as I'm about to learn.

"Once they mature," she acknowledges, "the males become protective, they become dominant, and at times they can become aggressive. They show their strength. Any time there's a stranger, they'll puff up, and they'll display. It makes them look twice the size that they are. They want to show you, 'Hey, this is my house. You stay out there, and I'm staying in here. And these are my girls, so don't step on my territory.' Most of the time once their display is done, they sit down and suck their thumbs, and then they want to start interacting and stuff. It's no different than they are in the wild."

Not so, says primatologist Jane Goodall. "Chimpanzees evolved in the tropical forests of Africa," she wrote after the Travis attack, "and that's where they're suited to live, roaming in groups of their own kind. A house in Connecticut was a completely alien environment for a chimp."[73] The suburban environment likely added to his latent stress, and the attempts to cajole him back to his quarters for some reason triggered his wild response.

Connie Casey swaps grandparents for teenagers to explain rough chimpanzee behavior. "It's no different than teenage boys; their testosterone's goin', boys will punch or poke and try to impress the girl. The chimps are the same."

"But if the chimp is a pet," I say, "and many times stronger than its owner, punching and poking are problematic."

"Yeah," she agrees. That's why all but one of her chimps are locked up. That's why even she always protects herself from her chimpanzees, animals she's known all their lives. Animals she loves, animals she's convinced love her. "For their safety, as well as other people's safety, the only way to keep them is in an enclosure." Her voice becomes almost whisper-soft as she says, "It wouldn't be safe to have them out." Her own physical interaction with her beloved apes is limited. "I don't go in with my big males anymore. But it's not that I don't reach through and tickle and kiss 'em and hug 'em. One of the reasons is that they're bonded to me. If I go in, then they don't want me to leave. It's difficult to get out without them wanting to get out. They're stronger than I am."

That's an understatement by at least four times. Comparisons of chimpanzee strength to human strength vary. I've encountered citations suggesting it's from four to seven times human muscle power. By any calculation, if a two-hundred-pound chimp wants to tangle, you're in deep trouble. His sharp canine teeth alone ought to make you pause.

Connie Casey likens caging her chimpanzees once they become adolescents to a "tough love" approach to child rearing. "You gotta do it for their safety," she says adamantly. She believes that one result of the Travis attack is that any chimp on the loose will now be shot dead.

But what about the animals' point of view? Does she think her restricted chimpanzees are happy? "Oh, yeah," she says with enthusiasm. "They sit and they groom and they cuddle and they love and they sleep together and they'll play with each other." But it's not all fun and games at Chimparty. "There's times when they get in a squabble, so we slide the door and divide them for a while. Sometimes they get a little jealous of one another, just like kids." They're captive bred. They don't know the wild. They enjoy some limited freedom in her compound until they become too old and big to control. They're not housed solo; they live in social groups. The route to happiness for them, she says, is to keep their minds stimulated and to allow them to interact with other chimps.

"I've had crappy calls. People say, 'You need to turn them loose! You need to turn them back into the jungle!' Those people are stupid because the jungle's not safe. They're killin' 'em. They're eatin' 'em. They're tearin' down the rain forest. The jungle's not a safe place. There's animals that have gone extinct in the jungle." Nor does she believe her captive-bred apes would survive in the wild. "They could never compete with wild animals. They don't know how to fend for themselves." She figures wild chimpanzees would attack her captive-bred chimps and kill them.

What are her chimpanzees? They're not wild. They're not domesticated. They're not feral. They're not tamed. Perhaps we need to create a new classification: captive bred, untamable, and latently wild. It's awkward but descriptive.

Connie Casey cares for retired chimpanzees in her custody, but she is in business as well. She's hired out her chimpanzees as entertainers and as hucksters, and she breeds and sells chimpanzees. A healthy baby chimp can fetch at least $60,000. But years can go by without new offspring, and she insists she's not getting rich, that the money made goes back into "monkey chow." If there's not much profit, I ask her, what motivates her to breed the apes?

"I think people who really want one should be able to have one. I think they need to be responsible and dedicated and take good care of the animal. It's hard to explain to somebody who doesn't have one, and it's their loss."

"You think everybody should have a monkey?"

"I don't think everybody should have a monkey," she says, but those who don't live with an other-than-human primate never experience the "contentment and joy" hers provide her. "I've been around primates for over forty years, and there's not a day goes by that they don't amaze me."

She rejects the calls for businesses like hers to be closed down. She dismisses the insistence of academy-trained professionals that self-taught entrepreneurs such as Casey should not meddle in breeding and trading, let alone caring and feeding. "Living with 'em, experiencing 'em twenty-four hours a day, puts ya probably far past what you can learn in a book. I'm not a zoo. I don't put in my eight hours and say, 'See you tomorrow.' Or maybe the next day, it's my day off. When you have them, and they're yours, you're there twenty-four seven. There's stuff that goes on at night that people at the zoo don't even know."

Casey is about to take me to meet her chimpanzees, but first I ask her about Travis. Does she feel any responsibility because she was the breeder? Travis was born here at her Festus spread. Her answer is immediate.

"No."

"Why not?"

"Would you feel responsible for your child if he went out and killed somebody?" A rooster crows. "I'm not saying Travis was bad. I don't know what happened, if he was being protective of Sandy. I don't know if any of us will ever know. If he wouldn't have been out, it wouldn't have happened." She expresses great heartfelt sympathy for Charla Nash and for Sandra Herold's loss. "She loved that chimp with all her heart," she says. But again she worries about chimpanzees that may wander in the future. "I think it's shoot now, and don't even ask questions."

Look at the numbers, she says, before you demonize chimpanzees. "Every day there's people killing people. You got parents killing their kids, kids killing their parents—people killing people for no reason. It's really difficult to think the Travis incident has pushed this over the edge. It's one very, very unfortunate incident.

"I love these chimps," she says again, and again a rooster crows. In response, the ape across the driveway again thrashes the sheet metal in his cage. Casey says, "The biggest problem with them is they're so damn strong."

"This guy who is jumping and making all that noise, does that mean he's happy?" I ask her. "Or does he want to get out and swim to Africa? Does he want to come here and hang out with us? What does it mean?"

"He's trying to get our attention," she says, dismissing the action as routine. "He does that to say, 'Hey! Give me some attention. Look at me!'"

We've been sitting out on the porch for about a half hour, and, aside from the monkey enclosures I've been looking at, this could be any all-American porch. That sense of comfortable familiarity collapses as soon as I cross the threshold into Casey's ranch house–style living room. Toy apes cover the mantelpiece and the shelves that surround it; there must be thousands of miniature chimpanzees. Connie Casey apologizes for her housekeeping and the dust that covers the dolls. She points out the urns holding Coco's and Suzy's ashes and leads me from the living room around a corner to what might be the kitchen in a traditional home. Instead I'm faced with a wall of windows and a big room, two stories deep, with a cage under it. There are ropes to climb on, a tire swing, and a structure to clamber up. Casey knocks on the glass, and Kimmy, a tired-looking forty-two-year-old chimpanzee, stares up. She's gray, and her fur is spare with skin showing through it. A thin gray beard outlines her chin. She shares the accommodations with two other chimpanzees.

"Hey, Kimmy," says Casey through the glass.

Kimmy comes right up to the glass and begins making frantic-looking hand signals, a sign language Kimmy created and no one else understands.

"What do you want?" asks Casey. "Banana?"

Kimmy looks forlorn and continues to sign, her soulful eyes looking at us, imploring us to understand her message.

"What do you want?" Casey asks again. "Tell me."

Kimmy tells us again. It's impossible for me not to think she's asking to get out. Those big eyes stare at me, and I cannot help but feel that she knows she's stuck in there—as big an enclosure as it is, as well equipped as it is—and I'm not. I look away from her eyes and her hands and notice she's toothless. Casey tells me Kimmy is a retired Zippy chimp and arrived in Festus with no teeth—not uncommon for show business chimps of her era. A toothless chimp is not able to cause biting injuries. Zippy the Chimp was a television star in the 1950s and '60s. There were Zippy dolls and Zippy comic books. A troupe of different chimpanzees played Zippy. Casey talks at the glass again.

"What? Apple? Huh? Whaddaya want?"

Kimmy keeps up an intricate series of fast-changing hand signs. Casey keeps asking her what she wants. I find the act extremely difficult to watch. Kimmy seems one sad and frustrated animal and looks remarkably like Connie and me: similar hands, similar head, and similar sad eyes.

"I love you, Sweety-pie," says Casey, and Kimmy taps on the glass. "What, what? I'll get you something." She adopts a sing-song voice. "You already had breakfast. You want an apple? What? More? That's her sign for more," Casey tells me. Kimmy makes another gesture. "That's her sign for please."

Kimmy and the other chimpanzees at Chimparty live in an interconnected maze of enclosures, a system that allows the four extended family groups to roam from room to room and cage to cage, but only within their social group. The four families are segregated to avoid territorial and personality disputes. On the backside of the house is a huge enclosed outdoor playground for the chimpanzees, equipped with ropes and swings. The four groups take turns using it. Picture windows allow the animals to view the landscape outside their domain, the duck pond, and traffic on the road. The windows are three panes of quarter-inch tempered glass, laminated together. One of them is boarded up. I fantasize that a chimpanzee fashioned a tool, intent on escape, and broke it. But Casey says the damage was caused when a lawn mower kicked up a rock. Televisions glow throughout the compound in an effort to keep the corralled chimpanzees entertained. That's also the theory behind an aquarium full of mice, another full of fish, and the big windows. The chimpanzee still young enough to avoid a caged life is allowed to play in the house with Dustin and Spring, the monkeys I met out on the porch. Kimmy and other adult chimpanzees can watch their antics from their sequestered quarters on the other side of the glass. The outdoor playground is lavish—filled with rope nets to climb, plastic structures to play on, ladders to climb up and down, and a tire swing. If other captive chimpanzees with less space to play—like Roberta's—could experience such a vast and well-equipped outdoor exercise yard, their lives would be improved. But Chimparty is still a prison, a prison with a decent-sized yard.

Kimmy keeps signing. "Hey, what?" says Casey to her, tapping on the glass. "Okay, baby girl." Another tap as we leave the room. "Alright, alright."

We walk down the hallway, and she points to a couple of geckos, a tarantula, a snake, and some hissing cockroaches. We pass Gabby and five-year-old Crystal, mother and daughter chimpanzees, in their enclosure. "She's a beautiful little girl," says Casey about Crystal. Crystal stares through the glass at me with her captivating eyes, cute—much like the toy chimps up in the living room. I find it hard to look and hard to look away. She is trapped, and, as was the case with Kimmy, I feel she knows she's trapped. Dusty sits in another room, rocking back and forth, knocking his head against the wall.

Under the house are cages and cages filled with chimpanzees—the cages connected to the play yard. But on this rainy day, the occupants choose to stay inside. As we walk past, they're not shy about checking out the stranger in town—me. "He might spit water," Casey says just in time, pointing out a massive fellow coming toward me on two legs. I step back as a mouthful comes shooting through the bars toward me. It barely misses. "He doesn't do it to be mean," she says, "just to get attention. No big deal." I've just met him, but it seems to me the spitting is a variation on the lonesome, longing eyes—an overt response to captivity.

In a room across from the spitting chimp, an ape is throwing bedding. At the next window is another of the massive animals, this one marching in circles around the room. I'm introduced to fourteen-year-old Conner. "That's when the testosterone kicks in," says Connie, about his age. Conner paces, circumnavigating his room, and as he comes around a far corner to face us looking at him from the other side of the glass, he whacks his forearm against the room wall with a force that makes an ominous loud bang. Over and over again he makes his rounds. He stops and stares. He climbs up on a rope swing and starts to pump, still facing us, swinging back and forth, then jumps off, smashing front first right up against the glass, facing us, all two-hundred-some pounds of trapped chimpanzee muscle. The three panes of laminated tempered glass hold, I imagine much to Conner's frustration. He looks as if he'd like to come out and, what? I'm not sure. But I'm glad the glass didn't break. He sits and sucks his thumb, and he looks at me. Confused and sad is how I interpret his intense stare.

"I wouldn't trade my life for nothing," Connie Casey says as we shake hands good-bye. It would be better were they in the wild, she says, but that can't happen. I imagine she's treating the animals as well as she can, with decent, if selfish, intentions. "I love these guys." She strikes me as a misguided, tragic figure, an unfortunate woman who may mean well enough and is as trapped and as broken as her chimpanzees.

CHAPTER TEN

Travis's Mother

Gunned Down

JASON COATES AND CONNIE CASEY WERE NEIGHBORS IN 2001 WHEN SUZY, Coco, and Gabby managed to jump the fence at Chimparty after slipping out of their unlocked enclosures. The three chimpanzees wandered down the road to the Coates place. Jason encountered the trio in his driveway, ran up to his room, and fetched his gun. Three shots later Suzy was dead, and Jason was in jail, convicted of felony property damage (Suzy as property) and misdemeanor animal abuse.

Jason Coates got what he deserved, Connie Casey told me. "He shot her twice in the back and then in the face. She wasn't even close to him. Suzy would never have hurt him. She was the most mellow chimp in the world. It was nothing but deliberate murder." She choked up. "That was deliberate, cold-blooded. I think he has a bad seed in him. I don't wish him no harm. I know it wasn't right what he did to Suzy." But the chimpanzees were out of her control, off her property, on his. "Even though I did have three chimps out, they weren't being aggressive to anybody. I wanted to get them back to safety as soon as I could."

After Travis, Suzy's son, went on his rampage in Stamford, almost killing Charla Nash, Coates felt vindicated. He wants breeder Casey—and all other private chimpanzee keepers—shut down. We meet at a café on Euclid Street in the gentrified Central West End section of St. Louis. Coates is taking a break from construction work. He's a wiry and intense man in his midtwenties. His smile is sweet; his polo shirt is Ralph Lauren. A subtle silver chain hangs from his neck. He politely asks if I mind when he reaches for the first of several cigarettes. Chimparty, he says, "sells these monkeys to anybody who's got the money to pay for them without regard to what they're doing with them or how they're cared for. It seems to me that's just wrong, especially being as how they're attacking people and practically killing them. Me and my friends are very fortunate that wasn't the case with us, and nobody wanted to hear it."

Coates was characterized by the prosecutor and some news reporters as a boy gone wrong, victimizing the defenseless chimpanzees.

"I'm put in the category with the worst of humanity in our society," he says about the felony on his record. "I'll be the first to admit I was never an A student, I never made the honor roll. I was always in trouble. But it was *Leave It to Beaver* stuff. Just being a mischievous kid. They painted me out as some drug-dealing, whacked-out kid that was like Jeffrey Dahmer out torturing kittens and stuff. Nobody wanted to hear me, this seventeen-year-old kid. They put on this smear campaign to totally tear me down and humanize these chimps." But humans they're not. "They don't have the moral standards that people have. We're not tame, but we have moral standards. You could press my buttons, and I could jump up and bash your head off the window, but I know that's wrong, and therefore I won't do it, because of my moral standards and the law. Animals have no concept of that. All they know is, you made me mad, I'm going to bash your head off the window."

❧

"Insane," says evolutionary biologist Marc Bekoff when I relay Coates's dismissal of morality in other-than-human animals. An emeritus professor at the University of Colorado and a working colleague of Jane Goodall, his research focuses on animal behavior and how other-than-human minds work. Bekoff draws on his years of research to state without hesitation that there is overwhelming evidence of empathy, trust, reciprocity, fairness, sharing, and altruism in the animal kingdom.

Animals have morality," he concludes. "Morality is a broadly adaptive strategy for social living that has evolved in many animal societies other than our own."[74] Not just in chimpanzees, he emphasizes, pointing to morality he's recorded in animals from rats to apes.

❧

"Because of this chance encounter with Suzy, you've become a chimpanzee expert?" I ask Jason Coates.

"I can't say I'm an expert," Coates counters. "Jane Goodall is an expert. I'm informed more than most, I think, but an expert I'm not."

"Do you find them intriguing?"

"To a degree. I think their intelligence is very interesting. There was that one at the zoo who would hide rocks from the zookeepers in strategic locations. Every day when they opened the gates, this chimp would be grabbing these rocks and chucking them at the people who would be looking at him." The story makes me think about Conner, bashing at the wall and slamming himself into his glass window. But when Coates takes his young sons to the St. Louis Zoo, he shies from the chimpanzees in the ape house. "They'll be up on the glass, and the kids will be cool with them, but I've got to stay back. They freak me out. They give me an anxiety attack. It's like a flashback. I've still got an image burned in my head of Coco baring his teeth, screaming, and shaking this Chevy Cavalier we were in. Holy crap! The spine-tingling fear of this thing busting the window and getting in the car." That fear, Coates tells me, drove him to make a break for his house when Coco was distracted and come back shooting his 20 gauge. By that time Coco had left the car, and a crew from Chimparty was rounding him up. "It was an act of God that thing didn't break that window, and I wasn't going to sit around and be subject to a second chance. I was a quarter-inch piece of glass away from being in the shoes Charla Nash is in." Suzy, Coates says, was fighting with his dog. He called his dog and distracted the chimpanzee. "She turned at me, and I shot her. Plain and simple."

His is an endearing, rapid-fire patter, a combination of good ol' boy from the Ozarks and thoughtful, sophisticated analysis. "Pimp her chimps," is his term for making money with the apes. "Uncontrolled and pissed-off about something" is how he characterized twenty-eight-year-old, 115-pound Suzy and the other two escapees in his driveway. Since that afternoon he's studied not just chimpanzees but also those who choose to live with them. "Most of these people have a desire to be famous. It's kind of like a guy walking down the street with a puppy, and all the little girls go, 'Oh, oh!' It's a chick magnet." The chimpanzees are the same type of deal, he says, "only it's an attention magnet. Another thing I have found is that they have a hard time with relationships with people, so they get a false sense of companionship, love, and emotion out of this animal up until the point that it regresses back to its natural state." Not that he is cozy with those he calls "chimp pimps." He engages some on Internet chats and observes the activities of others from reports he encounters. "Most of these people don't want to talk to me. They hate me. I'm the Antichrist to them because I don't love chimpanzees like my own child. But from their general behavior, it's one of those two things. Either they need the companionship, or they're desperate attention seekers who have no way of getting the attention they desire on their own, so they enlist the abilities of these big, scary animals."

—◦—

Big and scary they are when they're adults, just as they're cute and cuddly as babies. That cute-and-cuddly reality fuels the pet trade. Some of these cute babies end up as adults at sanctuaries like Chimp Haven in Louisiana. There, in an environment that allows the animals some room to roam in a natural habitat, behavioral primatologist Dr. Linda Brendt and her staff take in chimpanzees whose buyers realize they made a mistake. "Being a pet and being raised with humans," she told *Inside Edition* after reporter Paul Boyd feigned interest in buying a chimpanzee from Connie Casey, "they're really set up for failure, I hate to say."[75] Chimp Haven is a retirement home for what Brendt calls "surplus chimpanzees," former pets, animals no longer used for scientific research, ex-entertainers.

"Wild animals do not belong in human homes, they can be highly unpredictable, consider other attacks by famous animals on their handlers, and they should be allowed to live at sanctuaries that are dedicated to respecting their lives while minimizing human contact," wrote Marc Bekoff after Travis attacked Charla Nash. The evolutionary biologist railed against Travis's lifestyle. "Chimpanzees do not typically drink wine or brush their teeth with a Water Pik, and while it may sound 'cute,' asking a chimpanzee to do these things is an insult to who they are." Bekoff debunked reports that identified Travis as a domesticated animal. "Domestication is an evolutionary process that results in animals such as our companion dogs and cats who undergo substantial behavioral, anatomical, physiological, and genetic changes during the process. Travis was a socialized chimpanzee who usually got along with humans but not a domesticated being. He still had his wild genes just as do wolves, cougars, and bears who live with humans, and tragedies occur because these are wild animals despite [the fact] that they're treated as if they're humans. To say there was no known provocation is to ignore this basic fact."[76]

The debate between the exotic pet lovers and those opposed to their relationships with their animals polarizes participants and observers. Like abortion, capital punishment, and the viability of Sarah Palin as a presidential candidate, there seems to be precious little middle ground or room for compromise among the participants.

CHAPTER ELEVEN

Shambala

Are Wild Things Forever Wild?

THE VISIT TO CHIMPARTY LEAVES ME UNSETTLED. WHILE I'M PLEASED I GAINED access to Connie Casey's story and her bizarre animal farm, the visit haunts me. The images of her confined chimpanzees reappear in my mind as the Midwest slips toward the Rockies 30,000 feet below on my flight home, especially Kimmy, with her frustrated signing, and Conner, the monster chimp I'm sure would have loved to break free and do what to us? I don't think a kiss and a hug were first on his list. I find myself struggling with the sight of their soulful, pleading eyes—almost human, almost one of us—trapped behind glass. The sympathy I'm feeling now is the sympathy I would feel for a helpless human, or maybe any fellow creature pleading for help from a cage. But I do recognize that some sort of kinship exists— Kimmy and Conner and the other chimpanzees aren't quite siblings (my own blood sister will be pleased I'm noting that here!), but they're close. I keep contrasting those caged animals with the sad-eyed human who runs Chimparty and is their fellow inmate, a woman who has devoted her life to these animals. I have sympathy for her as well; she is trapped by her responsibilities (and apparent love) for the apes she has collected and bred, a gang of so many that even if she wanted to close up shop, it would be all but impossible for her to find adequate homes for her ape dependents.

I find myself revisiting my exchange with Tippi Hedren, a movie star using her influence, hiring people who are experts in their respective fields and who deal with this very issue: what to do with the surplus of captive-bred wild animals. Hedren's pride of cats lives out their lives at her canyon enclave just north of Hollywood. Her Shambala reserve is one model, an old folks' home for wild animals unequipped for the wilderness and a base from which to lobby for laws against breeding further generations of wild animals for private fun and profit.

"You can bottle-feed him. You can cuddle him, hold him, take a little nap with him, play with him." Tippi Hedren knows the appeal of the Bonzos and the Thrillers and the Sabus. "He doesn't care," she says about the mentality of wild animals. "As far as he's concerned, you're either a littermate, or you're another lion or tiger." She is talking big cats, but the example works for great apes and other wild things. "If he hurts you or kills you, so what?" She shrugs, taking on the point of view of the wild cat. "That's what we do." She is perplexed at the naïveté of any wild animal owner who would think otherwise. "That's their job. That's the job of a predator."

This is the woman who days before we talk sat with Michael Jackson's cats, attempting to inform them of his death, the woman I watched tirelessly and patiently sign autograph after autograph for demanding fans—raising money for the wild animals living on her reserve. "You must have developed some rapport—or at least think you've developed some rapport—with the cats you spend so much time with," I say to her. I keep wondering if caretakers of abandoned animals such as Hedren, as well as scientists who preach against keeping wild animals even as they manage a menagerie themselves for research, use their good works as an excuse to enjoy the exotic pets in their custody. Perhaps because of their intimate relationships with the animals, they let their own guards down, think theirs are special cases, that they can nurture connections with their animals that are the exceptions to the rules.

"We have fabulous relationships with them," Hedren says. She's ready to tell animal stories. She made that evident when she excused one of her handlers who was clock watching as we first talked, worried about the dinner schedule, and told her to come back and fetch her in an hour. She sips more wine and smiles as she launches into a memory. "The first little lion that we raised was a rescue, and one of the first accidents was with him. We were doing a movie scene; it was a lion fight. It's easy to arrange a lion fight," she informs me in the matter-of-fact manner of an experienced expert offering a primer to a newcomer. "You don't even have to try. All

Shambala

you do is bring in two lions who don't know each other, and they'll fight. Or two tigers, they'll fight. That's what they do. My then-husband, who was playing the scientist in the film, went to break up the fight, and the little lion who we raised bit him so badly that the canine tooth went right through his hand." She laughs again as she recounts how the lion bite missed the tendons and muscles. "He was lucky, but our director of photography was scalped, I was bitten on the back of my head, our daughter was scratched across her beautiful face, my stepson found his head in the mouth of the lion. There were all these horrible things that went on during the filming."

Not that Hedren and her crews don't feel an affinity for the cats. "Some of them will come right up to you and say, 'Gee, I'm glad to see you.' They make all these cute sounds."

"I bet it makes you feel good to have a big animal come up and rub up against you."

"Of course! And that can happen. They have a great capacity for love. They have a sense of humor. They have their inferiority complexes, dominancy problems." A dramatic pause and she adds, "Like *that* it can just switch."

"What happens at that switch point?"

"You can see it. It's very evident." She relates an example from just a few days before when the television show *Entertainment Tonight* sent a crew out to Shambala to shoot video of Michael Jackson's cats. "There were Sabu and Thriller head to head and just adorable. You just want to go in and hug them and tickle their tummies." One of the crew members moved a big camera toward Thriller. "All of a sudden she goes," and Hedren makes an attempt at a tiger sotto voce roar there in the Tides bar, "and rises up on the fencing. The sounds are horrendous. It's scary." Her voice is breathless now as she describes the scene. "Very frightening." She smiles. "I always love it when they do that because it says: Look what this sweet animal can become. It's worth a million words." She pauses again for half a beat. "Or should be."

That wildness never goes away, Tippi Hedren is convinced. "There's nothing you can do to take that away. Nothing."

That conclusion is what led Hedren to establish Shambala as a sanctuary for abandoned and mistreated wild cats, and what motivated her to work for laws designed to protect cats (and their keepers) from the abuses of private ownership. She wants private captive breeding of big cats outlawed by the federal government.

"We were acquiring these animals because people couldn't control them and couldn't handle them. They didn't realize they would get so big."

Ignorance is unfortunate, but it exists. Some owners just don't do their homework. But others revel in the idea of the King of the Jungle living in their homes. I return to the question of motivation, trying to get a better understanding of what Hedren thinks is the psychology behind choosing a lion or a tiger as a "pet," especially when it takes just a few clicks on the Internet to learn that lions and tigers turn on the most experienced trainers, and that chimpanzees, once they're adolescents, are many times stronger than humans of equal weight.

"They think that they are different, that this wild animal they have is different from the others, and that it couldn't possibly happen to *me*." She continues to theorize about how exotic pets are rationalized. "And it will," she says with the resignation that comes from years of dealing with wild cats and their victims. "It's just a matter of time. Who knows what went on in that chimpanzee's brain," she says about Travis. Of course, we can't know. Our interspecies communication from chimp to human and back is inadequate to the task of figuring out what made him snap, why he went from famously sipping wine to a frenzied attack. "There's no way we could ever know. As much as we anthropomorphize, there is no way we could ever understand what went on."

She has zero tolerance for the wild animal captive-breeding business. "It's like your butterfly book. I'm sure most people are not aware of the breeding business." Wild butterflies are captive bred and turned into a commercial commodity. It's a similar story with big cats, great apes, and long snakes. Except that butterflies can't hurt you. In the exotic pets business, the breeders make money. Those middlemen who buy and sell the animals make money. Money is made showing the animals in circuses and at roadside attractions that use caged animals to lure tourists to junk stores.

The result of all this breeding is a growing population of captive tigers, some of which (probably even *most* of which) will prove to be too much for their owners. It is Tippi Hedren who first tells me the statistic she knows will amaze: There are more tigers in captivity in Texas than in the wilds of India. Since breeding and trading are essentially unregulated in Texas, it is impossible to ascertain the Texas tiger population. Or the Ohio tiger population, or Missouri's. There are no databases. Who knew Texas was crawling with tigers? Certainly not me until I started researching this book. Captive breeding of wild animals for private ownership doesn't make the headlines until there's a crisis—or a curiosity. Witness the splash across newspapers when feed store owner Vanderholm put a FOR SALE sign on his tiger, Lilly.

       ━ ━

But if *Panthera tigris* is in jeopardy worldwide, isn't there a solid argument that captive breeding is healthy, that it's successfully propagating an endangered population? No, say scientists and activists working to protect the planet's remaining wild tigers. Captive breeding is expensive. One critical concern plaguing tiger lovers is the harvesting of tiger parts for traditional Chinese folk medicinal purposes. If tiger bones (pulverized to treat ulcers and rheumatism and typhoid) and eyes (to fight epilepsy and malaria) and tiger penises (to make tiger penis soup at over $300 a bowl to enhance virility) are available from legally captive-bred tigers, that supply likely will fuel the worldwide market for tiger-based cures. If the same potions can be made from illegally killed tigers with the raw materials available on the black market at a better price than the captive-bred parts, demand probably will encourage poachers to hunt protected tigers, especially since tigers roam in those parts of the world where poverty is endemic.

The TRAFFIC report on tigers in the United States forecasts that tiger farms in China are producing almost a thousand cubs a year. TRAFFIC is one of the leading nonprofit organizations focused on protecting wildlife. "Reintroducing a legal supply [of tiger parts] into the market will lead," its report states, "to the resumption of a latent demand for tiger products. There is no guarantee that such market stimulation would be fed only from farmed tigers in China. More probable is that any such action would increase demand for tiger parts from all sources, including possibly captive tigers in the United States and, of course most worrying, from wild tigers."[77]

In her film *The Tiger Next Door*, producer and director Camilla Calamandrei proves the TRAFFIC report worries true, at least in one case. She profiles the undercover work of U.S. Fish and Wildlife Service Special Agent Tim Santel. He exposes a creative criminal enterprise that took advantage of a market so flooded with captive-bred tigers that it is difficult for owners tired of their cats to give them away, let alone sell them to compensate for the money they've invested in years of care and feeding. The conspirators roamed the Midwest states offering to take "unwanted tiger pets" off the hands of frustrated owners. These they killed, selling the parts for a price Santel determined was $1,000 a tiger. "This whole cat craze is really being driven by money," Agent Santel tells Calamandrei. "I don't want to paint everybody with a broad brush, but, in the end, the reason people are breeding and buying and selling is money."

Tippi Hedren rejects the proposition that commercial breeding can be rationalized as morally responsible out of her concern for individual cats. "For what purpose, to have them born to be in prison? Is this conservation? I don't think so. I think it is profit." It's a conclusion that goes with her analysis of human beings as animals: "I think we're the worst predators on the planet."

The actress takes another sip of her wine as she launches into an aspect of the captive cat breeding business she loathes: raising lions and tigers for slaughter in order to provide meat for exotic menus. "Every creature has been born with a brain, with a reason to be here, and they all have a job to do. For us to assume that we have all the power is very naïve of us, and I think it will eventually be our ending. We will do it to ourselves.

Meanwhile I feel the need to protect animals. I think there are some things that are just wrong."

And she feels a need to protect *us* because big cats—especially as cubs—look so appealing.

"The powers that be, when they designed the predator," she says about big cats, "did a very bad job because they look so adorable and so beautiful."

We agree to meet again, this time in Southern California, at Shambala. There I will see for myself her old folks' home for big cats, far from the glitter of Hollywood.

Several weeks later I'm watching the TV news in a Castaic, California, motel room. Castaic is a strip along Interstate 5 just north of Santa Clarita on the outer northern reaches of the Los Angeles sprawl and the last stop before the wilds of Soledad Canyon, home to Shambala. The local Fox 11 News is droning the usual "if it bleeds, it leads" superficial stories, when my attention is caught by the tease "Happy ending to the tale of a missing snake." Just down the road, in Riverside County, I'm told, a Burmese python "escaped from a long-distance trucker's house." The good news: It's been found in a neighbor's yard, and I'm treated to video of an animal control officer opening the python's mouth. It looks vicious.

"Where does he live?" asks the cute well-coiffed anchorwoman. "Burma," answers the smiling Ken-doll anchorman, as the two dismiss the story with TV happy talk, ignoring the invasive species story while injecting themselves—apparently unknowingly—in Burma/Myanmar politics by using the premilitary coup name for the country.

⚊ ⚊

The next day I travel a dozen miles from suburban Santa Clarita to rural Soledad Canyon. The landscape looks like the locales of the typical Hollywood westerns that were shot nearby: scrub-covered hillsides, sagebrush, cottonwoods in the draws, and dramatic rock outcroppings. High cyclone fencing marks the Shambala border, along with the ominous sign at the gate: WARNING: SAVAGE ANIMALS. KEEP OUT. DANGEROUS AREA. NO VISITORS NO

EXCEPTIONS. The Metrolink train snakes past on the far side of the canyon, treating commuters from Palmdale and Lancaster to a look at wild cats.

"This is a prison," Chris Galluci tells me as we begin to tour Shambala. "This is a prison, and it's filled with serial killers." Not that the cats in his custody have all killed. He's referring to their role in the animal kingdom: apex predators. "We are a preserve that doesn't want to be in business. But it doesn't look like the laws are going to change anytime soon." Galluci runs the sanctuary's day-to-day operations; he's been working for Tippi Hedren much of his adult life, trying to keep retired show business big cats and other rescued animals as happy as possible while they live out their lives in captivity.

Galluci's training has been on the job. He's learned to take care of Shambala's charges from the preserve's consulting veterinarians and from careful trial and error. Now he manages the staff, a staff that no longer engages in hands-on work with the animals. After one too many injuries to workers, he and Hedren instituted a policy that keeps the wild animals segregated from the humans at feeding time and when their enclosures are cleaned.

There's a story to go along with each cat in the complex. How Zeus ended up in Shambala typifies the out-of-control big cat trade. We're looking at the lion, his long, wild, golden mane a contrast to Galluci's mostly white hair, which is tied back in a neat ponytail. Galluci's wearing a black T-shirt adorned with the image of Zeus. He speaks fast, detailing the bizarre pedigree of the lion on the other side of the fence from us. The phone rang at Shambala one day in 2002, and Galluci found himself talking to a woman who needed to unload a lion. "Her son, for his eighteenth birthday, wanted a Lexus or a lion. She bought him a lion." Years after the call Galluci still sounds incredulous as he relates the story to me. "The lion turned into Zeus, this big, huge lion. They couldn't handle him." Mother and son managed to get Zeus into a U-Haul and drive him from Texas to California.

"What kind of a guy wants a lion for his eighteenth birthday?" I ask Galluci.

"What kind of a guy? I think any kind of a guy." Galluci understands the lure of the strange and dangerous. His own background includes leaving home at twelve and spending his teenage years in the Los Angeles motorcycle gang subculture of the 1960s. He spent his first night in jail before he turned eighteen. His life changed when he hired on as a welder to help build the set of Hedren's movie *Roar* in 1975. He's worked for her since that day. "You're young, you're dumb," he says about the Lexus–lion boy. "You don't really realize everything and anything. It's a cool thing. That's what I found out about a lot of these animals. People want them as possessions."

"Why?" I ask. I think Galluci's opinion, with his past and the years he's spent in intimate contact with the cats at Shambala, is well worth knowing. "What do you think makes humans want to own a wild cat that could kill them?"

"It's 'This is mine, I'm more powerful than you, I'm more of a man than you, I am the possessor of the king of beasts.' Maybe it's wrong to put youth into the equation," he corrects himself. "Some people are just that way. It's an extension of puffing out their chest and showing the world, 'I can do this, and you can't. Look what I have, and you don't.'" He recounts the provenance of a tiger on the grounds. A wealthy man bought the cat for his girlfriend, and it lived in their Malibu mansion until the neighbors complained. "That possession was for pleasing Miss Beautiful. With these animals it's just an extension of the look-at-me thing."

A dry Southern California wind rustles the cottonwood leaves. Ominous tiger chuffs add to the canyon soundtrack, along with a periodic cautionary, low lion roar. The enclosures are sprawling and pristine—I smell the summer foliage, not the animals. But the animals are confined, and confined for life at Shambala. The sanctuary does not buy, sell, breed, or trade cats. It is open to the public only on a limited basis, for specific fund-raising activities. Chris Galluci points out Patrick, a liger—half lion and half tiger. His father was a lion and his mother a tiger. When such hybrids are the result of a tiger father and a lion mother, they're called tigons. They're bred for display. "He's an old man now," Galluci says.

"He's useless as a show animal." But Galluci considers him a prime example of Shambala's mission: Keep Patrick alive as long as there is a decent quality of life available for him. Euthanizing Patrick or the other old cats on the grounds—former pets and exhibits—is not an option unless their lives turn to misery. "It would be like killing Grandpa. Don't kill Grandpa, man, just because he's old! Leave him alone."

I'm struck by how often my sources in the exotic pet world use human analogies. He's Grandpa, she's my baby, he's a member of the family. It's typical of the transference that occurs with household pets. But an aging lion-tiger mix as Grandpa? Are Galluci and the others grasping for a way to account for our relationship to these wild creatures? It's a relationship that probably didn't exist in the long prehistory of our mutual species. Safe bet that hunter-and-gatherer tribes didn't take tigers as pets—maybe as a periodic meal after a lucky kill, but not as a companion. As animals ourselves, how do we deal with incorporating apex predators into our social fabric? One device is to humanize them in our minds. Galluci gets excited as he talks; he is an excellent ambassador for Shambala's role. "Until the animals start urinating on themselves, defecating on themselves, can't take care of themselves, lose all their dignity, can't eat, there's not even a hint of a thought of putting them down. Patrick can live as long as he is fine, and he is fine. He's just old."

There is no hands-on interaction with the cats at Shambala since one of them bit a cage cleaner, an attack that didn't surprise Galluci. Captive-bred big cats may coexist with their caretakers, but that doesn't make them tame. "You get it as a cub. If you're lucky, it bonds with you, and it doesn't eat you. But it's going to eat Aunt Martha. That's the problem. These people bring Aunt Martha in with the animal, and Aunt Martha is prey. Their perfect animal does what an animal does and bites Aunt Martha, and everybody's shocked. It's a wild animal! It's a predator!" The surprise owners often express perplexes him. "What the hell did they think it's going to do?"

"You can't breed the wild out of them," I say. "A captive-bred big cat is still a wild cat, don't you agree?"

"They're wild. That's why I say this place is full of serial killers. That is what they do. They're opportunists." He points to a couple of tigers frolicking with each other. "They have claws that are like knives, and their teeth are like spikes. There are hundreds of pounds of power there. So they just make rotten pets."

Galluci joins Hedren in lobbying for a nationwide ban on the captive breeding of big cats. "No human being," he's also sure, "can give a wild animal what it needs." The next stop on my quest will take me to a Missouri auction house filled with animal buyers and sellers convinced that they, in fact, can do just that.

CHAPTER TWELVE

Servals, Spider Monkeys, and Zedonks

An Exotic Auction in Missouri

VINE STREET TEES OFF OF MISSOURI STREET. IT'S THE OLD MAIN DRAG OF Macon, Missouri. Macon is the home of the Lolli Brothers exotic animal auction. The scene there is famous with exotic pet lovers, animal rights activists, and the Fish and Wildlife Service as an ultimate public marketplace for trading everything from aardvarks to zebras. And zedonks. Zedonks, for those unfamiliar with the breed (and I sure was until I found myself in the Lolli Brothers sheds looking at a corral full of them), are a cross between a zebra and a donkey. The result is a funny-looking yahoo with the upper body of a donkey and the distinctive striping of a zebra on the animals' legs. They look nothing like the donkeys in Tijuana painted to look like zebras posing for pictures with gringo *touristas*.

As I learned prior to visiting Chimparty, Missouri is one of the states virtually free of laws interfering with the trade and ownership of exotic animals, making it attractive for auctions of just about any animal you could imagine bringing home. The Missouri Alliance for Animal Legislation, one of the groups trying to change the state's reputation as a haven for exotic animal trafficking, cries out about the absurdity of the sole regulation in Missouri: "The only current Missouri law affecting the owners of exotic animals is a largely un-enforced requirement to notify the local county sheriff about such animals."[78] Year after year, lawmakers introduce bills designed to restrict and regulate the exotic animal trade, and year after year they fail to pass.

Vine Street looks like America frozen in time and in an arrested state of decay. Elsewhere, Macon has been Wal-Marted, much of the business district and its nineteenth-century storefronts eviscerated by the strip malls on the edge of the city. It's home to Toastmaster toasters, a notice on the city water tower proclaims, and it calls itself The City of Maples. I come into Macon from Hannibal, on the Mississippi River, boyhood home to Samuel Clemens. I spent the night in Hannibal, luxuriated in the sweeping view from my hotel room of the river, and the next morning ate at the Mark Twain Dinette. After breakfast I walked past a wooden fence—a fence kept stark white to remind passersby of Tom Sawyer's entrepreneurial skills. The highway west to Macon is US 36, the route I took on my first pre-interstate cross-country road trip. The prairie sky is huge, deep blue with white cotton clouds over harvested stands of corn, the cornstalks often marked with signs acknowledging which corporate brand provided the proprietary genetically engineered seed. Interstate 70 flanks US 36 an hour's drive south, leaving cities like Hannibal and Macon off the beaten path for most travelers crossing Missouri. Traffic is sparse on bypassed 36; it connects faded market towns with lonely looking farmhouses. Stark and vacant—or vacant looking—white farmhouses face the highway looking like the iconic Robert Frank lonely photograph from the mid-1950s, "U.S. 30 between Ogallala and North Platte, Nebraska."

Before I head over to the auction yard, I stop off at the Macon Rexall drugstore and take a stool at its soda fountain. A milk shake comes with welcoming patter from the soda jerk: "I can make it with mint chip, but I'm not sure the chips will go through the straw," a trip back to the 1950s.

The Lolli Brothers complex looks like a county fair. Sheds cover corrals of animals. Stands sell all types of books about animals. Hand-tooled leather belts and holsters are on display. And head after taxidermied head can be had, along with whole stuffed animals posed as they may look in the wild: bears, lions, deer with multipoint racks of glorious antlers. The auction hall's steep bleachers are filled with cowboy hats and trademarked gimme caps, broad-brimmed straws over Amish beards, along with a scattering of skullcaps over Islamic beards. A man sitting in front of me is holding a lemur. He's letting the diapered prosimian play with a plastic card. When it tires of chewing it, the cute, tiny thing—smaller than a human infant—crawls over to a little girl and places itself, to her delight, in her lap. It's impossible not to be captivated by its humanlike antics. It uses its hands to grab. It climbs over the bleachers, inspecting whatever strikes its curiosity with its sentient-appearing big, round eyes.

As I approach the barnlike auction arena, the murmur of the crowd cannot compete with the auctioneer's amplified chatter, a farmer's rap of incessant unintelligible glottal riffs mixed with come-hither lines like "I've got a nice set of camels for you today, zebras next," and "This camel ought to bring $5,000." An American flag hangs on steer horns. A sign on the wall reads ENJOY BEEF. REAL FOOD FOR REAL PEOPLE. As animal after animal is bid on and sold, I contemplate the slave trade. I know there is a difference between human beings and camels, or even monkeys. But at the same time, it strikes me as odd to see these other beings sold as commodities. If it's okay to sell a monkey, just how much of a stretch is it to rationalize selling a human?

This is where Linda Bilbrey bought her new love two days ago, a tiny, twelve-day-old captive-bred African serval that is going to grow to be much bigger than a typical house cat, even while it will look much like common pet cats. She is cradling it to her bosom when I catch up with her.

"It's my first time at the auction," she gushes, "but not my last." She's taking a break from the auction hall, but a camel and a zebra are still on her shopping list. Bilbrey and her husband run an eighty-acre exotic animal farm at their bed-and-breakfast across the Mississippi in Illinois. But the serval is not destined for show-and-tell at the farm; it's headed for their home.

"He's not going to live outside. He's going to live in my house," she says. And she knows she's soon going to face a challenge. "He's going to get about knee high."

I pet the cat. The downy fur is so soft and so fluffy, it's almost like petting air. Its face is round and innocent looking, about the diameter of an orange slice. Innocent looking, but he's already causing some trouble. Bilbrey's hands are victims of his sharp claws. Well scratched. She knows his sweet disposition may change with age. "He might get a little hissy, but I'm going to be very, very hands on with him. I've raised my parrots from two weeks old, so they know me as Mom, and the same thing is going to happen with him."

Out in the dusty Lolli Brothers parking lot, Linda Bilbrey is beaming, kissing the serval, then kissing him again and again. "I always wanted animals, and I always wanted to live on a farm," she says. "I'm living my dream!" She smiles at me but looks with adoring eyes at the kitten. Her blond hair is pinned up, with falling strands framing her content smile. A Lolli Brothers sticker identifying her as a buyer is pasted to her blouse. She heads for her car. "I just came out to get his bottle."

The tiny cat mews with its tiny voice.

"He's mewing!" I say about the obvious. But there's no question his vocalizing adds to his charming allure.

"He'll suck on my face," Bilbrey tells me.

Which leads me to ask, "Do you think it matters that he's separated from his mother so early?"

"No. It'll be fine. I'm taking very good care of him. Lots of interaction with him. It's something I've always wanted to do, and I've been lucky enough to live my dream."

He mews again, a high-pitched and brief meow. Bilbrey grew up poor; she and her husband started their marriage with no frills.

"We were so poor, we couldn't afford meat. Now we're living our dream," she says again. She understands that her dream is a nightmare for Tippi Hedren and others opposed to big cat pets. "I want to live my dream. I'm a good mom. I should have been born in Africa. I've been there twice. I should have been born in Africa and lived with the animals." Her explanatory sentences come fast and short as she pets the cat and answers my queries. "My husband has taken me to Paris, he's taken me to Italy." She sighs. "He's taken me to Africa and, oh my God!" A rooster crows as she considers her African memories. "It was my dream. It was amazing."

I snap some photographs of the two of them. "I love him so much," Linda Bilbrey says as I depart, and she tells me again that she understands the complaints against exotic pets. "But I'm good to them. They're already captive born. I've been to the rain forest. I didn't bring any animals back." A bovine moans a deep moo from its pen as she tells me that there is nothing wrong with breeding, selling, and owning exotic animals like her serval. "Not if you're good to them. These are my children." Her voice trembles. "I had cancer when I was nineteen. I had one child, and I can't have any more. These are my children." The serval, the camel, and the zebra she intends to take home to Edwardsville, to the menagerie at Bilbrey Farms.

I pet the kitty one more time as she prepares its formula—he is so soft, he looks so innocent—but I know how such cat looks can be deceiving. Back home Schrödinger is purring one minute and lashing out with his claws the next. I head back to the auction hall.

The auctioneer is pitching the crowd like a monotonic yodeler full of methamphetamine. I sit in the bleachers watching camel after camel get paraded to buyers and fetch thousands of dollars each. I want to see the zebras, but the march of the camels seems endless. I get up and wander around the stalls and find the bizarre zedonks and a striking, stately, gorgeous zebra-horse cross. Imagine a rich-looking brown horse decorated with black zebra striping. Eye-catching and elegant. A cowboy saddles up a little zebra, mounts it, and rides off toward the auction hall.

I spot a woman I overheard the day before wondering if her motel room was too cold for her monkey. She is cradling a diapered fur ball, and I ask her what she bought.

"It's a little spider monkey," Teresa Shaffer says and smiles. She's wearing a tan billed cap over her blond hair and a loose blue hooded sweater. The monkey is up against her chest looking over her shoulder. He's looking out at the Lolli Brothers parking lot with wide-open, big brown eyes. They glisten like mirrors. Later, when I study the photographs I took, I can see myself reflected in those eyes, eyes that look almost human in contrast to its doglike black nose.

"So cute," I say about her monkey.

"Yeah, she's a baby. Just six months old. She doesn't think she's a spider monkey." Shaffer and her husband didn't just buy the monkey this day; they've had her for two months. They breed, raise, and sell African servals, savannahs, caracals, and chausies near Kansas City and call their business Exotic Cats-R-Us. But the little spider monkey is not for sale; it's for them.

"What does the monkey think she is?" I ask.

"A person."

"What makes you think that?"

"Because when she goes with his monkey," she points at a fellow holding another spider, "she doesn't like it."

"What are you going to do with her?" I ask.

"We're going to keep her as a pet. Oh, yeah," she coos at the monkey, "she's going to be our baby." She cuddles the monkey and says matter-of-factly, "She'll probably get mean some day. It depends on the monkey. But we're prepared for her to get mean."

"And then what happens?"

"She'll stay in our house. We just probably won't handle her as much."

This means she'll be relegated to much more cage time. I want to know the appeal. Why spend thousands of dollars on a high-maintenance family addition that could turn into a permanent teenager from hell?

"I think a lot of people get them because it is like having a child. I love her, but I would never have another one. They're just a lot of work, a lot of work."

The monkey is clinging to Shaffer.

"This is how I'll be until I physically pull her off. She will not let go. She's got a death grip on me." The monkey's hands are around Shaffer's neck. "She isn't going to let go, and if I do try to pull her hands off, she'll squawk and scream." That may be because of the auction ruckus. "At home she's fine. She gets down and jumps around."

Shaffer isn't a twenty-four-hour-a-day nurse to the monkey. She leaves her alone in her cage for a few hours at a time, and she left her in a kennel in the motel room.

"She was fine. She yells a little bit; all the maids said they heard her yelling some. But she's okay, she's a good girl," she pats the monkey and plays with its tail. The tail curls around her finger like a miniature Burmese python. "They're the only monkeys with a prehensile tail. She can pick up a dime with this tail." In fact, other New World monkeys enjoy prehensile tails.

Shaffer extracts her finger and admonishes her new love like a mother to a favorite child with a baby talk voice. "You are just a stinker!" She turns back to me and repeats, "She does not think she's a monkey. I do not know what she thinks she is, but it ain't a monkey."

"What do you think she is?"

"I think she's a monkey, I think she's a spoiled monkey."

"What made you decide to get her?"

"Crazy," she says, and then, "I really don't know." What she does know is that her monkey is no toy poodle. "Wild animals are wild animals. People shouldn't act like they're a pet, because they're not. Monkeys don't stay nice." She and her wild animal continue to cuddle.

"Good luck with her," I say to Teresa Shaffer and to the monkey she calls Ayla.

"We'll see. We love her. She's staying with us forever, no matter what."

"No matter what?"

"Yup." She strokes Ayla, murmuring, "Sweet thing, sweet thing. She is a good girl, a good girl."

I leave the two of them hugging in the parking lot, convinced from what I've learned about exotic pets that there is a problematic future in store for both human and monkey. Compared with the often unpredictable antics of human beings, I'm quite sure I know what that monkey will be doing in the next few years: tearing up the Shaffer household until the couple lock her in a cage.

CHAPTER THIRTEEN

Zeus by the Side of the Road

The Myth of the White Tiger

WHILE EN ROUTE TO THE SPOKANE AIRPORT AFTER VISITING LILLY THE TIGER IN Oldtown, I stopped off at a roadside private zoo named Cat Tales. What I was learning about captive tiger breeding made me realize that my casual tour of Cat Tales was, in fact, an example of how the worlds of exotic pets and roadside zoos intersect. I paid my $8 admission charge and was ordered to sign a release form.

"Why?" I ask the ticket taker.

"It's for liability," she says. "If you do something and get hurt, you can't sue us."

I sign, enter the grounds, and find myself face-to-face with big cats trapped in what look to me like too-small enclosures. I linger at one called Zeus. Zeus is a popular name for top-of-the-food-chain exotic pets; there seems to be a propensity among owners to play up the dominant animal kingdom role of their charges. The white tiger is labeled a descendent of Mohan, a "royal white Bengal tiger" captured by the maharaja of Borada in 1951. The maharaja, goes the story, knew poachers were after Mohan and the few white Bengals still wild. He captured Mohan to save him, according to the sign at the compound, and with hopes of captive breeding enough Bengals to keep the species from joining the extinct list. Wearing the green Cat Tales uniform, a pert Lisa Small was happy to break the monotony of guard duty to chat about the tiger I was looking at and about her work. Small (I've changed her name here in order not to jeopardize her job) is studying at Cat Tales, earning a certificate from its "Zoo Training Center" and hoping to graduate into a job at a zoo as a keeper.

Zeus was captive bred, as are all white tigers in America.

"Unfortunately," she acknowledges, "a lot of them that you'll see nowadays are inbred. It is very difficult to get a white tiger."

It is a striking-looking animal; he looks to my novice big cat–spotting eyes as if a regular tiger had been washed with Clorox. Instead of an orange background, his black stripes are on white fur. We admire Zeus together. "He has a clean bloodline. He's a direct descendent of Mohan, the last known wild white tiger."

"Really?"

"Yeah."

"Bullshit," Ron Tilson says when I describe Zeus to him and relate my conversation with Small. "I know this world," he says about the proliferation of captive-bred tigers that look like Zeus, "and it is full of deceit." Dr. Tilson is in charge of conservation work at the Minnesota Zoo, and he coordinates the American Zoo and Aquarium Association's tiger captive-breeding program. His expertise includes years of fieldwork studying wild tigers, along with pragmatic efforts to sustain a captive population without cross-breeding subspecies. Research by Dr. Tilson and his colleagues shows that there are no living descendants of Mohan in North America. White tigers are extraordinarily rare in the wild. There is no such thing as a unique species called "royal white Bengal tiger." Their color—when they occur in the wild in India—is caused by a rare double allele (an alternative form of the gene for the yellow color) that both parents must carry. That original import from India was mated with his daughter so breeders could gain another white tiger, and that bloodline for white tigers ended with the resulting generation. All extant white tigers born in captivity since, according to Tilson, are inbred hybrids of subspecies, a cross between Amur and Bengal tigers. Many suffer from debilitating birth defects and are not exhibited. To get a Zeus—a cat that appears normal—means littering breeding farms with feeble sibling cats. The private trade fuels this breeding frenzy.

Apollo, another white tiger, lives in an enclosure adjacent to Zeus. They were donated to Cat Tales, Lisa Small tells me, by "another facility." They don't much like each other these days. "As they're getting older, they're getting more aggressive and more territorial," says Small. The two are eight years old, well along in years were they wild, but in captivity Zeus and Apollo could be on display at Cat Tales another decade or more.

"Everything is controlled here. They're not searching for their own food. There are no poachers."

"He looks relatively content," I say. And Zeus does at the moment. "He looks like a big house cat." He is white, like my cat Schrödinger, who is probably napping in my living room as I speak with Lisa Small.

"Oh, definitely!" she says. "He is very content, except when the flies are bothering him." He swats at them.

"He looks like a kitty when he does that," I say. A 550-pound kitty.

"They do have a lot of the same characteristics as a regular house cat," she tells me. "Unfortunately, that's what a lot of people see. They say, 'Oh, he looks like my cat at home, only a lot bigger, that's the only difference.' It really isn't." She turns serious. "These guys become extremely aggressive during feeding time. They still have natural instincts. You can't breed that out of them."

As I collect stories about exotics and their owners, I'm becoming convinced that it's true of all animals: You can't breed the wildness out of them.

"They will always have a natural instinct about them," she says about captive-bred tigers. "Even house cats do. They're always out catching birds and mice. These guys," she points to Zeus and Apollo, "they're affectionate. They'll rub on the fence."

But the humans on the other side are not all affectionate. Small's guard duty includes stopping onlookers who throw rocks at Zeus to wake him and preventing visitors from jumping the secondary fence to get closer to him. I think I can begin to understand the lure. I look at Zeus, glad that he's sequestered, but at the same time it's an appealing notion to rub his nose and scratch his ears.

Curiosity and risk are the motivators for the fence jumpers, figures Small. "There's that potential risk, and a lot of people like taking risks. I'll tell you one thing. You step on the other side of that fence," she points to the secondary barrier, "these cats get so much bigger. From here," we're standing maybe twenty feet from Zeus, "they're huge." She estimates his shoulder height at four feet plus.

"So, isn't this pen too small for Zeus?"

"Yes, in the wild they have a lot of space. They're used to more roaming territory. We don't have that kind of space for them here." But she doesn't think that this is necessarily bad for the cats. "We like to say if these guys were not here with us now, they would be dead. A lot of these guys," she gestures to the cat collection, "have come from worse, really horrible conditions. They'll get up," she says about Zeus and the others, "they'll pace back and forth. They'll play in the pool. Most of the time they'll just lounge around, doing nothing." She smiles a sweet smile. "They'll get fed. They're happy."

"You think?"

"They are," she says without hesitation. "You can see it."

"How can you tell?" I wonder aloud. "How can you see it?"

"They're used to it. They just have a look in their eye. When you get to know them on a personal level, they'll come up, rub on the fence, and chuffle at you. Tigers make a sound called a chuffle. These guys can't purr like house cats. They're roaring cats, they roar. So they chuffle; it's like blowing air through their nose. That means that they're happy. It's an affectionate sound."

"Zeus does that to you?"

"Yeah!"

She scratches him, she says, and Zeus leans on the fence, looking like one happy cat. I'm struck by how often the owners and caretakers extrapolate contentedness from pet body language and verbalization. As I watch them being scratched, cuddled, and sweet talked, the animals usually do appear content to me. Perhaps they are, or perhaps the attention they're receiving at the moment distracts them from the frustrations of their confined life.

Lisa Wathne from PETA disagrees with Small, calling Cat Tales "nothing more than a pseudo-sanctuary and roadside zoo," the kind of a place where Zeus could not be happy. Sanctuary purists reject the term for a reserve that's open to the public and charges admission and buys, sells, trades, or breeds animals. Roadside zoos and self-styled sanctuaries are common tourist attractions along America's highways. Nobody knows how many exist—they range from the disturbingly tawdry to the relatively clean, like Cat Tales. Regulations are minimal: The U.S. Department of Agriculture requires the easy-to-obtain license for exhibitors, and it mandates basic standards for enclosures. Cages can be as small as Lilly's feed store home and simply must be kept clean.

Ron Tilson opposes not just the captive breeding of white tigers, but also the unregulated captive breeding of yellow tigers by private owners for the pet trade. Such offspring cannot compensate, he says, for the loss of wild tigers in their natural habitat. "Captive-bred tigers are not wild predators evolving and carrying out significant functions in their natural habitats," he writes in his book *Tigers of the World*. They've lost what he refers to as their "tigerness" and end up as "tiger soup." The abundance of these mongrel tigers makes wild tiger conservation efforts more difficult from a public relations standpoint because the surplus of captive-bred tigers makes it appear there is no tiger population crisis. Tilson embraces the potential value of scientifically managed captive breeding to augment conservation in the wild. Managed breeding for conservation keeps tigers genetically distinct. Still to come are techniques for introducing such captive-bred tigers successfully into the wild, as are controls over catastrophic tiger habitat loss.

— ⁓

As I continue to probe human interaction with big cats, great apes, and long snakes, I keep contemplating that line that demarks wild versus "domesticated" in the animal kingdom. Years ago I lived in the old mining camp of Silver City, in the high desert within sight of the east slope of the Sierra Nevada; it's in the heart of Nevada's wild horse country. A common sight was a few of the wild horses grazing in the city park across High Street from our house. These horses were descendants of ranchers' and Indian horses let loose or escaped, horses once considered domesticated. They now live on their own in the wild, protected by federal law, and they are thriving. No one "owns" these wild horses (although the Bureau of Land Management culls the herds and offers horses for adoption in an attempt to keep herds from growing too large for their environment; they suffer from no natural predators).

Should we own animals? Admittedly, I come to this argument with some prejudices. I've not eaten red meat or fowl since Ronald "Bedtime for Bonzo" Reagan was president. I don't eat dairy products or eggs, and I only eat fish (no crustaceans; why, I'm not sure) because my wife threatened to stop cooking if I further restricted our menus. She also worries I'd fall over without some protein from animal sources. Yet despite the exquisite taste I can still enjoy from a fresh-out-of-the Pacific (I live right on the ocean) salmon steak barbequed with a splash of olive oil, lemon slices, and a sprinkling of dill, even the fish I eat—lots of sardines, probably too much tuna considering the mercury, halibut—can make me uncomfortable when I contemplate them beyond cuisine.

Even were I to stop eating fish, my footprint would continue to squash other animals. "The cost that consumer society imposes on the planet's fifteen or so million non-human species goes way beyond either meat or eggs," Elizabeth Kolbert points out in a *New Yorker* review of Jonathan Safran Foer's book *Eating Animals.* "Bananas, blue jeans, soy lattes, the paper used to print this magazine, the computer screen you may be reading it on," she writes, "death and destruction are imbedded in them all. It is hard to think at all rigorously about our impact on other organisms without being sickened."[79]

I'm not quite sure why I stopped eating meat. I used to be a pretty cavalier diner; a lunch stop for a burger at McDonald's was not out of the ordinary. But over time the meat stopped appealing to me, and it was only after I quit eating it that obvious reasons for eliminating it from my diet—beyond just my lack of desire for it—started adding up. I seemed to feel cleaner inside without meat. I knew the fat was not good for me, not to mention whatever junk was administered to the animals to fatten them up quickly. My hay fever attacks lessened. I signed on to all the usual health arguments against meat eating, and then I started thinking about the animals. Again I bought the party lines. How could I justify the abysmal lifestyles animals are subjected to on factory farms? Why should an animal die for my dinner when I could eat beans? If I were to eat meat, was

I ready to hunt for it, kill it, and dress the animal—or just buy it wrapped in Safeway plastic? Finally, raising animals just for our meals is, of course, an extraordinarily inefficient use of resources.

Nonetheless, I'm not a fanatic. As I told monkey smuggler Fran Ogren, I still carve the Thanksgiving turkey at our home. It's a tradition. The bird is already dead. I do the best job of it in the family. But I'm sure my vegish lifestyle inflects my attitude as I try to understand the lure of exotic pets. I find my rejection of meat as a foodstuff extending to growing concern for animal welfare. Confining Zeus by the side of the highway, where, for an $8 ticket to Cat Tales, passersby can gawk at him and taunt him as he paces his minimal enclosure, seems an offensive abuse of a helpless animal brought into this world by profiteering human beings.

When I look at our cat Schrödinger, it's difficult for me to relate to him as something I own. And it's easy to see him as all-but wild. He's an outdoor cat who freely uses his own door to join us in the house when he wishes. His personality seems schizoid to me. One minute he'll vocalize, sounding almost like a pleading child, seeking attention, and then purring nonstop as long as the ear scratching, stomach rubbing, and back petting continue. The next minute he'll act aloof and skittish, or he'll curl his lip, showing off those teeth not so distant from a saber-toothed tiger's, and adopt a threatening stance. Were he the size of one of Tippi Hedren's tigers or lions, I'd want him in a secure cage, not roaming around my living room. We feed him, but he's fed himself plenty of mice and birds, once bringing down one of the big Bodega Bay crows made famous by Alfred Hitchcock. Ownership seems like an out-of-place concept for the relationship between humans and animals—at least in my backyard.

CHAPTER FOURTEEN

Rampant Trafficking

You Can Get Anything You Want

A BLUSTERY SUMMER DAY IN YORKSHIRE, ENGLAND. I'M AT THE MANCHESTER airport wandering around. I've got plenty of time; my flight to Charleroi is delayed over five hours. The flow of foot traffic in Terminal 1 is forced by the interior design of the terminal past kiosk after kiosk selling perfume and other stuff promising to make you look, feel, and smell sexier. The display for a product called Rare catches my eyes. Whatever it is comes in a bag adorned with a leopard skin print.

A poster for Rare is on the case holding the product. The poster shows a vamping woman—her pouting lips a high gloss—looking off into the middle distance. She's wearing a long gown, its print motif echoing a leopard skin. Her raised right hand is resting seductively against a wall, showing off her bright red nail polish. Her left hand holds a leash connected to a wide, sparkling, diamondesque collar—a collar around the neck of a fine specimen of a leopard. An intense look is in the animal's eyes as it, too, gazes into the middle distance.

What is the message? What is the product?

The clerk comes over and asks me why I am scribbling in my notebook. I start to answer and then stop to ask him, "What do you think of when you look at this advertisement?"

He looks puzzled by the question, his face taking on what we in our family call the Amigo Look. When our dog, Amigo, did not understand something we were trying to communicate to him, he often would tilt his head slightly to one side, cock one ear up while the other flopped down on his head, and look at us, his eyes asking for help in understanding. Interesting: Just as we attribute human characteristics to animals, so am I foisting my dog's expression on this clerk. This cross-species morphing

I engage in may well fuel my growing moral obligations to other-than-human animals. "I don't know," the clerk finally says.

"What does the ad mean to you?" I try another tack.

"I don't know," he says again.

"Come on," I encourage him. "Just tell me what you think the message is supposed to be."

Finally, he offers, "Just as the leopard is defending the girl, you always want a styler with you to defend your hair—to keep it looking good."

Ah, the product is a device to fix your hairdo.

The clerk asks me the same question I ask him.

Just the day before I was farther south in England, in Cambridge, meeting at the TRAFFIC headquarters. I'm thinking about all sorts of questions about the ad because I'm immersed in the research for this book. Who is its keeper/owner? What motivated the advertising agency to use the leopard? Is it photoshopped, or was the leopard really held on a leash by the model? Was she scared? Was she trained? Was the animal sedated? How is it treated? What was its fee for the shoot?

I tell the clerk that when I look at the ad, I wonder about the leopard. What is it doing in the ad? How does it feel being in the ad?

He smiles indulgently and offers, "Everybody thinks different."

Indeed. And when it comes to the wild animal trade, I'm learning that there are multiple nuances. After considering animal smugglers and the cops who chase them, captive breeders and the pet owners who buy from them, the diligence I find at TRAFFIC helps put the exotic trade into a global perspective.

Soft-spoken Dr. Richard Thomas oversees TRAFFIC's work against the illegal trafficking in wild animals, a portfolio that extends to the legal trade in captive-bred tigers in the United States. "We're very concerned that the parts from these animals might stimulate demand among the Asian community; there might even start to be trade back toward East Asia of tiger parts from the United States," he says. "The U.S. really doesn't know how many tigers they've got or where they are or what happens to them. There are no requirements to dispose of the bodies." Trade in tiger parts is illegal, but the Chinese government is under pressure from tiger farmers to lift that ban, a reversal Dr. Thomas considers would have disastrous consequences. "Hang on," he says. "What's the cheaper alternative? If you open that trade, you're going to restimulate demand. People are going to want to use tiger parts again, and inevitably it's going to lead to increased poaching. We're very much opposed to any reopening of the tiger trade."

Of course, as is the case with any banned illegal product, the ban alone does not end trade.

The TRAFFIC offices are in a nondescript one-story building a couple of miles from the charming university town along the Cam, a place crammed with students and tourists. Here at the Cambridge headquarters and at branch offices wherever there is a perceived threat to wildlife, the TRAFFIC staff pores over computers, compiling reports from statistics and field studies in order to buttress their lobbying efforts. TRAFFIC doesn't engage in debates about animal rights; it simply promotes sustainable and legal animal trade. Its reports indicate, for example, that demand for tiger parts in China is declining because of the ban. That's why TRAFFIC researchers refute arguments that legalizing trade in the remains of captive-bred tigers would take the poaching pressure off the wild populations. Instead, they believe, legalizing tiger penis soup and other tiger derivatives in various balms and potions would only embolden poachers and the retailers who flaunt the law.

Richard Thomas looks and acts unassuming ("Oh, blimey," he says when I ask him about his background). He's an average-size, middle-aged man with short hair and a short salt-and-pepper beard. His PhD is in chemistry, but he describes himself as "a bird nut for years" who worked to protect birds and their habitat. It was an easy transition to join TRAFFIC and add all endangered fauna to his workload. He's wearing a T-shirt adorned with a Brazilian macaw protected by TRAFFIC; it's a casual office. But that low-key appearance proves of value when TRAFFIC does its undercover work. "We have evidence," he tells me, "that demand for tiger parts is actually declining in China because people are aware that it's illegal, and it's harder to get hold of the parts. We go into shops and ask if they've got any tiger parts. We've seen a marked decline in shops that say, 'Yes, we've got them.'" Such undercover work in China is done by a TRAFFIC operative whose identity is kept secret, and whose photograph—understandably—is never published.

Shops in the United States, where captive tiger breeding is legal and there are no restrictions on the sales of the animals, could theoretically peddle tiger parts. But selling the bones and organs and skins across state lines would violate laws, and selling them internationally without permits would violate CITES laws, the international treaty to which the United States is signatory. (CITES stands for the Convention on International Trade in Endangered Species of Wild Fauna and Flora.) CITES is a landmark agreement that allows the international community to work together to prevent international trade in animals and plants if such trade threatens the survival of the species being bought and sold. It regulates more than 30,000 species, and each of the nations signatory to the agreement (171 as of this writing) is responsible for its own enforcement, a complex bureaucracy that results in a byzantine pile of rules, regulations, and laws, along with the penalties for violating them. CITES Appendix I lists the most endangered animals and plants in the world. These are species on the verge of extinction, and almost all trade in Appendix I species is prohibited. Appendix II species are not quite as vulnerable, but trade is monitored, and a permit is mandatory for legal exportation and importation out of or into the United States and the other countries that have agreed to the terms of the treaty.

That some U.S. intrastate tiger commerce exists without regulation is difficult to understand. Imagine: You're cited by the cops if you fail to wear a seat belt across America, but in Ohio, it's okay if there's a tiger in the back of your station wagon.

In addition to tigers, TRAFFIC priorities include a lesser-known animal that's being hunted relentlessly for its medicinal and ritual use, the pangolin. The pangolin looks like a Transformer cousin of an armadillo, or maybe, from a distance, a design for a streamlined car from the 1930s. This little nocturnal mammal is equipped with a body covered by scales that make it appear reptilian, but the scales are a variant of mammal hair. That streamlined look comes from the small head, followed by the bulk of the body, and finished off with a long and wide prehensile tail. Its long, sticky tongue works wonders for searching out and grabbing tasty termites and ants. The scales are sharp defense devices and work in conjunction with anal glands that generate a disgusting smell. When a threat is imminent, the pangolin rolls itself into a ball—like the roly-poly bug (*Armadillidium vulgare*)—a ball difficult for predators to unroll. Mothers protect their babies by rolling up around junior. Pangolins live about twenty years if left alone, but humans rarely leave them alone.

"They're targeted for traditional medicine in China," Richard Thomas tells me, and to such an extent that TRAFFIC is concerned about their survival despite the fact that they are a CITES-protected species. "We have anecdotal evidence that hunters can't find them anymore in neighboring countries to China and even in China itself. They've just been wiped out." In parts of Africa, the pangolin's use is ritualistic. If a woman manages to bury one at the door of a house belonging to a man she wants, she is said to gain power over him. The scales are used to obviate evil spirits and for witchcraft and to keep lions from villages. Sacrificed pangolins are offered in exchange for rain.[80] The number of animals involved in this illicit trade is staggering. Thomas says just one seized shipment of pangolin in Vietnam weighed in at twenty-four tons. That's a lot of pangolin, considering they weigh only thirty to forty pounds each. "We're very worried about that. I feel it is the forgotten animal." He sighs as he describes pangolins; we were talking about pets, and pangolins are not sought for companionship. "They're not gorgeous. The odd person might keep them in a cage as a pet. But that's not the reason they're being traded. They're mostly shipped frozen." The trafficking in pangolins is a parallel commerce to the tiger trade and the trafficking of great apes and other protected species. Smugglers learn techniques from one another; their skill sets (and personnel) are interchangeable. It's typical to simply shroud the contraband with similar-looking legal material. Masking illegal animals with surrounding dangerous (like venomous snakes) cargo is another device. And Vietnam often is a common denominator.

Vietnam is a major source of wildlife sold on the international black market, and it suffers from an all-but-insatiable domestic appetite for poached animals. Literally. The country is rife with opportunities to eat bush meat, a sure sign of a flourishing illegal trade. "Considering the number of wildlife meat restaurants in Vietnam, it is clear there is a serious conservation problem," reckons Tran Quang Phuong, a specialist in small carnivores at Cuc Phuong National Park.[81] Monitor lizards, cobras, pythons, macaques, tigers, and bears are among the creatures smuggled into the pet and traditional medicine trade via Vietnam. "Vietnam is getting richer," says Edwin Wiek, "but people also believe in ancient medicine and showing off their wealth and power by eating these endangered species." Wiek rescues captive wild animals from his base at Wildlife Friends Foundation Thailand, an organization he founded and heads. He retrieved, for example, a couple of poached orangutans from a private, illegal zoo in Vietnam. "For some people," Wiek now understands, "having a Ferrari outside their front door is not enough. You have to have a chimpanzee or an orangutan in your backyard as well. Then you're really the man."[82]

I ask Dr. Thomas what he thinks motivates the collectors, and he equates it to a childish compulsion. Without buyers, there would, of course, be no illegal pet trade. "Some people do want something that they know is naughty, just because they know it's wrong," he tells me. There is a lust to fool the authorities. But there is a further lure. "Another big influence is the rarity factor. People want something just because they know it is very, very rare, and they are the only ones who have it." It's a succinct appraisal. "I'm not interested in owning this kind of stuff," he says, shrugging, but he is interested in stopping those who are. The illegal pet trade is an insidious tangled net stretched around the globe. The United States and Europe are the world's biggest importers, and the Third World countries are susceptible to plundering. Their poverty often makes the value of the Yankee dollar and the euro more compelling than obeying the law or worrying about local endangered animal life.

I left Richard Thomas at his TRAFFFIC office, but not before he told me about a case he likened to *Mission Impossible*. The Australian Post confiscated an illegal shipment of geckos en route to the Czech Republic (a favored European entry port for reptile smugglers). The geckos were stuffed into a hollowed-out book. When Dr. Thomas wrote the story for the TRAFFIC Web site, he couldn't help himself. "Geckos Posted to Czech Mate," was his headline. His attempt at humor offers momentary relief from the Sisyphus-like struggle he and his colleagues face daily.

Tarantulas, I learn from TRAFFIC, are in high demand as pets. Richard Thomas introduced me to Carlos Viquez, curator of arachnids at Costa Rica's National Institute for Biodiversity. His worries are an example of how even an animal not on the wish list of most pet owners is in jeopardy because it intrigues a subculture of collectors. Costa Rica is home to forty-three different types of tarantulas, and Dr. Viquez informs me that hustlers are poaching them for the international pet trade. "Smugglers come to a rural place," he writes, "pay a little money to local guys, who in most cases have a poor job or no job, and they help find the spiders in the forest." It's a low-risk business, he reports, and one with high rewards. Some prized tarantulas can bring hundreds of dollars on the pet market. What's their appeal? Owners think tarantulas look cool, and they enjoy watching them. Viquez tries to educate his poor rural countrymen that *Megaphobema peterklaasi* (one of the most popular "pet" tarantulas) and the forty-two other local tarantulas are a national treasure and illegal to plunder.

I'm sitting at my desk. It's a crisp summer morning, and the blackberries are ripening on the overgrown bushes in the backyard. I'm contemplating the psychology of exotic pet owners. What types of emotions trigger the desire to own a great ape or a big cat or a long snake or a killer arachnid? What motivates the owners? A desire to dominate must be a factor, as Tippi Hedren suggests. Intrigue with the rare, the unique. I can relate to that; I have a 1974 Austin FX 4 London black cab in my garage. Some collectors, it's easy to conclude, keep dangerous animals to scare and impress the neighbors (along with competitors and employees). That would explain the propensity for drug traffickers to stock private zoos. To anthropomorphize—an attempt to create a relationship across the species divide by making the animal seem human—obviously is another factor I can relate to as well. Once we put a pair of my boxers over the hindquarters of our dog, Amigo, and pushed his forelegs through the sleeves of one of my shirts. He was, as usual, patient with our antics. That attempt at humanizing motivates some ape owners; the image of Travis the chimp sipping wine out of a stemmed glass recurs in my mind.

⤙ ⤚

Drug traffickers famously dabble in private zookeeping. A-list cocaine smuggler Pablo Escobar kept a lion, giraffe, kangaroo, elephant, camel, rhinoceros, and hippopotamus at his Hacienda Napoles in Colombia until he was put out of business, gunned down in Medellín in 1993. His animals were given to zoos, except for some African hippos. Three escaped from his compound and spent a few years roaming wild near the Magdalena River with their wild-born calf. Farmers complained of damaged crops and worried about their own safety. The state responded with a death sentence. By the summer of 2009, hunters finally shot and killed one of the hippos, a decision rationalized by the country's environment minister, Carlos Costa, who said, even as two of the hippos still roamed free, "It was only a question of time before those animals hurt someone. The decision was a sound one."[83]

Before public zoos became common, royal families and dictators had a reputation for keeping exotic animals of their own. In 1927 William Randolph Hearst (by some definitions, an American equivalent of royalty), flush with cash from his growing newspaper empire, hired the former San Diego zookeeper, one Richard Addison, to come to San Simeon and curate the Hearst Castle zoo, a menagerie he'd begun assembling three years earlier. Why did the press lord collect animals? Addison had a theory. "It was because of his fondness for them, maybe as a little boy's love for his pets. It wasn't just for show or part of the setting; he actually liked those creatures and was always concerned for their comfort."[84]

But Hearst was also looking for kicks. The iconic California architect Julia Morgan was his San Simeon designer, and the year before he hired Addison as zookeeper, he wrote to her with an idea for landscaping his animal kingdom. "How about a maze in connection with the zoo," he wondered. "I think getting lost in the maze and coming unexpectedly upon lions, tigers, pumas, panthers, wild cats, monkeys, macaws and cockatoos, etc. etc., would be a thrill even for the most blasé."[85]

Thrill the blasé the animals wandering around the maze did, according to author Marina Belozerskaya, who, in her book on extraordinary relationships between man and beast, *The Medici Giraffe,* cites actor Ralph Bellamy's memory of spending the night in a San Simeon guest room.

"When I came out of the bathroom," remembered Bellamy, "I found my wife petrified in the room saying, 'There's a lion outside that window!' And I said, 'Oh, come on, it's late. We had a drink or two. Go ahead and get your face washed and get to bed.' When we woke up in the morning and I went to the window, there was a lion!"[86]

Hearst, just up the coast from Michael Jackson's Neverland Ranch, championed animal rights, yet he kept chimpanzees, an elephant, a tortoise, a variety of bears, giraffes, and a slew of other animals—all under conditions harshly criticized by George Bistany, the first director of the Fleishhacker Zoo in San Francisco. Cash-strapped as the Depression wore on, Hearst quit his collection, shipping his animals off to zoos, including Fleishhacker.

Fleishhacker Zoo. As a youngster I lived just a few miles from it in San Francisco. The zoo—now called the San Francisco Zoo—was named for its founder, Herbert Fleishhacker, a banker and Parks Commission president. The San Francisco Zoo is where the tiger Tatiana jumped out of her enclosure Christmas Day in 2007 and killed a zoo visitor, a visitor who—evidence suggests—taunted and teased her. But it didn't occur to me until I was compiling this history of my hometown zoo's founder that his name translates as "meat chopper." How appropriate.

From the time of Kubla Kahn through the relatively recent days of William Randolph Hearst, harboring exotic animals remained, for the most part, an expensive dalliance of the idle rich, self-regulated because of the cost and the logistics: Apes and lions came from Africa, tigers from Asia, snakes from South America. Cheap international airline tickets and freight services make shipping animals easier these days. But domestic captive breeding is what brought exotic pets to Everyman. Whether it's a chimpanzee, a tiger, or a Burmese python, it's available homegrown. And with two, anyone can go into the breeding business. Such easy accessibility, combined with the fact that so many owners quickly tire of their novelty pets, put the purchase of wild animals within the range of most family budgets (the long-term upkeep is a more expensive commitment). In response to the ever-increasing exotic pet population, more and more jurisdictions are passing laws regulating and prohibiting animals of all types in our midst. At the same time, our cultural zeitgeist is becoming more sensitive about the use of animals for human amusement. The days of attracting positive attention from most bystanders by holding hands with a monkey or walking a tiger on a leash or wearing a python like a necklace may well be numbered.

CHAPTER FIFTEEN

A Conscientious Merchant

Selling New World Snakes in the Old World

"A FRIEND OF THE FAMILY HAD A SNAKE. I WENT AND SAW IT, FELL IN LOVE. I was ten years old." That's how Charles Thompson explains his fascination with reptiles and snakes in particular, a fascination that led him to his life's work: He owns and operates Snakes 'n' Adders, an emporium in suburban Sheffield, England. He and I are chatting in the backyard of his shop shortly after John Ord Clark was sent to prison for operating an illegal pet store in his home, just up the road in Manchester. There the Royal Society for the Prevention of Cruelty to Animals found an estimated one thousand exotic species—not native to Great Britain—living in what an RSPCA inspector described as "appalling conditions." There were lizards and frogs in the bedrooms, parrots in the living room. The charges against Clark were specific: causing unnecessary suffering to geckos, failure to meet the needs of water and bearded dragons, and the like. Guilty on all counts, ruled the magistrate, sentencing Clark to three months and forbidding him from keeping animals for five years.[87]

The house was a mess, according to inspectors, with vivariums stacked throughout the place. "Fungus was growing in a tank which housed one of the snakes," testified an inspector, "and the rat was living in a small plastic box which meant it was sitting in its own urine and feces." Clark denied the charges, but the judge was not impressed, especially considering his record: In 2003 he was convicted of housing two unlicensed caiman crocodiles and causing a tortoise to suffer.[88]

John Ord Clark is not alone. The BBC calls the United Kingdom a "magnet" for the illegal animal trade—not just live animals but also artifacts, such as elephant ivory and tiger skin. One factor encouraging the trade may be the relatively light sentences for criminals. Clark's three months is not unusual. Nonetheless, British customs agents seize over 150,000 illegal wildlife products in a typical year, suggesting an enormous amount of contraband, living and dead, crossing successfully into the country. That means there is a demand for the illegal stuff. Without buyers there would be no smuggling.

That first snake Charles Thompson met when he was ten years old was an American broad-banded water snake. Eighteen years later his shop is teeming with its relatives. Floor to ceiling the immaculate tanks are stacked with some four hundred serpents. "You look around at these tanks. None of them have got dirty glass," he points out to me. "We work very, very hard to keep the animals in a way that we think they would like to be kept." Thompson is a charming fellow, quick to smile and passionate not just about his snakes but also about where they will call home once he sells them. He's wearing a polo shirt with the shop's logo emblazed on it, camouflage-patterned shorts, and a short goatee to match his close-cropped hair.

"I think the public perception has changed vastly over the past few years," he says when I ask him why someone would want a snake for a pet. He credits television wildlife programs "showing these animals for the wonderful creatures they are." Not that he personally needed help. "I just knew instinctively, straight away, the first time I saw a snake, that this was a magical, wonderful creature. They are pets, same as any pets, and you can get attached to them."

I've already told him I'm puzzled about their appeal to his customers. A snake doesn't come when you call it; it won't bring you your slippers and newspaper.

"They don't have the brainpower to recognize you," he concedes, "but they recognize your scent as not being a threat, so you can go into a tank with an animal, and it won't react in an offensive or aggressive manner. That's as close as you get."

That you can manipulate them and they are passive in their response impresses him, especially since many of his captive-bred snakes are only a few generations removed from their wild ancestors. Some of his stock in trade are caught in the wild.

"The fact that we can go into a tank and pick up an animal that was out in the Iranian desert six months ago, and it doesn't react in an aggressive or flight manner because we've set the tank up right, and it doesn't feel threatened is a strength that promotes it as a pet."

It's still hard for me to appreciate it. What do you do with it? Just look at it, or pick it up once in a while and appreciate that it's not aggressive, or watch it eat a mouse? It won't chase a ball or a stick. It won't shake hands/paws or come when you call it. But Thompson is convinced that generations of captive breeding do change snake behavior. His favorite example is the American corn snake, a constrictor.

"Corns have now become very lazy with their constricting. Instead of biting it," he says about their prey, "wrapping their rings around it, and squeezing, same as a boa or a python would, the corn snakes now just grab hold of it, mouth it, and swallow it almost as if they're used to the fact that it's dead."

Used to the fact that it's dead? He feeds his snakes dead stuff for food? That means as pet entertainment his snakes don't even offer a show of grabbing live food. My wife tells the story of an acquaintance of hers in Berkeley with a pet king snake. He would frequent the old co-op supermarket community bulletin board searching for notices advertising mice. Often, she says, they would be scrawled in the handwriting of what appeared to be children, children with fast-reproducing pet mice. "Mice to a good home," they would offer. Her friend would buy two and let one go, not because he cared about the other mouse, but because his king couldn't eat two at a time. He would put the mouse that lost the coin toss in the tank with the snake, and the king would drop its jaw and lunge at the mouse, swallowing it whole. It would then pass through its body to come out as a stripped skeleton.

The corn snakes at Snakes 'n' Adders don't wrap themselves around their dinner, at least in part because there is no danger that it will escape them. It's already dead. "Over time," Thompson tells me, "they get used to the fact that they don't need to fight their food. They'll still strike at it, and they'll still attack it with vigor, but they won't constrict. If they were wild snakes, they'd have to immobilize and suffocate their prey through constriction." In America and on continental Europe, pet snakes often are fed meals they need to chase, but not at Snakes 'n' Adders.

"In England it's deeply frowned upon to feed live prey," says Thompson.

I find the custom strange. What difference does it make if you provide your pet snake a dead mouse or a live mouse? In fact, it seems a better deal to give the snake a live mouse so it can at least engage in a mealtime somewhat like its wild cousins. As for the mouse or rat, it's a goner no matter how it is presented to Mr. Snake.

But Thompson sees it otherwise. "I buy into it because the prey can actually be a threat to the animal. If your snake decides it doesn't want to eat, you've got prey that's going to get hungry itself, at some point. Or it's going to feel threatened when cornered, and it may lash out." It's not just his concern for the poor snake, but also for his pocket book. "I sell snakes for five, six thousand pounds. Do you really want a rat in the tank with it that can do real damage? If the snake is not hungry, it will not eat. The snake may just crawl up to it, maybe having a look, and the rat can lash out. By feeding defrost, we're removing the risk. If they take it with vigor, what difference does it make?" The frozen rodents come from the same type of suppliers who contract with scientific laboratories.

The snakes I'm looking at on display sell for as little as twenty-five pounds to as much as 1,600 pounds—close to $3,000 (something I could imagine paying a specialist to get a snake out of my house if I found it in the basement). For the top price, Thompson will sell me a constrictor he calls a sunglow boa. It is an amelanistic breed; selective breeding has resulted in the absence of black pigment, leaving the bulk of the snake yellow. At the same time, the sunglow exhibits hypomelanism, which makes the saddles—those segments of the snakeskin that appear between the yellow parts—bright orange. The result is a yellow-and-orange curiosity that is dear for some collectors. When Thompson shows his sunglow to me, gently lifting his prize out of its tank, I can't help but admire its warm appearance, reminiscent of sunshine. But it also makes me think of those sickening marshmallow peanuts I used to eat too many of after Halloween.

"Some people say it's exploitation," Thompson says about the work he and other breeders do to manipulate abnormalities, "but they're naturally occurring. If there weren't a market, people wouldn't buy them. People make Ferraris, people buy Ferraris."

True enough, but with a difference. Ferraris are, despite their sleek looks and high speeds, inanimate objects. He and his suppliers are taking a natural anomaly and perpetuating something that would not live on in succeeding wild generations—playing dead-end evolution or a temporary god.

"But the living animal," Thompson argues, "isn't going to go back out into the wild where there is a chance of these genes being passed on."

That's certainly true in the United Kingdom, where, even if a pet owner decides to discard a python into the local woods, it won't survive the winter. Exotics that would not survive in the wild are the only snakes legal to trade in the UK. The same is not true in Florida, where abandoned pet Burmese pythons are thriving in the Everglades and decimating local fauna.

"There always are going to be irresponsible keepers," Thompson agrees, and tells me he tries to spot them before they buy. "Part of the job of a shop owner is fathoming whether you are a dickhead or not." He laughs his hearty laugh. I like this guy: self-didactic, bursting with enthusiasm for his charges, well-spoken in that precise English style so often appealing to those of us from the Colonies, and quick to inject an unexpected profanity.

"You'll refuse to sell?" I ask the merchant. Connie Casey, too, claimed she vetted her customers.

"Oh, yeah!" he says without hesitation. "I probably turn away thirty-five to forty percent of the people who come in."

"What types do you refuse?"

"They want to feed it live prey, that's one example. They show no respect for the animals. I'm giving them information, telling them how to keep them correctly, and they're blasé. They say things like, 'It only costs a hundred pounds; why should I care?' or 'It's only a snake; if it dies, I'll buy a new one.' We come across that a lot. They put no importance on these animals. They don't want to set the tank up right. If they don't want to put a thermostat in to control the temperature, and they just want to put a lightbulb in, then it's 'No, sorry, this isn't suitable. This isn't up for negotiations. You do as you're told, or you're not getting it.' I'm a hard ass with people. I respect the animals. I love the animals. I live for them. I would hate to think I've sold somebody an animal that they're going to mistreat."

"What happens when you refuse to sell to a punter? There must be some heated reactions."

"That's half the fun!" Thompson gives another long, loud laugh combined with a friendly smile. But he recognizes that his refusal to sell does not mean the irritated guy on the other side of the counter is denied a snake. Other shops do not insist on customers showing the same level of expertise and responsibility, and shops can be bypassed. There is a vibrant, Internet-based snake exchange, ready to sell to anyone who can flash the cash. "There are always idiots in every walk of life," Thompson says.

Snakes 'n' Adders does sell the big snakes: Burmese pythons, reticulated pythons, anacondas. But these Thompson sells only to what he calls his advanced-level customers: "You've got to come in and dazzle me with your knowledge. And if you don't, you don't get it." Still, he doesn't take responsibility for what happens once the snake is out the door of his shop. "I breed the big snakes. I understand the interest. Who am I to tell somebody that they can't have it if they have prior knowledge, if they're adept with the species? But if someone comes in with a pram, and they say to me, 'I want a Burmese python,' I say, 'No, you don't.' If he's a single guy, or a young couple, I've got no issues. But if they come in with toddlers, I'm not about to sell them a snake that's going to get to twenty-five feet. It won't be sensible or ethical. Or small pets. If they have a Jack Russell terrier, they don't want a python."

Charles Thompson knows that his business is disturbing to some onlookers. "They look at you like you're mad, or a serial killer," he tells me. But snakes do give a lot of us the creeps, an aversion he traces to the Bible.

The Bible calls the serpent "more subtle than any beast of the field which the Lord God had made," and, of course, it was the serpent that told Eve not to worry about eating the apple. "Ye shall surely not die," he encourages her as she eyes the forbidden fruit. "For God doth know that in the day ye eat thereof, then your eyes shall be opened: and ye shall be as gods, knowing good and evil." She ate the apple, Adam ate the apple, God evicted the couple from the Garden of Eden, it was the snake's fault, and so Charles Thompson dates some snake phobias to Genesis.

There are those with no biblical problem with snakes but who find his business wrong because they believe it is unhealthy for wild reptiles to be caged and bred. He counters with the calm argument that were the animals stressed and unhealthy, they would not thrive and breed. Big cats and great apes need more room, he says, but snakes? Hey, they just lie around all day. Give them a nice place to lie around, and they don't care if it's a tank in Sheffield or the wide-open deserts of Iran. "We're aficionados of reptiles. We're not keeping them to be cruel. We're not keeping them to kill them. We're keeping them because we love them, and we find them attractive." He offers a neat example. "Lizards are reasonably sedentary. They're territorial, so they'll protect a specific rock that receives a certain amount of light. That's their prime basking spot, that's their prime mating spot. It's got a good food supply. If we provided this perfect environment in the wild, the lizard would fucking stay on the rock. It wouldn't run away. Do you know what I mean? Because it's got the perfect environment there." We're both laughing at this point. "He's the daddy, all the girls come to him. He's going to stay on the rock." There's no difference, he's convinced, if that rock is in a tank, as long as the conditions equal what the lizard would seek in the wild.

As we chat I learn that, although I'm no particular snake fan, we do share other interests: Thompson and I both fancy the music of The Who and The Kinks. I think about The Kinks hit from 1964, "You Really Got Me." It neatly sums up my concerns as he dangles constricting python and venomous adders too close to me for comfort: "You really got me now, you got me so I can't sleep at night."

We go back into the shop and pass Barney—the shop pet—an iguana from Barbados and a clear expert at rock sitting. The size of a hefty Jack Russell terrier, he eats carrots and bell peppers, and he wanders around Snakes 'n' Adders when he's not hanging out on his rock. He's not for sale. I pet him; he feels like a combination of shoe leather and sandpaper.

The shop door chimes, and a young couple walk in with a snake in a box. They look to be in their early twenties. She sports a sparkling stud in her upper lip, huge hoop earring, and a concerned, serious look on her face. He's a skinny guy with tattoos on his arms and neck and two studs in an earlobe that nicely complement his girlfriend's lip decoration. He offers a concerned half-smile as he suggests that the corn snake Thompson sold him is a dud.

"I'd like to exchange her," he says in a quiet voice. "Every time I go to pick her up, she does bite."

"Let's have a look," says a convivial Thompson. "Come here," he reaches into the box and speaks softly, coaxing the snake. "There you go." Just as he did with the python and adder, he takes the corn snake into his hands with a calm and fluid grab. She doesn't bite, she doesn't look bothered, and she acts content. "It's the way you handle them," he explains, putting the snake back. "If you stay nice and slow, don't show that you're scared of them, then they won't bite. It's nearly all about territory. This is her environment," he says about the box. "When you go in and pick it up," he takes the snake out of the box again, "as long as you don't show any fear, the snake's got no threat."

"Every time I pick her up, she does nip, she does snap," says the customer.

Thompson demonstrates again, moving his hands confidently, smoothly, and without hesitation as he grabs the snake. "If my hands are going like this," he reaches toward the snake with rapid and jerky hand movements, "that will irritate her, and she'll not like it. As long as you're calm, the snake stays calm. She's a big softy." (Not that big, maybe a little over a foot long, but she'll grow to four or five feet.) "She'll not bite you now, now that I've calmed her down."

The timid customer tries for himself. "It's just picking her up I have a problem with," he says, making a case for not being afraid of his pet.

"Uh-huh," Thompson affirms. "You've got nothing to fear once the snake is out. It's going to become submissive because you're holding it. In the tank, that's *its* environment." And in there you must approach it with cool confidence, he says. If you hesitate, and your hands are going in and out, the snake will eventually look up and think (Thompson speaks for the snake), "You're not fucking coming in this tank. You're starting to irritate me now. I don't know what your intentions are. Your intentions are to eat me, to kill me, to attack me."

The novice snake owner nods.

"They're persecuted everywhere," Thompson lectures. "They know that they've got enemies. They're going to react. So you need to just go in," he takes her out again. "As soon as she comes out, then you can calm her down because she's not going to react to you once she's out of the tank."

"Yeah," says the customer, but without conviction, watching Thompson repeatedly lift his charge out of the box.

His girlfriend asks, "You want to have a go?"

Thompson tells him to hold the snake from the midriff down, not to approach the head. "If you're worried about snakes, regardless of what snake you choose, even if it is another corn snake, you'll potentially get the same response from that corn snake. There's not necessarily anything wrong with this snake. You just need to get over it and get in there. As soon as you do that, you'll be fine."

His customer looks somewhat reassured, and he grunts agreement and tries again.

"See how it tries to skip over your fingers?" Still he's not lifting it out directly and with confidence. "Give it some support. As long as it feels supported, it will be slow."

"But even when I pick her up, she gets away. You know what I mean?"

A cherubic smile from Thompson as he says, "Be quicker!"

"Yeah," says the customer as he tries again.

"About halfway down," Thompson guides him. "Other hand ready. Scoop it under her. That's it," he coaxes. "Done." The snake is out of the box in the hands of her pleased-looking new owner. "That's it."

The snake's tongue is darting rapidly in and out of her mouth.

"All she's doing is sniffing. You don't need to fear that. She doesn't sniff with her nose. She sniffs with her tongue. She's just a teddy bear. A big softy."

We leave the young couple to bond with their snake, and Thompson tells me he is convinced snakes exhibit unique personalities. "That corn snake there is maybe a little aggressive with this gentleman, and we could find fifty corns that are totally tame. And you could find one that, regardless of the style of handler, it's going to bite. It's going to try and eat you every time you go in. Across a thousand animals you'll get fifty different personalities."

"So are those guys," I ask, "that snake and that fellow, ever going to be pals? Or has it been established—"

"Yeah." He interrupts me. "I don't think the snake is the issue."

"It's him being skittish," I offer.

"Yeah, and he realized that, too."

"If he's skittish, why does he want a snake? Why doesn't he get a puppy?"

"They're like jewels," Thompson says about the beauty of the snakes. He understands the appeal, and he understands the downside of the competition. "If you've got a puppy, you've got to walk it twice a day. It's going to chew your furniture. It might crap on your rug. Whereas the snake, you feed it once a week. It poohs once a week, so you clean it once a week. This is suited for the modern lifestyle."

Perhaps the skittish snake handler wanted the snake to impress his girl. It seemed to me she was quite anxious for him to interact with the reptile. He practices, and after just a few minutes he's now picking his pet out of the tank with ease. I ask him why he chose a snake.

"I just like them."

"What do you like about them?"

"I just do."

"She certainly seems to like you now."

"A bit, yeah."

I leave Charles Thompson and his client, looking back on his shop and the banner advertising THE RIGHT LIFESTYLE FOR YOUR REPTILE.

"I just like them," is a refrain I've heard from several owners of exotic pets, and what's wrong with that? Why do I cohabitate with Schrödinger? In part I feel an obligation to him since he showed up at the door abused. I've toyed with the idea of finding another home for him. But when he disappeared for several days, I remember how happy I was to hear his cat door clatter and the patter of his paws coming up the stairs into the living room. I realized then how much I missed him. He vocalizes with vigor. I like his various greetings and complaints, from a typical meow to what really sounds like, "Watch out! Don't step on me!" Or at least it does to me, after hearing the same sounds so many times at the appropriate times. I now know I feel comforted when we doze together on the couch. And when he strides up to me while I'm working and seeks a pet or a pat, he appeals to me in an almost doglike manner that reminds me of Amigo.

Charles Thompson enjoys his jewel-like snakes. Nothing wrong with appreciating beauty. Fran Ogren claims the monkey she smuggled was like a grandson. A little weird, perhaps, but—aside from the felonious provenance of the ape—adding a member of the family seems a reasonable motivation, too. David Vanderholm likes the majesty of his tiger, Lilly. He likes to sit in the cage with her, experiencing her massive—and potentially deadly—presence. That is understandable (even if I don't share the desire). I head back across the Atlantic to Florida as I continue to collect explanations for odd (to me) pets and the havoc they can cause.

I'm still hoping to find more substantive explanations for keeping exotic animals as pets other than "I just like them."

CHAPTER SIXTEEN

Florida's Python Plague

A Snake Seller's Perspective

I'M OFF TO FLORIDA TO INVESTIGATE WHAT SOUNDS FROM THE POINT OF VIEW of the temperate and bucolic California coast I call home like an extremely creepy crisis: Tens of thousands of Burmese pythons are said by government biologists to be on the loose in the Florida swamps. They're the progeny of—well, no one is sure, although quasi-official speculation is that they're either abandoned pets or snakes let loose when Hurricane Andrew whacked the state. I'm going to locales with intriguing names such as Crocodile Lake on Key Largo, the place where the U.S. Geological Survey is trying to create a firewall to stop the nonnative pythons from devouring the few remaining Key Largo wood rats and the Key Largo cotton mice—both endangered native species—even as the snakes continue to migrate south.

The news from Florida is predictable. The python-smothering of two-year-old Shaiunna Hare a few weeks earlier in Oxford motivated government regulators and politicians toward action. Julie Jones, the director of law enforcement for the Florida Fish and Wildlife Conservation Commission, is informing the governor that her agency is looking into a ban on pythons. Senator Bill Nelson is pushing for a federal prohibition on importation of the Southeast Asian native. Given the numbers of snakes already on the loose and the complexities of trying to enforce such a ban, it seems from my vantage point a prime example of closing the proverbial barn door after the snakes have left. State legislators announced they were working on laws against keeping pythons as pets. Python aficionados contested the crises talk, insisting those who were responsible snake handlers should not be penalized. "We're coming up on an election year, and this Burmese python issue won't go away," said Andrew Wyatt, the president of the United States Association of Reptile Keepers. He sees opportunistic politicians as a problem. "All these Florida politicians want their little piece of the pie." The impressive statistics continued to pile up. I found a newspaper article advising that the Burmese pythons can easily attain twenty-six feet in length, weigh over two hundred pounds, and lay up to a hundred eggs at a time.[89]

My friend and colleague George Papagiannis, a journalist working for UNESCO (he specializes in the establishment of independent media in postconflict zones), was about to move from his Paris home to a Baghdad tour of duty. I wrote a note reminding him to watch his back in Iraq and suggesting he come join me in Florida; he had a few weeks leave before his new assignment. He rejected the invitation with a terse "You think I am crazy to go into Iraq. Why not read your own note. You are in search of two-hundred-pound snakes that can eat you in one gulp. No thank you." My previous experience with exotic snakes was limited to watching charmers encourage cobras out of baskets in Karachi and in Marrakech.

It's August, not just hot in Florida but hurricane season. Local TV weather forecasters talk about a storm developing off Cape Verde and what it may mean to the Florida coast. The thunderheads that build up in the afternoons are white and fluffy, a nice contrast to the deep tropical blue sky. Weather like this presaged Hurricane Andrew, the catalyst—according to one school of thought—for Florida's plague of Burmese pythons. Restaurants are empty, as are the stores. The snowbirds are safely ensconced in their northern habitats, leaving South Florida to the full timers. The condo in West Palm Beach I borrow from friends is in a ghost-town complex; the beach is empty. I've got the building almost to myself. One Florida full timer is Aaron Joyce, the owner with his wife, Hillary, of Wild Cargo, a pet store in nearby Lake Worth. He catches my attention because before my arrival, a couple of boxes were left on his store doorstep, each box containing a long and suddenly homeless Burmese python.

Wild Cargo is on the endless sprawl of Military Trail just south of Gun Club Road. The one-story building is a bright yellow, and there's a man-size model of T-Rex—or something that looks like the dinosaur—out front. Signs in the window promise EXOTIC PETS and warn NO

UNATTENDED CHILDREN PLEASE, STAY WITH YOUR CHILDREN AT ALL TIMES, and REMEMBER, IF THEY BREAK IT YOU BUY IT. Despite the signs, the atmosphere in Wild Cargo immediately feels friendly. I walk in, and Hillary greets me, pointing at the Tropicana lemonade I'm drinking; I grabbed it at the gas station next door in my continuing effort to beat the Florida summer heat. She smiles and then points to the same brand lemonade in her other hand. Aaron and I adjourn to a quiet corner in the back of the store to talk, as quiet as can be expected in a store lined with cages of squawking, tropical birds.

Shark attacks a few years prior to my visit dominated Florida headlines for a summer; now it's Burmese pythons. I offer Aaron Joyce the opportunity to blame us journalists for trying to cash in on a few loose exotic snakes as a sensational story, but he responds with due caution. "From an environmentalist's standpoint, there is a problem anywhere man leaves his footprint." At first he speaks slowly, either choosing his words carefully or because we're in the South, where the pace tends to be slower than where I come from. Or both. "We've got a cattle egret out in front of the store," he says. I saw it when I drove up. It was parading on the sidewalk, showing off its gorgeous snow white plumage, brilliant feathers highlighted with the distinct accents of its orange bill and legs. "His name is Igor. He's a great little guy, and people can feed him by hand." Aaron and Hillary don't feed him, but passersby come into the store, buy crickets, and feed Igor. "That's not an indigenous species. They're native to South America and came up here, they think, via hurricane. My whole life they've been here." Joyce was born in 1982. "My dad's whole life they've been here. There are hundreds upon hundreds of nonnative species here, not only in Florida, but in America." Joyce is speaking faster now, aiming to debunk propaganda against pet Burmese pythons. "The Burmese python is from Southeast Asia. They love the wet, tropical climate. Everybody's just up in arms about this huge, scaly, no-arms-no-legs, big-toothed snake that ate a little girl. Or tried to."

He takes a breath, and I suggest the animal in question is easy to demonize. A huge snake may appeal to him, but it probably panics—or at least scares—plenty of his neighbors.

Affable and forthcoming with his opinions, Aaron Joyce—just like his counterpoint at Snakes 'n' Adders in Sheffield—looks the part of a python purveyor. He's a stocky fellow with buzz-cut hair and tattoos. Wild tattoos. He pulls up the sleeve covering his left bicep and shows off a multicolored octopus stretching from the top of his shoulder toward his elbow. He's wearing shorts, so it's impossible not to notice the intense snake head exploding out of a seascape on his left calf.

No question the Burmese pythons loose in Florida devastate local fauna, Joyce concedes, but from his perspective as pet shop owner and self-taught herpetologist, he sees no crisis. "Burmese pythons do have natural predators, unlike what people have reported," he insists. "King snakes, alligators, birds of prey, and now humans." Just two weeks prior to our meeting, the Florida Fish and Wildlife Commission licensed thirteen wranglers to hunt the pythons on state-owned land, and as we talked a federal government Burmese python search-and-destroy mission was under way in the Everglades. No laws restrict killing them on private property.

"Is it your fault?" I ask Joyce about pet shop owners and the python infestation.

"No. It's not our fault, for sure," he says firmly. "It is irresponsible pet ownership." One result of all the publicity about abandoned pythons breeding in the swamps is that some irresponsible pet owners are now choosing Joyce's doorstep instead of Florida's wilderness when they abandon their growing serpents. The delivery days before our chat came in an unmarked cardboard box with tape around it.

Joyce's first thought when he arrived at the shop that morning was, "What's this in the box?" he tells me. "Feels like a snake when I pick it up."

"What does a snake in a box feel like?" I ask.

"Just heavy, and dead weight to one side. I pick it up, and it feels like a snake, a big one. I bring the box to the back and open it up, and I'm like, 'Oh, shit!' because Burmese have a nasty disposition."

Not that Joyce was worried. He knew the worst thing the snake would do was bite him—no big deal for an experienced snake handler. It doesn't have a venomous bite, but it's not a bite he wants. "I don't like to be bit," he tells me, "whether it's a bull ant or a snake; it doesn't matter to me." He checked the snake, probing with tongs, trying to determine if the snake was "nice," and decided it was. "Nice" is relative. "He does have some kind of retarded bite. You'll be handling him." No I won't, I think, as Joyce explains the snake's antics. "He opens his mouth and starts going at you, which is a good sign of a domesticated snake. It means it's been fed dead things its entire life. Live eaters will look at you from a distance and strike at you."

Two snakes were dropped off that day, snakes he passed along to a colleague with a Burmese python–peddling license; they went back into the pet market. Joyce doesn't sell the species; he doesn't want to deal with the burden and expense of the required license or with the expense of "chipping the snake"—implanting a microchip into the animal that identifies the owner.

Satan is Aaron Joyce's pet ten-foot-long Burm, as aficionados call the snakes. They've been pals for seven years. "He's actually the nicest snake in the world, he really is." His little boy wanders over to us. "Want to be in the interview, Wyatt?" asks Joyce. Satan and his other python live in the store because of Wyatt. "The kids are too small," Joyce tells me. "I don't really want the snakes in the house. Yeah, I could have an enclosure in the house that I couldn't get into without a hammer and a torch. But just for safety reasons." Understandable concern, I think. The little girl near Orlando, killed by a python a few weeks before we talked, was not much older than Wyatt. Keeping such snakes in a private Florida home without violating the law now requires a license; it means building enclosures that meet state standards for security and implanting chips to help escapee trappers find snake owners.

Nonnative invasive species are common in Florida, as they are throughout the world. Sometimes their arrival in a locale is benign; they coexist with the native plants and animals, and everyone lives happily ever after. The Burmese python is evolving as the poster child for the opposite scenario: the voracious habitat-destroying baby eater. Live and let live, is the attitude Aaron Joyce adopts regarding the Burms, although he approves of an adequate amount of control to keep them from taking over South Florida.

"It's important to know the numbers so that we know the severity of the situation," Joyce says. "Is it severe? In my opinion, yes, just because it is a nonnative species."

Aaron Joyce knows where to find the Burms: the same place he looks for any snake, a nice and dry, warm and sunny spot during the summers, and in the rainy season up on the islands, dry land where they spend their time when they're not in the water hunting fish. "Mainly, the Burmese python eats fish," he says with authority. "Same thing as big gators. The fifteen-foot gators you see out here? They're eating fish. The little ones are the dangerous ones. The little six-foot and ten-foot snakes are the dangerous ones. But these big ones that they're catching? They don't really eat big, enormous meals." Don't worry about the snakes, he advises. If you want to worry about Florida wildlife ruining your vacation, worry about the alligators. "They're much more of a threat. They hang out right at the docks where people fish, right where people give the gators fish. Gators look to humans for food, and if the humans don't give it up, they become the food." We're not the only wild apex predators in Florida.

—— ~

"This guy is a complete ass," Joyce says about the python owner whose snake got out of its enclosure and smothered his girlfriend's daughter. "He was owning a snake completely illegally. It really just puts a bad name on everybody. The Burmese python—you keep them well fed and well housed, they pretty much leave you alone." But these pets he sells, when they grow up, they can kill adults. "I'm six foot, 255 pounds, and a sixteen-foot snake could very easily strike me on a vital point and wrap around me and constrict me."

I ask Joyce to explain the attraction. Why do his customers lust after these killer snakes? Why does he keep Satan? And what a name to choose for your "pet" python.

He answers with a question, after suggesting the draw is merely preference. "Why does somebody drive a Mitsubishi Gallant rather than a Ferrari if they can afford a Ferrari?"

"A killer snake is different than a favorite car," I point out to him. I find it intriguing that so many exotic pet owners compare their animals to fast automobiles.

He doesn't buy my argument. "Not really," he says. "I can take you right down the street to meet a very wealthy man. He drives a Ford F-150. Nice truck. He could very well afford to go down and buy a couple of Maseratis."

"But the Maserati or the F-150 isn't going to strike you in a vital part and wrap itself around you."

"You know what? Some people have pit bulls. Some people have tea-cup Chihuahuas. It's just personality."

"Exactly," I grab at his last word, "and can you explain what the personality type is who comes in here and wants to buy a killer snake? What kind of person wants a big cat that could bite his head off or a great ape that could rip his face into pieces?"

"I just think it comes down to personal preference," he says again. "I've got a mastiff right out back. Sweetest dog in the world to me, and if I bring you out there, he's fine, but if you break through the gate, he's going to have problems."

"It's a guard dog. He's got a job to do. That's different from choosing to keep a snake in a glass box that can kill if it gets loose. What makes someone want a pet that is potentially lethal?"

"People who have large animals," Joyce speaks slowly again, perhaps because he realizes he must include himself in that group, "want to demonstrate some type of power not just over nature, but over their world. They have a desire to be in charge." The pronoun changes to the first person. "Society we can't really control, but we can control our own world. We have dominance over our animals."

This desire to dominate animals, this need to demonstrate power by controlling monsters, extends beyond pet ownership. Bull riding is an example Joyce offers. "That animal can kill you, wants to kill you. Unlike the snake. The snake, if it is full, will leave you alone. The bull will just charge."

His mastiff is sniffing around in the yard behind the store; his two Burmese pythons are lying latent in their vivaria. I suggest that Joyce may be a control freak, and he readily agrees. "Oh, sure. Yeah. Absolutely." But such a mentality is what makes for good leadership, he tells me, and that's why plenty of movers and shakers own exotic pets. "You'll also find nut jobs, like the lady with the chimp." That's why, he says, he reserves the right to refuse service to anyone. He insists that if he feels a customer just wants to buy an animal for flash and doesn't exhibit an adequate sense of responsibility, there's no sale.

Next in Aaron Joyce's sights is Senator Bill Nelson. The month before Joyce and I talked, Senator Nelson asked Interior Secretary Ken Salazar to authorize a python hunt in the Everglades National Park. The senator estimated the number of Burmese pythons in the park to be at 100,000 or more and in his letter to Salazar warned, "Lord forbid, a visitor in the Everglades ever encounters one."[90] The warning came as the senator was pushing his federal legislation to ban the importation of Burmese pythons into the pet trade. "It's just a matter of time before one of these snakes gets to a visitor," he told his colleagues as they debated his proposed ban.[91]

Give me a break, is Joyce's response. "Senator Bill Nelson is this old guy [the senator was sixty-six when we talked] we looked at as a figure of authority. Really, he's blowing facts in the air like it ain't nothing." Joyce knows pythons from personal experience; his politics he's studying from others. "I'm kind of new on the political scene, listening to [Rush] Limbaugh and all those guys. And I listen to the guys on the other side and try to stay somewhere educated in the middle." And where is that middle? "I'm more toward the right wing," he acknowledges, "but I've got to be careful of going to the extreme." He seeks guidance for finding that middle ground from his favorite pundit. "I like Limbaugh a lot, he's pretty even keel." Not Senator Nelson. "Nelson, if he had his way, he'd ban everything besides dogs, cats, and goldfish."

The sign outside the Wild Cargo store advertises exotic pets. What constitutes an exotic? What's the difference between keeping a mutt or a tiger, a house cat or a python? It's an easy definition for Aaron Joyce: anything nonnative. But it's more. There are animals native to Florida most of us would consider exotic pets. Alligators come to mind first. I'm a wordsmith, not a biologist, so I'm taking the license and the liberty of deciding that the vernacular use of the term *exotic pets* means unusual pets. I appreciate the specific definition of an exotic being a nonnative. But in the weird pet world, exotic extends to mean the unexpected, the dangerous, the chick magnet. Look at me and my pet alligator! My boa is wrapped around my neck! Isn't my monkey cute? My tiger just lacerated my scalp! Not that there's necessarily anything wrong with showing off and enjoying the attention. We're social animals, and we like to attract others of our kind. I've walked around Georgetown with my friend Jeff Kamen and his huge, lovable, doe-eyed dog, Yukon. It's rare that we pass anyone without stopping to hear, "Oh, what a beautiful dog! What is he?" He's a Great Pyrenees mountain dog. "Can I pet him?" Yes. "Is he friendly?" Very. "Does he bite?" Not unless you assault Jeff. I know Jeff has met and become friends with passersby and neighbors he would not know were it not for Yukon. Jeff is gregarious by nature, and Yukon is his passport, allowing him to meet and greet strangers who otherwise might find it off-putting if Jeff just strode up to them and initiated a conversation.

The more time I spend studying so-called exotic pets and their keepers, the more I find myself questioning the concept of pet ownership, and of animal ownership in general. Does Jeff really "own" Yukon, or are they companions, taking care of each other?

I continue wrestling with the term *domesticated animal*. The usual definition of a domesticated animal is one that is tame and bred to coexist with humans. Wild animals we tend to identify as untamed and existing in a natural state. But is an animal really ever domesticated? Isn't it just controlled, prevented from returning to wildness? Man's best friend when abandoned or escaped runs in packs of what we call wild dogs. Feral cats fend for themselves.

"The only thing that can be domesticated is yourself; that's the only thing that you can control," Aaron Joyce says with certainty, surrounded by the animals he offers for sale—a sage statement. "You, right now, could jump up and slash my throat. The same thing with any animal. There is no such thing as domestication. Chickens are the most brutal animals that this store sells, believe it or not." Feces can stick to the posterior of a chicken, he tells me, and then cause a tear that results in bleeding. "The other ones kill it," he drops his voice, "eat it from its ass first. It's the most horrible way to die. Animals, no matter what you do, are wild. I think that's what draws us to them. It's being in control. We can dominate."

Even dogs and cats?

"Absolutely dogs and cats."

Aaron was a firefighter when he and Hillary decided to start a family. She walks back to talk with us at the rear of their shop. He joined her family's exotic pet business, and now the store is theirs. "When reptiles weren't cool, my daddy was," she says, but now reptiles are mainstream. "It used to be only tattooed, scummy people would buy them," she adds. I point to the tattoos adorning her husband. "That's what my dad said. 'You got a man with tattoos? That's horrible.'" But she knows the draw for owning a potentially dangerous pet is unchanged for a significant segment of her clientele.

"Oh, to be cool," she says with dismissal and disgust, "that's what they think. You know when you see a young guy walking in here, he's in here to look cool, like, 'Check me out, lady.' That's what it's about. When I see people walking around with snakes on their shoulder, I'm not, 'You're so cool.' That's what they want you to do. A snake isn't a cool magnet. It's an animal you should have respect for. The idiot that had the Burmese python that killed the two-year-old, he wasn't thinking. He didn't lock it up properly. He didn't feed it properly. He didn't have the right permits. They just have it to be cool and to be manly, and that's not what snakes are about."

What are they about? Why else would someone want a Burmese python?

"For their beauty," she says without hesitation. "I've had them since I was little. They're so beautiful." Her merchant side adds, "You can make a lot of money off them, too."

Aaron cites $179,000 as the highest price he's seen asked for a ball python adorned with rare coloration, the markings that breeders develop as they seek to bring out recessive genes. He offers a litany of other, less expensive, collector's items, including eyelash vipers, green tree pythons, green tree boas, and panther chameleons. "That kind of stuff is what is desired once you get past, 'Hey, I got a big snake.'" Their toddler, Wyatt, wanders over to us in the corner of the store and tosses a ball. "Ball," he says with an endearing smile, "ball." Aaron and Wyatt and I head over to the vivarium where his Burm lives, locked up as state regulations require. I take out my camera, and Aaron shows off Satan. "Satan has struck at me, but he's never bit me." He wraps the long snake over his shoulders.

"Want to touch him, Wyatt?"

The little boy reaches out to Satan.

"You guys are nuts," I tell them.

"Yeah, we are," agrees the cheerful Hillary.

Aaron reaches out to Wyatt, and the three of them pose, Aaron controlling Satan while draping him over a bemused Wyatt, who continues to offer his winning smile to my lens.

"Do you want to hold him?" Aaron asks me.

No.

He and Satan kiss. Satan starts to wrap around Aaron's neck, but Aaron says that's okay with him unless Satan starts squeezing. In that case, "I take his tail and unwrap him." And if Satan doesn't unwrap? "Hot water, vinegar, or alcohol will make him release."

Satan draws customers to the store. But before Aaron and Hillary met, he kept Satan because he was one of those guys who thought it was cool. He remembers his old self, while acknowledging that he figures part of what appeals to him about owning Satan is that he controls an animal that could kill him.

"Excitement," offers Hillary as another explanation for keeping exotic pets. "Why did I have a squirrel monkey?"

Why did she?

"A passion for animals, I guess. I grew up around exotic animals. I dunno," she says. I ask again. "I dunno," she repeats.

"I think it really has to do with our primal urges to control things," says Aaron.

"No, not for me!" protests Hillary, offering a distinctly different motive. "Beauty."

I suggest the monkey wasn't beautiful.

"Yes, he was. He was a little angel. I got up every hour and bottle-fed him and took care of him."

But she got rid of him.

"Because I didn't want him attacking the baby. He wasn't raised around Wyatt." And the monkey was aggressive around Aaron; Aaron was competition. "Would I ever own one again? No, because now I've learned to respect the beauty of a real exotic in its own environment. Now I have a different view on exotic. I'd rather help conserve them and keep them where they're supposed to be."

Oliver the monkey lives nearby, at McCarthy's Wildlife Sanctuary. Hillary visits him. "I go, 'Oliver! Oliver!' when we see each other, and he goes, 'Eeeeeee!'"

Hillary and Aaron Joyce don't just peddle exotic pets. They moralize about their business and philosophize about their animals. When the two offer to introduce me to the sanctuary operator who now takes care of Oliver, I accept. In my effort to learn more about exotic pets and their owners, it seems likely that any friend of theirs must be another adventurous character worth meeting.

CHAPTER SEVENTEEN

Mark McCarthy's Tigers

The Best of a Bad Scenario

THE NEXT AFTERNOON MARK MCCARTHY WELCOMES ME TO HIS ACREAGE EAST of Palm Beach, almost where suburbia ends. The array of signs affixed to his front gate does not forecast hospitality. They warn, DO NOT ENTER. DANGEROUS ANIMALS, and joke, TIGER PARKING ONLY, and perhaps also offer a glimpse into McCarthy's personality, NO TRESPASSING. VIOLATORS WILL BE SHOT. SURVIVORS WILL BE SHOT AGAIN. They contain specific warnings, VENOMOUS REPTILES, and advice, NO TRESPASSING. KEEP OUT, and instructions, CLOSED. My favorite is illustrated with the image of a Doberman and reads, THIS DOG CAN MAKE IT TO THE GATE IN 3 SECONDS. CAN YOU? And a bumper sticker directs passersby to one of McCarthy's pet peeves: PETAKILLSANIMALS.COM. It's a crowded gate.

As I check out the signs, the gate slowly opens. McCarthy points me to a place to park on his drive as he corrals the Doberman in its doghouse. We briefly get out of the heat into his air-conditioned kitchen before heading out onto his five acres, five acres filled with caged wild animals, many of them ex-pets he's housing because they would otherwise be homeless. Repo and Slammer, for instance, a tiger and a cougar, were confiscated by the Fish and Wildlife Service from a room in a Motel 6 in Orlando. An itinerant troubadour used the cubs in an act he performed from his truck on International Drive. Inspectors followed him back to the Motel 6 and relieved him of his cats. McCarthy's Wildlife Sanctuary is licensed by the Fish and Wildlife Service to provide a legal and safe home for rescued animals. He drove to Orlando and fetched Repo and Slammer. Five years later, they're still with him. "They're out back, just eating and hanging out," he tells me. McCarthy is permitted to rehabilitate injured wild animals, to exhibit animals, to breed captive wildlife, and to use animals for shows, from educational exhibits for schoolchildren to entertainment for kids' birthday parties.

The kitchen looks like a typical suburban one. Aside from the signs on the front gate, there's been no hint of what's kept out back. I ask McCarthy who's out there besides Repo and Slammer.

"We have Hillary Joyce's monkey. We have some lemurs, a lot of parrots, kinkajous, four or five sulcata tortoises." Sulcatas came to Florida from Africa, for the pet trade. Abandoned or escaped (they like to burrow and efficiently dig out of enclosures that don't take their tunneling into account), they thrive and breed in the wild Florida climate. Sulcatas grow two feet across and a hundred pounds, easy. They live long.

Before Mark McCarthy continues to list his menagerie, he tells me the short version of his life story. Florida was an annual winter family destination when he was a child, and one year his father took him to the Miami Serpentarium, where he watched its founder, Bill Haast, work with cobras and extract venom. "I thought, 'This is the coolest guy on earth!' I bought his book, and I was hooked. I started to collect snakes."

Bill Haast does seem a pretty cool guy, still active at the age of ninety-eight when I was talking with Mark McCarthy in the summer of 2009. At his Serpentarium, audiences paid to watch him extract venom from live snakes, venom he then sold to the pharmaceutical industry. To protect himself, he practiced mithridatism, subjecting himself to ever-increasing doses of various snake venoms in a continuing effort to develop tolerance to and even immunity from snakebites. He's spent a lifetime studying snake venoms, convinced they offer untapped medicinal value. "Occasionally, my wife will give me a shot of snake venom," he said, when still a spry and healthy ninety-seven. "Just a little bit. It burns when it goes in. I think without fail it'll help me make one hundred easy. I think what it might do, and I don't have any proof, is it makes the heart function stronger and longer."[92]

After watching in awe as Haast worked his magic, Mark McCarthy convinced his mother to buy him his first boa constrictor. He joined a reptile club in Detroit, and, along with some professional collectors, he took a road trip out to Arizona just after he turned sixteen, coming home with a mess of rattlesnakes. "My mother said, 'No way are you bringing that stuff on the property.' In the middle of the night, I got up, packed all of these snakes in cloth bags, and packed them in my backpack. I walked out to I-75 and hitchhiked all the way to the Miami Serpentarium."

Sixteen years old, he was three days on the road wearing his suede fringed jacket (it was 1972) and a raccoon hat with a tail further adorned with snake rattles. He showed up at Bill Haast's door and asked for a job. Haast expressed little interest in the youngster until his backpack moved.

"What's in there?" McCarthy tells me Haast asked him.

"I've got my snake collection in there," McCarthy answered.

"Why would you bring your snake collection to a job interview?" Haast wanted to know.

"Because I just hitchhiked down from Michigan."

"You hitchhiked all the way from Michigan with a backpack full of rattlesnakes just to come to work for me?"

"Yeah," said McCarthy.

Haast said, "You're hired," offering the teenager $1.60 an hour.

It's a grand story, and McCarthy is an energized storyteller, anxious to talk about his coming-of-age arrival in Florida from his middle-aged vantage point, smiling at his memories, his wife nodding with approval from across the kitchen. The two met in Tanzania, and when I offer my business card, she smiles and reads *mwandishi* aloud. On my card I identify myself as a writer in a dozen languages. She's the first professional contact I've encountered to recognize the Swahili.

"I've always worked with animals," he says about the years since his Serpentarium teens. The animals help pay the bills at his sanctuary. He takes them to schools for shows, to photo shoots for advertisements; he charges admission for tours of his facility; and he accepts donations to help with the care and feeding of his charges.

McCarthy speaks in staccato bursts of information and opinion, full of enthusiasm for his animals and his work. He's a congenial fellow, the kind of regular guy I would expect to find sitting next to me at a baseball game.

I test my wild-versus-domesticated theory on McCarthy, suggesting to him that wild always is latent in an animal, including the three of us, talking in his civilized kitchen. He readily agrees. "There are more people killing people than there are tigers killing people. Nothing is ever one hundred percent tamed. If it's got a mouth, it can bite you. I tell this to people at my shows. I tell the schoolkids, 'I could bite you. You treat me nice and properly, I'm a great guy. You be an idiot to me, I'm going to bark at you and bite you.'"

Animals may seem "lovey-dovey," McCarthy says after over thirty-five years of handling a zoo full of them, but if something goes wrong, "they don't care." He offers the Siegfried and Roy attack as an example. He calls Roy "the best cat guy ever, and he got bit." That Travis the chimpanzee ran amok doesn't surprise him. What surprises him is anybody keeping a chimp as a pet. "I've worked with apes before, and I wouldn't keep one in captivity as a pet just because of their strength and their power." This from a guy who looks plenty strong himself. McCarthy is stocky and broad. But he knows he's no match for a chimpanzee. "Once they get sexually mature," he says of animals, "they're trouble, regardless of who you are. Things go wrong. I've got a cat out here I could kiss all day, but one day she might go off for whatever reason."

Owning a long snake or a great ape or a big cat just to show it off offends McCarthy. Those who acquire exotic animals not because they understand and appreciate them but because they want something unusual and can afford the purchase price he dismisses as being on "a power trip." He offers a Hollywood heavyweight as an example. "Sylvester Stallone hired me. He wanted a cheetah. I said, 'You should start small.'" McCarthy says he convinced Stallone to test a serval. After the cat was delivered, goes McCarthy's story, Stallone called him, threatening to throw the serval out through the window of his hotel room because it bit him. I said, 'Why did it bite you?' I'd showed him how to bottle-feed it. But he's the kind of guy who wants everybody else to do things for him. You want to be tight with your animals, you've got to clean their shit. You've got to be out there with them, you've got to feed them. If you say, 'I'm Mr. Ten Million Dollar Movie Man, I want to play with my tiger now,' that's not how it works. You've got to put in the time. He was filming some movie and came back to his hotel room and took the cat and was just trying to hold it. The cat is all fired up; it's been in the kennel all day long. It bites him. He freaks out and calls me up and says, 'I'm going to throw this goddamn cat out the window!' I said, 'Send it back.' He was a nightmare to work with."

He rejects the term *pets* for his animals, instead calling them a collection. "I've raised a lot of them up from babies. I love them. They're my life. I work with them all the time. But I would not tell you, 'Come on, Peter, let's go pet the black leopard.' It's putting you at severe risk. Bites don't always mean the animal wants to kill you. They nip each other all the time, but the cats have really thick skin like dried leather. They bite each other, and it doesn't hurt. They bite you or me, it's tearing stuff wide open."

"My house cat scratches me and draws blood," I say, "and he's tearing the couch wide open."

"Exactly. They don't have to want to kill you to kill you. They're just playing with you, and they can kill you. They've got sharp claws."

Mark McCarthy takes me into his backyard: five acres of enclosures filled with exotics and rescues. We start at the birdcages, big cylindrical structures several feel high and a few in diameter.

"This is a turkey vulture," he tells me, stopping in front of one cage. I recognize the bird; I've watched vultures circle for carrion over Bodega Bay from my office window. "This guy got hit on the turnpike over by the dump. He lost the upper part of his wing, so he can't fly." McCarthy doesn't just tend to the vulture; he uses the bird as an exhibit when he teaches schoolchildren. In the next cage is a white-tailed hawk. "This one I got from a drug smuggler in Miami after he got busted." His flock of parrots came from pet owners who tired of the noisy birds or were forced to rid themselves of a favorite companion because the squawking bothered the neighbors. "Some of them are crying their eyes out," McCarthy says about the emotions he sees when owners drop pets with him, "and some of them are saying, 'Thank God it's gone.'" Some of the former owners stay in touch with him and return to his place periodically to visit their parrots. He introduces me to vibrantly colored Snowball and Norma

Jean. Amid the cacophony of squawks, Norma Jean softly croons a sultry, "Hello, baby." McCarthy points out a parrot that came to him with the moniker Bubba. But Bubba turned out to be a female, a female that liked to mimic a sound unique to a particular mobile phone company's service. McCarthy renamed her Nextel.

We move from the parrots to the monkeys. I meet Hillary Joyce's monkey, Oliver, the pet she was forced to give up because he was jealous of her husband, Aaron. His almost-black eyes are big and round, like marbles. He stares right at me, and those eyes seem humanlike, looking at me from his side of the cage, pleading it seems, and for what? Perhaps for a visit from Hillary? Or maybe I'm just reading that into his look because he appears so familiar, the baby head, the little hands grabbing the cage wire. He's almost one of us. These are the same emotions I've had so often when facing caged primates, but I can't help myself. Nor do I want to. I find it strangely appealing—if a bit disconcerting—that the apes tug at me with a familial pull I don't quite understand. I meet a silver fox dropped off at the sanctuary by a neighbor who had grown tired of keeping it as a pet because it stunk up her house. They smell like skunks, says McCarthy.

The well-groomed grounds are home to all sorts of cats: tigers and lions, panthers and lynx, an old black leopard named Baxter, and a white tiger named Natasha, who starred with a *Penthouse* Pet in one of the magazine's "Pet of the Year" videos. "Do I feel sorry for them?" McCarthy asks rhetorically about his charges. "Yeah, I feel sorry for all of them." He gestures across his compound. "But I'm giving them the best possible care that I can give them." The cats roar an accompaniment to the birdsongs.

Slammer, one of the cubs rescued from the Motel 6, is now a full-grown tiger, and McCarthy rubs Slammer's nose through the cyclone fence that keeps Slammer from roaming the neighborhood. Although the animal was captive bred and raised by McCarthy, he keeps a respectful distance, convinced the massive cat could switch from tame to wild in a moment. "I love them. I think they're beautiful animals. But I don't trust them," he says of the tigers and lions, cougars and panthers, and other cats surrounding us.

"Why don't you trust them?" I ask.

"Because they're wild animals!" he says in a tone of voice that suggests the answer should be obvious. "This animal," he points to Slammer, "weighs four or five hundred pounds and is six times stronger than a man. There's nothing I could do to stop him physically. It's like the lady with the chimp" (he's referring to Travis and Sandra Herold). "She did not have control of that animal when it attacked. I don't like those chimps. They remind me of humans. That's why I don't like keeping them."

McCarthy is no purist when it comes to animals. "I've killed animals, I've saved animals. I've eaten animals, I've worn animals. I've had animals as pets, I've euthanized animals, and I've released animals. And, yes, I have a love for them. But I'm not sleeping with them. There's nothing in our house; we don't keep an animal in the house." He claims no animal as a pet. His Doberman he calls a guard dog, not a pet. His candor is refreshing, and his actions remind me of my friend and business colleague Peter Morris, who likes to brag that his favorite color is gray because he does not see things as black or white. "A pet," says Mark McCarthy, "is something you're hanging out with, that's jumping in the car with you, you're going fishing with it. It sleeps at the end of your bed, or it sleeps in your bed." He's describing my dog, Amigo. And that's okay with me. If Amigo didn't want to come home, he could have run across the unfenced deserts of Nevada as far as Utah looking for a better place to live. Schrödinger has his own door and the run of Bodega Bay. I know he eats elsewhere if I neglect to keep his dish full, and he often comes home with his fur freshly combed. But come home he does via his own free will. That's a far cry (or screech or roar) from Sandra Herold caging Travis or David Vanderholm's box for Lilly or Aaron Joyce's locked vivarium for Satan.

Last stop on the tour is McCarthy's snake room, a spotless bunker lined floor-to-ceiling with vivaria, many of them labeled with a skull and crossbones, and containing deadly venomous snakes. Snake collecting has been a hobby for him since his Michigan days. Included in his stock are a couple of Burmese pythons, dropped off by owners who could not afford to keep feeding the ravenous nonnatives and chose McCarthy's Wildlife Sanctuary instead of dumping the snakes in the Everglades.

"His we classify as a pseudo-sanctuary," says Lisa Wathne of People for the Ethical Treatment of Animals. She considers Mark McCarthy an opportunist preying on the big cats he keeps in his compound. "We oppose the private possession of wild exotic, potentially dangerous animals absolutely." It's just a ploy to elicit sympathy and donations, she says, when McCarthy identifies a cat like Slammer and claims he rescued the tiger. As an example, Wathne tells PETA's version of Sabi's life story. Sabi, she says, came to McCarthy when she was two weeks old. "This little tiger cub was torn from her mother and handed over to Mr. McCarthy, who then exploited her by taking her to public photo shoots and TV commercials." PETA joins Tippi Hedren in lobbying for laws against breeding exotics and favors sanctuaries like hers where there is no breeding, no buying, no selling, no trading, and no turnstile for ticket-buying customers.

In 2008 McCarthy was commissioned by a music video production company to bring Sabi to a set in Miami, where the rap musician Rick Ross was shooting a video for his song "Here I Am." The fee, McCarthy told me, was $5,000 for Sabi to make an on-camera appearance. "She got tangled up in some chains," says a disgusted Wathne, "and Mr. McCarthy was bitten very badly trying to get the chains from around her neck." From her point of view, it was an accident that should not have been allowed to happen. "Why is a tiger, an endangered species, in a chain, on the set of a rapper video? This is completely wrong. It is inappropriate for the animal." She rejects claims by McCarthy that when he makes presentations at schools, he teaches children that exotics make poor pets. "Kids see a gorgeous animal. They see someone handle and hug and love it, and they think, 'I want one of those.' This promotes the exotic animal trade."

Nonsense, Mark McCarthy tells me. He gets apoplectic when he talks about animal rights activists. "We get to the shoot, and I put the leash on Sabi. She comes out of the cage on the leash, and I walk her to the mark where they want her to lay down. I'm walking her, and she smells the ground, and she starts to roll. When she stood up, the chain tightened up, and she started to choke." Sabi struggled with the chain and was on her back as McCarthy intervened, trying to cut the chain with bolt cutters. "As I was trying to cut the leash off, she bit me in the leg." He's convinced Sabi wasn't attacking him, just trying to bite off whatever was bothering her. "She didn't even know she was biting me. As soon as we got the chain cut off, everything got back to normal, and everything goes fine." Sabi was secured with an additional emergency leash. McCarthy's leg was hurting, and he was bleeding, but he waved off the crew and told them to get on with the show.

"As we were driving home up 95, we heard on the radio, 'White tiger savagely attacks animal handler on the set of Rick Ross!' It wasn't a savage attack, but next thing you know, PETA gets a hold of this, and they immediately attack me without knowing who I am." He calls PETA's criticisms of his operation "slanderous" and says, "They just want to take away people's freedoms. It's un-American. I think you should have the right, in this country especially, if you take the proper steps, to keep exotic pets. PETA's thinking is bizarre. It goes too far. What right do you have to tell me that I can't own an animal? They're just encroaching on people's rights." I ask him if he has a message for Lisa Wathne and other animal rights activists working with organizations like People for the Ethical Treatment of Animals. His tone of voice is packed with abject disdain and sarcasm. "You're polluting the air, you're overheating the planet, because you drove your car to work, PETA girl. I hate those people. Tell her to take that stuff to other countries where people are starving to death, and preach that bullshit. They'll cut 'em up and eat 'em. I'm not kidding. If she wants to practice it, great." He takes a breath and surveys his compound, reflects on his work. "I think I've helped a lot more animals than any of them have. Physically, personally."

McCarthy walks me over to Sabi's enclosure, and I look through the cyclone fencing separating me from the enormous cat, an intimidating beast. "It wasn't something that was a deliberate thing. She's friendly," he says. He calls to her and puts his hand out for her to lick or smell, but the fencing keeps her from biting, were that her inclination. She makes a guttural noise, her chuff. "That is a friendly greeting," he explains. "Now she's licking my hand." He interprets what the chuff and the lick mean. "This is, 'Hi, how are you doing, buddy? Everything is fine.'" But he quickly adds, "That doesn't mean if I go in there that she won't, out of love, knock me to the ground, play with me," the pause is dramatic, "and kill me. She doesn't have to want to kill me. But one bite in the wrong spot, and I'm dead." When he takes her out for a show, he hedges his bet with leashes, and he uses special restraining devices to ensure the safety of other performers and their stage crews.

There are more than two sides to a story. What did the rapper see the day Sabi took a bite out of her owner? "Forty-five minutes into the shoot," Rick Ross told MTV, "the trainer is doing his thing with the tiger, and the tiger just grabbed his ass! Did his thing. You could tell they have their own little relationship. It wasn't his first time being bit—he got bit pretty good. I wasn't too far from it." Ross figured McCarthy was in control of Sabi right after the bite. "It was all good—the tiger was on the chain," Ross clarified. "You had to be there to see that it wasn't out of control. It wasn't crazy. He wasn't getting mauled. It was the owner–pet thing. He plugged him good! I let [McCarthy] know he had to finish my video. He wiped the blood off, it was all good. Trilla!" In Ross speak, *trilla* means "real enough," a word derived from the Michael Jackson song "Thriller."

Ross said McCarthy told him before the shoot started that Sabi was irritated. "One of my homies let him know, 'If the tiger gets out of line, we gonna shoot it,'" the rapper told the music video TV network, staying in character.[93]

Sabi's cameo in the video is just a few background seconds, a chain in clear evidence in the shot. Hard to imagine those few seconds of big cat were worth $5,000 to Ross or a bite to McCarthy.

As Mark McCarthy's sign-posted gate closes behind me, I drive back to my beach condo with an understanding of the middle ground he treads. Purists vilify him, but he serves some wildlife in need while he earns a living and enjoys messing about with his animals. I enjoyed his candor when he denounced the "PETA girl" who criticized his role on the rap video set, and I decide to head up to Washington to hear another side of that story from the belly of the PETA-beast's main offices.

CHAPTER EIGHTEEN

No Kissing the Cats

The PETA Girl and the Cheetah Lady

THE CHIEF "PETA GIRL," AS MARK MCCARTHY WOULD CALL HER, IS PETA'S founder and president, Ingrid Newkirk. We meet in the organization's elegant headquarters building on Sixteenth Street in Washington, just a few blocks north of the White House. Newkirk's soft and crisp British accent is intact after years living and working in America, a life dedicated to animal rights. She chose her career after reading Peter Singer's seminal book *Animal Liberation*. On her to-do list is shutting down the exotic animal pet trade. "It's not good for exotics to be bred, shipped around and housed, and kissed by somebody. It's people who are not thinking very deeply about animals," is how she characterizes the breeders, sellers, and buyers of wildlife.

Proper is the word that comes to mind as I look across the desk at Newkirk in her sparse office, this nemesis of McCarthy and so many other exotic fanciers who want to be left alone with their animals. Polite and poised, her bobbed hair adds to her very serious appearance. She comes up with a litany of things the animals would prefer rather than life in an enclosure, no matter how clean and spacious. "Birds want to fly. Birds want to be in flocks. There are many animals sold in pet shops that want to swim. They want to climb. They want to be in trees. They want to call and be answered. They want to raise their own families somewhere. They want to dig. Parrots scream and scream because they don't have mates. They scream because they don't have friends. They scream because they want to fly. They scream because they have no room. They scream because they have no freedom. People then get angry because they scream. They say things like, 'Be quiet! Shut up! I've told you to shut up!' I've been in people's homes when they've done that, and they love their parrots in their own way. This is not in the parrots' best interests."

I tell her about my trip to the Lolli Brothers auction and meeting Linda Bilbrey and her newborn serval. Bilbrey loved the delicate baby serval, but Newkirk is disgusted, calling it theft that the kitten was taken from its mother. When I asked Bilbrey about the trauma early separation might cause the mother serval and its offspring, she was unworried, insisting her love for the kitten was compensatory. When I asked her about the negative aspects of keeping in her home what would grow to be a big wild cat, Bilbrey was unconcerned, saying her hands-on attention would mitigate difficulties for her and for the cat. Ingrid Newkirk calls that response sheer ignorance combined with selfishness.

"I wonder," she says. "Perhaps in your posing those questions to her, it may be the first time she had a glimmer of thought about them. I could put myself in her shoes at one point. A salesperson has said to her, 'Look! Isn't this beautiful? He doesn't have a mother, he's perfect for you.' This is a shiny, beautiful, living, animated gift-toy on a shelf that she's going to possess. She's going to be the envy of everyone. It's irresistible unless you've had other thoughts or someone has helped you have other thoughts."

"But she was thinking ahead," I say about Bilbrey. "She told me the grown cat would love her and not be problematic because she was nurturing it from birth, and loving it."

"Wishful thinking," is how Newkirk dismisses Bilbrey's optimism. "We all have wishful thinking. People don't think they're going to die of cancer if they carry on eating the way they eat. Young boys in Texas think they're never going to be impotent." She laughs. "We're just a hopeful species that wants something and believes we'll make it work somehow. That's how we've conquered nations and done everything else we shouldn't have done. I don't know. Is this too psychological?" It is an unusual grouping: exotic pets, eating habits, impotency, and world domination. I neglect to ask her why she singled out Texans.

But I enjoy talking with her. She's challenging human attempts to dominate wildlife that go back to antiquity, and she readily acknowledges that there is no black and white in her fight for animal rights. Compromise is a tool. She points to a sparrow outside her window on the fire escape as an example of how animals should live free. It's pecking at a tortilla chip she left for it, and she quickly adds a caveat: It ought to be eating natural sparrow food. Our big cat talk returned to sex.

"There is something sexual with women and some of these animals, for sure." Newkirk answers my questions with stream-of-consciousness replies that bounce around the room before she deftly manages to anchor them to animal rights. "I suppose just as a woman used to want to lie on a bearskin rug, it's another projection," she says about women owning tigers. "'Look at me. I'm a tiger with exotic, gorgeous skin. I'm powerful. You can possess me. Don't you want to possess me?'" Her voice takes on a matter-of-fact tone, as if the motive is obvious.

"Owning a tiger is an extension of wearing tiger and leopard clothing?" I ask.

"I believe it is. Lying on bearskin, wearing the fur is, 'Look at me. Don't you want to touch me? I'm a little bit wild and exotic,'" she purrs the words. "Control is a big part of it, I think, sexual control. Domination. I don't know, I'm not a psychiatrist. I'm not a psychologist. I'm just guessing."

Newkirk frames PETA's role as one that opportunistically seizes events, such as the Travis attack on Charla Nash, in a continuing effort to change society's attitudes toward animals. Michael Vick and his abuse of fighting dogs is a perfect example. She believes his criminal conviction, combined with his notoriety as a football celebrity, means fewer dogs will be trained to fight for sport, and harsher penalties will face those who violate the laws against such matches.

"If you look into the eyes of another animal, you should be able to see a reflection of self," Newkirk says and joins philosopher Mark Rowlands in sharing personhood with other-than-human animals. "Absolutely. It's just a conceit to think that we're it. We're God. The rest are trash. If they feel pain, if they have thoughts, even if the jury is out, if they can see themselves in the future, who cares? They can see themselves now. Personhood, absolutely."

As we say good-bye, Ingrid Newkirk tells me a joke, my first exotic pet joke. She says it was voted 2009's best British joke. Here's the joke: Hedgehogs! Why can't we share the hedge?

There is a photograph in the *Gulf Times* showing a woman petting a cheetah sitting in the passenger seat of a car. "A cheetah being driven around in a local car, an increasingly regular sight," reads the caption in the Doha, Qatar, newspaper, "but one that is frowned upon by experts."[94] One of those experts is Laurie Marker, the founder and executive director of the Cheetah Conservation Fund. We meet far from her cheetah reserve outside Otjiwarongo, Namibia. It is a glittering autumn afternoon in Marin County, California, and the view of Richardson Bay off toward the Bay Bridge is spectacular. Dr. Marker is about to speak to a group of supporters at this fund-raiser for her cheetah conservation work in Namibia, where more cheetahs run wild than anywhere else—over three thousand of the world's fastest animals.

The hostess is pouring wine from the Cape of Great Hope Wine Company. A cut of the sales price of their special cat line goes to support the Cheetah Conservation Fund. The wines are named after rescued cheetahs living on the reserve. The Cabernet Sauvignon is Chewbaaka, after a cat Marker raised from a cub and calls the fund's ambassador. "Like the noble and dignified Chewbaaka," reads the label, "the Cabernet is the ambassador of wines with its subtle layers of blackcurrant flavors, evolving into velvety vanilla undertones with firm lingering tannins." The winery suggests drinking it with venison, lamb stew, meat pastas, or rare beef. Guests arrive, many sporting a purse or a scarf or some other accessory adorned with a cheetah skin motif.

Dr. Marker and I find a quiet corner to talk about the lure of the endangered cheetah as a pet—an animal that chases prey like venison, lamb, and rare beef at speeds of up to seventy miles per hour. The cheetah pet trade from Africa to Doha and the rest of the Middle East is a growing problem. Two interrelated factors are at play: Since the 1970s the habitat in the Middle East no longer supports native cheetahs, and the historic role the cheetah played in Middle East cultures makes the cat a prestigious status symbol. There is a long history of both falconry and coursing—hunting with animals that spot and then chase down prey—among the region's sheiks. Cheetahs excel at coursing. Sheiks would go out into the desert with a falcon on their arm and a cheetah riding on the back of their horse. Smugglers catching cheetahs in lawless southern Ethiopia and Somalia sell them across the Red Sea for as little as $5 or $10 a cat, and attempts are being made to limit commercial cheetah captive breeding in the Middle East. Trouble is, unlike the easy-to-breed tiger, cheetahs do not reproduce well in captivity. There is talk of reestablishing cheetahs to run wild in the deserts of the Middle East. But for them to survive, their decimated prey must also be reintroduced.

"The illegal cub trade from that war zone up in Somalia and Ethiopia is pretty bad," Marker tells me. She works with whomever she can to help when cubs are confiscated from smugglers, and she offers an example of a crisis call. "It was Thanksgiving, and I happened to be in the United States. My phone rang, and it's this guy in the middle of the Ethiopian desert saying, 'I can't tell you where I am, but there are cheetahs here.'" Her crews were able to secure the cubs, but it was too late for several of them; they died. The publicity from such events helps conservationists rally governmental and popular support for their efforts, and a reserve is under construction in the Horn of Africa region as she and I talk. But demand is a powerful market force. "If there's a buyer, there's somebody who can smuggle them out."

Cheetahs are easier to tame than other big cats. "They're delightful," says Marker, and that adds to their appeal as pets. "A nicely hand-raised animal will purr to you." They are the smallest of the big cats, which makes them more manageable even while still offering the lure of the wild. "It's man versus nature," she says about those who seek cheetahs as pets. She reiterates that buyers rarely understand the grueling work ahead of them as owners, and she says that as pets cheetahs often are kept in enclosures much too small for their characters and physical needs. "The cheetahs are built to run," and stuck in a kennel they'll be unhappy and are unlikely to warm to their captors and purr with affection. "Cheetahs have an extremely high metabolism. They go crazy in a small enclosure. Pacing, pacing. Looking, looking. Quite often they end up with renal disease, liver disease. We've seen a lot of gastritis problems. It's because the animal needs to be out running in a large area."

Dr. Marker's lush mane of curly salt-and-pepper hair sets off a winning smile. Her somber concern for the cheetah is balanced with an infectious enthusiasm for the animal that she's dedicated her professional life to saving from extinction. "And yet I'm not gaga over them," she wants understood. She cautions me to remember that her primary role is as a conservationist. "I keep the gaga people away from the cats. Cats don't want to be drooled over. They're aloof." It sounds as if she's describing my house cat Schrödinger. "Give them the proper exercise and food and acreage," she's talking about the cats rescued on her reserve, "and they really don't want to hang out with you. They have a life of their own, and they'd rather be out in the wild."

Yet because they tame with ease, since ancient Egypt cheetahs have served humans as companions—protecting thrones, hunting, and lending prestige to households. "I think it's ignorance to start with," says Marker about those who want an endangered cheetah for a pet. "There's something lacking in their own lives. I don't know what that is. I try to protect myself and the cheetahs from those kinds of people."

She shakes her head as she prepares to return to the gathering and make her fund-raising speech to a group that she knows may include a smattering of cheetah lovers gaga over the idea of communing with the cats. Dr. Marker takes on the voice of the cheetahs in her care, pretending that they speak to each other about her: "At least she's working for us, and she's not out here kissing us all the time because," she growls, "we don't want to be kissed!"

CHAPTER NINETEEN

An Absurd Infestation

The Everglades Amok with Pythons

"THERE ARE NO OTHER EVERGLADES IN THE WORLD," WROTE JOURNALIST AND environmentalist Marjory Stoneman Douglas in 1947, a time when the Florida wetlands' continued existence was in jeopardy from pollution and diverted natural water flows. "Nothing anywhere else is like them: their vast glittering openness, wider than the enormous visible round of the horizon, the racing free saltness and sweetness of their massive winds, under the dazzling blue heights of space. They are unique also in the simplicity, the diversity of the related harmony of the forms of life they enclose. It is a river of grass."[95]

It is that diversity of life Skip Snow is working to salvage. "At its simplest," he says, "my job is to preserve, protect, and conserve native plants and animals." He's a wildlife biologist at Everglades National Park, and he's convinced a rampaging Burmese python population is on the verge of wiping out animals unique to South Florida and animals critical to the Everglades ecosystem. "It gets challenging with some species that show up on their own accord," he says of his mandate, "but there are others, like the Burmese python, that were human mediated and are here by virtue of the pet trade. They did not find their own way here by swimming across the ocean. They didn't even stow away. For the last thirty years, we've imported something like 300,000, and that doesn't account for the captive breeding that's been going on in basements or what have you." He points to CITES documents as the source for the impressive number of imported snakes he references.

Skip Snow and I first meet in the Florida City Starbucks, the last pseudo-urbane stop before the wilds of the park's main entrance. Until I went Burmese python hunting in Florida, I assiduously avoided Starbucks for all the usual reasons: its predictable sameness combined with its predatory attacks on local coffee shop locations. But on the road in Florida, Starbucks outlets have become oases for me. Refrigerated against the stifling summer heat with free Wi-Fi and clean toilets, they offer me respite, and I have succumbed repeatedly to their convenient lure and their refreshing iced lemonade and green tea concoction.

Biologist Snow wastes no time before launching into a verbal attack on the pythons rampant in the park. "We've done this to ourselves," he says of the Burmese python invasion of America, "and now it's a component of the Everglades landscape."

The foreign python is a component he's intent on at least controlling since he fears it may be too late to eradicate it. Even were the python doing no harm to the Everglades, he says, his job description requires that he do what he can to rid the park of the nonnative snake. And whether it came to the park abandoned by a pet owner (an overt illegal act) or because a pet owner failed to secure its enclosure (an illegal act of negligence), his job remains the same: Get rid of it, it's a nonnative. He's appalled that the pet trade is allowed to peddle the snake. "Is it reasonable to bring in a high-risk species and disperse it to a whole bunch of holding facilities" (he's referring to owners' tanks) "that you have no control over, and expect them to remain captive? The answer is no."

I manage to interrupt his rhetorical speech for a second. Snow is an intense fellow, consumed with the python crisis, and after talking for just a few minutes with him, I can tell that this encounter is going to be more like a graduate school lecture than a casual chat. With John Lennon wire-frame glasses, blue jeans, and a gray T-shirt, gray hair to match the T-shirt, and a salt-and-pepper goatee, Dr. Snow looks professorial. He's been working the Everglades since 1988 and remembers when a colleague found the first Burmese python deep in the park in the mid-1990s. That find initiated heated debate. Did it represent a single abandoned pet or evidence that the Burmese pythons were already established in the park and hence a threat to native flora and fauna?

"This is an animal that people think they know a lot about because they've had them in captivity," Snow says. "It's a very popular snake. But what they learn about them in captivity is often not at all related to what they're like in the wild. It's either misinformation or downright wrong." He barely pauses and adds, "Or wish information, meaning, 'I don't want anybody to regulate me, so I'm going to wish that this is not as bad as it is.'" Great term: *wish information.*

Years were wasted, Snow laments, while the pythons thrived, wasted as debate dragged on: biologists, regulators, pet peddlers, and Burm hobbyists all arguing the potential danger or benign impact of the huge snake in their backyard; wasted because of the dearth back then of details available to him and his colleagues about the life cycle of the Burmese python, as well as the snake's habits. Not much was known about those Burmese pythons meandering around Florida, nor was there much literature about the snake's behavior in its home range in Southeast Asia. "We spent those first years trying to get people interested and trying to raise the level of concern," he says. Snow says his worries were pooh-poohed. He was told the snakes couldn't survive the Florida winters, or the finds he was making in the park were not sufficient to prove they were breeding in the Everglades. By the time most everyone agreed a problem existed, the Burms were out of control.

I offer sympathy. "This must make you somewhat crazy."

"Well, it does," he says, with what sounds like sorrowful resignation. "The precautionary principle should apply. The first time a nonnative animal shows up within the boundaries of the park should be enough for a moratorium on its importation or its sale until we figure out if it is just one animal or if it is breeding. But we don't have any of that in place. This is not unique to Florida." Snow believes techniques need to be developed to respond to what he considers nonnative species emergencies. He sees a template in firefighting. "There are lots of tools, people, and equipment staged in different places and funds that can be moved immediately. We have none of that when it comes to invasive species."

Meanwhile, Snow's challenge is to detect the Burms in the wild and to figure out how to get to them. The ones he and his team are killing (they prefer the term *euthanizing*) they more or less stumble over. Some snakes are picked up as roadkills or found during roadrunning hunts. *Roadrunning* is a local Florida term for a modern type of snake hunting. It means going out at night catching snakes that are out soaking up the heat on the blacktop. Others are caught in traps. Trap makers are experimenting with different designs and a variety of baits and other attractants, seeking the most efficient lures and traps. But if Snow's estimates are correct, and there are tens of thousands of Burmese pythons on the loose in his park, how can he hope to catch enough to make a consequential impact on the Burm population?

"Right," he agrees with more resignation. But he's not capitulating. "We need to know how to detect them, and we need to know how to catch them." If it's too late to eradicate the snake, Snow hopes at least to suppress its ranks, contain the environment inhabited by the foreigner, and minimize the impact they have on native Everglades animals like the round-tailed muskrat. "It really likes high water, the kind of environment we're trying to restore here in South Florida. We find a lot of muskrats in the bellies of snakes. If we find that they're having a disproportionately adverse effect on the species, maybe there's a way in that localized area," the restored high water habitats, "to remove pythons and suppress their numbers in and around that environment." Breeding grounds for wading birds may be candidates for similar targeted suppression, "if we think Burmese pythons are impacting wading bird rookeries negatively."

I realize Frank Sinatra is singing at us over the Starbuck's jukebox the Rodgers and Hart tune "Bewitched, Bothered, and Bewildered" from *Pal Joey.* "I'm wild again, beguiled again," croons Frank, and it could be Skip Snow—consumed about the invasion he's fighting—lamenting the Burms, as much as Frank swooning over a girl. And maybe celebrating the Burms at the same time? I ask Snow if the invasion of his park by the voracious snakes serves him and his cause. It's a huge animal, terrifying to many, and a killer not just of muskrats, but of pets and children as well. Does the worldwide publicity about the snake help him with his work even as it jeopardizes his park?

"You guys released these pythons," I tell him, "for the publicity to help gain better funding." He groans but concedes, "The benefit of all of this is that it attracts attention. We really are trying to use it as the spokes-snake, the poster snake, for this larger issue of invasive, nonnative animals. I want everyone to ask themselves, 'If we knew back then what we know now, would we have done something different, and what would that have been?'" He laments the fact that agricultural pest eradication is well funded, while securing money for Everglades restoration is a continuing battle. "Pythons don't have a direct economic impact; they're not eating oranges or strangling fruit trees."

Skip Snow understands why irresponsible pet owners would abandon Burmese pythons.

"You mean the shaved head and tattooed set," I offer him, my working shorthand for irresponsible snake handlers.

"I hate to stereotype them," he says, ever the scientist, but he concedes there's no question that because the snake is so big, "it attracts attention to its owner, and that's why there is a small segment that have found themselves interacting with these large snakes just because it draws attention to them. If you go to Miami Beach, that's what you'll see wandering the streets down there, people with their pet snakes. I would hazard a guess that a lot of those folks view them as an accoutrement." An accoutrement that they could bring home from a flea market for as little as $20 before Florida law finally restricted sales. But the thrill can get old fast. "They're really hard to clean up after, and they pee and poop like a horse. You've got to feed them rabbits when they get big. They can live twenty-five, thirty-five years in captivity. So what do you do when it gets too big for you to carry around, and you've exhausted the entertainment value?" Snow is picking his words carefully. Hillary Joyce was more direct when she made the same point at her Wild Cargo store, explaining that when the show-offs get older and fatter, big snakes are no longer enough to attract girls, so the owners want to get rid of them. "It isn't unique to snakes," Snow says. "You know how when you buy a car or a freezer, and it tells you how much energy it will use over its lifetime? You really need to do that with pets. Pets are living things. Here we are, dabbling with living things."

"The whole idea of owning another living thing is questionable," I interject. I keep thinking, as I consider the ownership of cats and apes and snakes, that the traditional concept of ownership of any animal is worth reconsidering.

"You're going to enter into a relationship with this animal," says Snow, and merchants should make it clear to buyers what the long-term costs and responsibilities are of that relationship.

"It's like bunnies at Easter."

"Shortly after Easter we find bunnies in the park," Snow says, confirming such abandonment. "People somehow think the park is a wild place, and it must be okay for the bunnies."

"Instead they're feeding the pythons their kids' Easter presents?"

"Most of the time they're feeding the alligators."

Skip Snow dissects and examines the snakes his team finds and kills, and after years of such duty, he is still amazed at the number of eggs each gravid female carries. For him to find five dozen eggs is not unusual. "It's frightening," he says softly. The words sound ominous in the benign Starbucks environment.

"Frightening not because you're afraid of the snake, but because all those eggs remind you of how many pythons are on the loose?"

"This is a large predatory animal running around so far from home. It's frightening to see how big their reproduction potential can be. Frightening in the potential for them to continue to sustain themselves and expand through favorable environments. We've found a number of pythons that have had alligator remains in them." His voice is rising with frustration, and he catches himself, trying not to sound alarmist, even as he tells me how hard it is to find the pythons: A 150-pound, twenty-foot-long snake can crawl into a space just two feet by two feet, easy to miss in the thick foliage that covers so much of Florida. "It's not like Burmese pythons will be the final straw that will break the Everglades, but it is another straw. The frustrating thing is, we did this to ourselves."

Snow calls the python infestation "absurd" and laments being forced to kill the snakes. But, he points out, "there's no old folks' home for snakes." There isn't, yet there are old folks' homes for the great apes and the big cats. Charity doesn't extend to animals so many of us dismiss as a pest, dislike, or fear.

"Humans have always regarded snakes with a mixture of inquisitiveness and fear, of awe and revulsion, but whether these conflicting tendencies reflect genetically based predispositions or cultural tradition has long been controversial," writes Cornell University evolutionary biologist Harry Greene in his study *Snakes: The Evolution of Mystery in Nature*. Widespread ophidiophobia, he says, suggests that fear of snakes among humans may be an evolved self-preservation tactic. Greene traces snakes' historic roles in culture beyond Adam and Eve, to prehistoric art, Eastern religions, indigenous South American rituals, and creation stories from aboriginal Australia.[96]

"I have almost a phobia of snakes," says psychology professor Judy DeLoache from the security of her office at the University of Virginia. She collaborated on a study that showed humans detect images of snakes much more quickly than those of frogs, caterpillars, or other benign animals. "When I see a picture of a snake, I'm like, 'Oh my God, eew!' The reason I got into this research was because I've always been fascinated by how it is that people develop it [ophidiophobia]. My intuition was that there was something that made me feel afraid of snakes early on." DeLoache and her colleagues theorize that throughout human evolution, those who see snakes first enjoy survival of the fittest status and pass on those snake-fearing—or at least snake-aware—genes.[97]

US 1 drops off the Florida peninsula and heads across the Gulf of Mexico toward Key West from the last mainland outpost, Florida City, toward Key Largo, the southernmost recorded outpost in the States of the Burmese python. This is where Dr. Ron Rozar, U.S. Geological Survey biologist and snake fancier, is busy designing traps in a desperate attempt to save the endangered Key Largo wood rat and the Key Largo cotton mouse.

In August the mercury in the Keys is pushing one hundred degrees. I find Rozar in his office at the Crocodile Lake National Wildlife Refuge, the site of a former trailer park, reclaimed by the federal government as protected wild land for the endangered species. Just as we shake hands, his mobile telephone rings.

"Oh, a little guy," he says into the phone. "A male? Very cool." He hangs up and tells me it was one of his interns on the line, reporting a python capture. Rozar and his team, a week before, set up python traps on the perimeter of the Everglades National Park, where he estimates 30,000 wild pythons are on the prowl. The caught snake was the first found in the traps; the "little guy" measured some six feet. Dr. Rozar is a strapping fellow in cargo shorts and a T-shirt with AMAZONIA spelled across the front of it in letters formed from snake images. His straight brown hair is held in a ponytail down his back.

The first Burmese python was spotted in Key Largo in 2007, and the arrival of the snakes caused immediate concern. The remains of two Key Largo wood rats were found in the belly of a caught Burm, alerting authorities to the fact that the voracious predator was targeting a rare protected species. Over the next several months, more pythons were found on the Key, most of them roadkills. About ten miles north on The Stretch, what the locals call the two-lane US 1 blacktop to Key Largo, researchers discovered a colony of pythons. War was declared to stop the snakes from establishing themselves in the Keys and to create a firewall against their spread at the north shore of Key Largo. As best as researchers can determine, there are only about two hundred of the Key Largo wood rats left in existence. With the mighty python the new kid on the block, the little rodents were in immediate jeopardy. "A large python," says Rozar, "could easily consume twenty of these in a day. So it wouldn't take terribly long to move through two hundred."

The government scientists' priority is to keep the Burmese python from becoming established on the island. They want to use Key Largo as a choke point to stop the snake from colonizing south toward Key West. If the python sets up housekeeping in the Keys, marsh rabbits and Key deer ("Bite size for a python," says Rozar) are at risk, along with the endangered rat and mouse.

Crews laced the Key with python traps, and when Rozar and I talk, the total count for Burms on Largo is holding at ten—both roadkills and live captures—with none yet snared by the custom-made traps. Traps were placed in the habitat of the listed endangered wood rat and cotton mouse and along The Stretch. The assumption was that the snakes were coming down from Florida City taking the same route I took: US 1. All snakes can swim, but Ron Rozar figures the waters around Key Largo are uninviting for the pythons. "This is brackish to saltwater. I don't know that they'd be too happy in saltwater, at least not for extended periods of time. Certainly, they could island hop from Mangrove Island." The tough snakes may indeed be able to swim to Key Largo from the mainland, though; their tolerance to saltwater is yet to be determined by scientists (yet another item on the intriguing list of unknowns confounding the experts). Rozar likes snakes; he raises them for fun when he's off the clock. Working on the front lines of an international snake challenge, I mention to him, must be the herpetologists' equivalent of hog heaven.

"It is intriguing! It's interesting to think about what to do with an animal that is such a generalist, that's well suited to so many different areas. You don't have to be a scientist to walk through the Everglades and think this is a pretty nice area for a big snake."

"And a big snake with no severe predator, as I understand it."

"Not really," he says, confirming Skip Snow's assessment of the python's place in the Everglades food chain. "Even the hatchlings are hatching out at about two feet long. Some of the big wading birds can take them, maybe a raccoon, and certainly the bigger cats." But otherwise the pythons are top dog. If a Burm is power fed to satiation, it can stretch to ten feet in a year and a half. "At that point, nothing is going to mess with it." Until they hatch, python eggs usually incubate worry free. "The females lay eggs and coil around them. Typically, predation upon eggs is rather minimal because you have Mom sitting there waiting to take a bite out of anybody who comes by."

We head out of his office, into the stifling midday heat, and within just a few paces we're in the thick of tropical hardwood hammock, the largest plot of contiguous tropical hardwood hammock in the continental United States.

"Be careful with this," he says, pointing out a plant. "It's poison wood; it has the same effect as poison ivy."

We tromp through the trees and brush toward one of Rozar's traps. He's set sixty-four of them along eleven miles of roadways. "We might find a python. I know this trap hasn't been checked yet today." We don't find a snake, but we do find a rat. The trap is equipped with one-way flaps that allow pythons to enter but not exit, escape hatches too small for pythons that enable native rodents and snakes to leave the enclosure unharmed. The rat is bait, locked in a cage within the cage, acting as a lure for the pythons but sequestered so a foraging python can't get at it.

The air is thick with both humidity and bugs, and I'd neglected to drench myself in DEET that morning. By the time I get back to the office, welts are already forming on my arms.

Ron Rozar knows from firsthand experience how big and nasty mama pythons grow. He tells me the story of encountering one during a lonely nighttime survey deep in the Everglades. On Park Road close to Flamingo, he spotted the monster crossing the road. She was caught in his truck's headlights, and he slammed on the brakes. His partner jumped out and started distracting the snake, acting as picador to Rozar's work as matador. Rozar grabbed the back end of the sixteen-foot-long, one-hundred-pound serpent (big enough to cause trouble, but only about two-thirds of what she could potentially grow to become). He embraced her.

"I started treadmilling," he explains. "You pick up the animal. You don't grab it. You just pick it up and support it, and it starts crawling." Rozar shows me with pantomime how he moves his hands under the snake, swapping left for right, so that the snake's attempt at forward motion in fact accomplishes nothing. Rozar stays in place just behind the snake's slithering midsection. It's like walking backward on an escalator making no progress. "One thing we have going in our favor is that they tire out quickly. The snake gets tired. This only takes a minute or so, and then you can grab it."

"Where do you grab it?"

"Behind the head."

"Then what do you do with it?"

"We bag it. Once it's that tired, the amount of fight is limited."

In captivity, well fed, the Burmese pythons tend toward passive and lethargic behavior. But Rozar says after adapting to a wild lifestyle, they change. "They remind me of hogs. You can go to a barn and walk around with them, but once they get out and are gone for a month or two, they go feral. That's how a lot of these pythons are. Sometimes you go to approach them, and they start lunging at you." They start the transition from a perceived tamed state to a wild state as soon as they're out in the wild. It doesn't take generations. The same individual that was calm in the vivarium at home is wild in the Everglades. It never was tame; it was adapting to a confined life, being fed dead rodents. There was no need to lunge and fight. Rozar stays focused when he's out in the field wrangling Burms, despite his love affair with snakes.

"A sixteen-foot snake is certainly capable of taking a human life. Once it is in the bag, and you tie it up, you can say, 'Wow, that was a beautiful animal.' But at the time it's as if you're driving a race car; you're making sure you don't screw up."

If the snake were to pin his arms, and he were alone, it could constrict him dead, then probably leave him by the side of the road, figuring he's too big to eat. That's why the snake hunters go out in pairs. If one hunter gets caught in a python coil, the other can simply unpeel him. The chances of a human being killed by a python—even for those handling them daily—are miniscule. A sign on The Stretch announces that this year ten fatal car crashes occurred between Florida City and Key Largo, and the year is only half over. It's much more dangerous to drive to Key Largo than to hang out in Key Largo and find yourself assaulted by pythons on the march.

The next day the sun is unrelenting again and beats into the rental car as I stop at the Florida City Starbucks for the habit-forming iced lemonade with green tea, soak up some air-conditioning while I read the newspaper, then head west on Florida Highway 9336 toward the Everglades, past billboards advertising airboat rides and, of course, alligators. I take a right turn at the Dade County prison, pass nurseries growing palm trees, and wait for my toast to get warm. It's almost one hundred degrees, and I've discovered that if I place pita bread on the dashboard, it's warmed through and stiff in about ten minutes, ready to be used as a shovel into my tub of hummus—along with a bag of baby carrots, it's quick road food. Flat is the distinguishing characteristic I first notice as I look out over the pita. The terrain changes from urban sprawl to flat with a huge sky, punctuated with white cottony clouds. A highway sign warns of panthers crossing the road. "Don't worry about the latest tropical depression," says a comforting radio voice, "it's not going to be a hurricane." In Florida City I left behind another type of tropical depression, shuttered storefronts and shattered real estate prices. The main drag looks desperate and feels like it's languishing somewhere between sad and angry.

Just a few minutes' drive past the sprawl and the palm farms is the Everglades National Park entrance. I get directions from the gatekeeper to Skip Snow's laboratory and head out on a desolate two-lane blacktop, seeing nothing but visions of alligators and pythons in the wilds of the impenetrable-looking foliage lining both sides of the road. Ahead in a clearing, I spot the block building that houses the Daniel Beard Research Center, the federal government's python war room (named for the first Everglades Park superintendent and son of Daniel Carter Beard, author of *The American Boys' Handy Book*, published in 1882, still in print, and a great guide for doing boy stuff, like mucking about in swamps looking for snakes). The building originally was a Nike missile base, but the rockets that were aimed at nearby Cuba are long gone. Instead of worrying about Fidel Castro, as did the previous occupants of the site, Skip Snow surrounds himself with bags of pythons trapped in the Everglades. He euthanizes them, studies the contents of their bellies to learn what they're eating, checks them for eggs to get a sense of how many are on the way, and samples their genetic material as part of a search for their origin. The stomachs usually yield just hair, feathers, and an occasional tooth. But that's enough for researchers to ascertain that the snakes will eat most types of animals in the Everglades. They're trying to determine if the snakes prefer any particular offerings on the Everglades prey menu in an effort to find out what species may be at greatest risk from the new bad boy on the block. Another worry is that pythons are better hunters than some native species that rely on the same food sources as the voracious snake. The local bobcat, for example, likes to eat the Florida hispid cotton rat, and that rat is showing up in plenty of dissected python guts.

When the Burmese pythons encounter a colony of foodstuffs, researchers are learning that they may power feed themselves. They fail the old Frito-Lay potato chip advertisement challenge, "Betcha can't eat just one." In one snake's gut, for example, Snow and his team found the remnants of fourteen hispid cotton rats. "It was stuffed from stem to stern with these rodents," he says, impressed—and worried that the snakes are cleaning their plates at the expense of the competing populations.

I realize as I write this I've succumbed to adopting the lexicon used by most of the animal handlers I've been hanging out with while researching this book. They shy from the stark word *kill* and prefer *euthanize*. But *kill* better describes the scene Snow shows me: freezer after freezer stocked with python heads. We talked about the killing the day before in the cool comfort of the Starbucks, and the biologist said he was seeking solace in folk traditions, hoping he could find some ancient prayer for the snakes that he could recite while doing his job, perhaps something from Australian aboriginal traditions.

"I don't hate the snakes. It's not their fault. I don't particularly enjoy the fact that we've got to figure out a way to eliminate them. Part of that solution," he pauses, searching for the word he finds difficult to say, "is euthanizing," then he blurts it out, "is *killing* snakes, because there really is no good alternative for the numbers that we're dealing with. You can't simply round up thousands and thousands of adopters." If the theory is correct, that the Everglades are full of abandoned pet pythons, few would line up to adopt the monsters. The lab is a killing floor.

"I've never felt comfortable with it," Snow says about killing the snakes. "In my alone time or having a beer with a friend, I start thinking about the bad karma points that may be racking up." He's yet to find an appropriate personal ceremony to offset the nasty python work that consumes much of his daily routine. "Where's my Get Out of Jail Free card?" he asks. Perhaps he and his colleagues need to create their own modern postmortem ceremony.

He shows me plastic baggie after plastic baggie of snake parts. Heads are stored as kill tally. Tissue is saved for mercury analysis. The apex predator pythons are chock-full of quicksilver. Pythons tested in Snow's lab show mercury levels higher than deemed safe by Florida authorities for regular human consumption, and higher than the amount found in another Florida game animal high on the food chain, the alligator.

I ask the biologist if he's tasted Burm. Of course, is the answer. He's a curious scientist. A colleague cooked one and . . .

"It's a very firm white meat, largely tasteless. It's not offensive in any way, somewhat tough and stringy."

They breaded and fried some medallions, and they grilled python.

"It needs to be tenderized."

"Marinated," I suggest from my no-meat-eating point of view.

"Marinated or slow cooked," he agrees, "like in a stew or a chili, but spiced up. It needs some flavor because it's bland."

Combine the mercury with bland, and it doesn't sound as if it's going to be a big commercial success no matter how many are roaming Florida, but Snow has studied peppered python and curried python recipes from Southeast Asia that he figures may taste much better than the scientists' ad hoc preparations. Add the exotic factor, and there may be a niche market for Florida python meat. Python from Vietnam is prized by connoisseurs and is advertised by importers as available in the States for as much as $90 a pound. Raw.

Of course, if python meat or the snakes' hides become valuable as a commodity, that could exacerbate the plague. Traders seeking products to sell would want to propagate the Florida population, not eradicate it. The same greed makes authorities hesitant about offering cash bounties for python kills.

Skip Snow shows me a photograph, evidence of a bout that's become a South Florida legend: python versus alligator. The snake swallowed a six-and-a-half-foot-long alligator, or tried to. The picture was flashed around the world, suggesting the Everglades equate to a python-infested horror movie. The grotesque exploded snake is severed midpoint, with the hind legs and tail of the alligator extruded from the python's open guts.

"It was a very large meal," Dr. Snow says with typical reserve. Very large meal? It was an enormous alligator! "It stressed the animal," he says about the snake. No question it stressed the alligator, too. "The hind claws are very, very sharp. That caused rips and tears, like porcupine quills or bird beaks." When pythons bite off more than they can chew, and it's sharp, their alimentary canals can puncture. Often the snakes will heal; some even slither around with quills or beaks creating peaks in their skins, sticking from the inside out, the guts coating the foreign object in new tissue. Other times, when they try to eat prey too big, and it's an animal equipped with sharp protrusions like antlers, the resulting puncture wound can kill. "It couldn't recover," Snow says about the snake stuffed with alligator. It slit open and died. So did the alligator.

A park helicopter pilot saw the floating victims from the air. He flew back to the lab and grabbed a camera to document the fight. Wearing waders, he climbed out of the airship, out onto its pontoons, then into the water, sloshing far enough from the machine and the animals to get a shot that showed all three together in order to make it clear just how big the snake and gator were. Snow went to the scene to perform a necropsy out in the water.

I look at the picture of the dead, killer swamp dwellers. "You're standing there doing inspections on these two guys in crotch-deep water that clearly contains both alligators and pythons. Are you concerned that one of their cousins may come after you for a bite?"

"No. I guess I wasn't at the time. The encounter rate is so slim that it's not likely to occur."

Alligator remains have been found by Snow's crews in about a dozen of the pythons they've caught. "It's not an isolated incident. We have detractors who suggest we're making it up. Well," he holds up a baggie of alligator claws and shakes it, "they're getting eaten." Added to the long list of things yet to be learned about pythons in the Everglades are details about the relationship between the snakes and Florida's most famous reptile. "We also have lots of incidents of alligators eating pythons." Otters, raccoons, owls, and red-shouldered hawks are among the native Everglades animals that prey on python eggs and hatchlings. But once they get a year or so old, and six feet or so long, Snow doesn't think any of his native animals stand a chance against the pythons. Except for the alligators or, perhaps, an adult panther.

Exotic wildlife is like oil, Snow says. It's valuable when it's held captive, but when it gets loose in the Everglades, it's a disaster. He thinks we should err on the side of caution and not import exotic species that easily get out of what he calls the pet pipeline until we know if they're benign or an ecological catastrophe.

Before I leave his isolated lab, Snow shows off some new catches, road finds that are still alive because the lab's "killing machine" is backed up. Each kill needs to be examined and catalogued, which is time-consuming work. The parts not saved for further study are dumped back into Everglades marshes to feed the local fauna. It's only fair, says Snow, to let the critters pythons eat get a chance to eat some python meat. Some of the males are turned into what the scientists dub Judas snakes. Outfitted with a wire like a turncoat spy or a Mafioso gone state's evidence, the Judas snake's new role is to lead hunters to the haunts of other pythons and to learn about the habits of the Burmese in the wild, information expected to help researchers figure out strategies to control the infestation.

Snow grabs a packed laundry sack out of a plastic box full of bags. He looks inside and takes hold of a python just behind the head. He holds it up for my camera, and the snake plays its role, opening its mouth wide, showing off its fangs, and looking at me with what I perceive is severe irritation and at least a latent consideration of me as potential snake food. While Snow holds the head, the constrictor starts to wrap his tail end around the biologist's ankle. He patiently unwraps it. His left hand is still secure behind the snake head, his right hand moves to the midsection. The snake wastes no time. It wraps its aft section in neat coils around Snow's right hand.

"I've got his head, and he's trying to figure out who's got him and what he can do to make me go away," explains Snow in his calm and professorial voice.

"You like this guy?" I ask.

"I'm not on a first-name basis with him," says Snow, "but I try really hard not to vilify this animal. I appreciate them. It's not their fault. They are amazing creatures."

The snake is vacating its bowels all over the lab floor, a natural response because it feels threatened, as is the release of a musk gland designed to generate a repelling stink.

Snow looks down at the python around his hand, and his voice quickens with some urgency. "It's pretty tight," he says. "I cannot get my hand out." He's yanking his right hand, and Mr. Python hangs on.

"You can't get your hand out?" This is an unexpected development. "Shall I help?"

"You may have to." He keeps yanking his hand. "It's pretty tight for a small snake." It's five or six feet long.

"You want me to pull?" I ask, just as with one more hard yank he frees his hand; he checks it and is pleased to pronounce it okay—he doesn't want tangling with snakes to put an end to his ukulele playing.

I am quite pleased he freed his hand himself. I didn't relish the idea of grabbing the python's tail and unwrapping him from Snow's hand. The snake was wet with urine, and I didn't much want him to exchange Snow's uke hand for my pen hand. But I was somewhat disappointed not to be needed to save the python expert from his quarry (especially while he held the teeth-baring head).

I wave good-bye to Skip Snow and head out of the Everglades, greeted by a sign for a roadhouse announcing, YOU'VE SEEN THE ALLIGATORS, NOW TASTE THEM. I imagine it won't be long before the restaurant adds wild python to the menu—grilled, breaded, and smothered in curry—no matter the mercury content.

Soon after I left Skip Snow at his Everglades laboratory, a Burmese python named Delilah made headlines near Orlando. Neighbors complained about Delilah, worried because she had escaped from her enclosure. Not much surprises Florida animal control officers, a state full of big cats, great apes, and long snakes, but Delilah was the biggest snake Lieutenant Rick Brown of the Florida Fish and Wildlife Commission Investigations Section had ever seen. "To me it's a Goliath. It's a monster of a snake." At eighteen feet long and some four hundred pounds, with a thirty-inch waist, *Goliath* is not a bad word to use.

Melvin Cheever was on the scene when officers hauled Delilah away; he had been caring for her while his brother, her owner, was out of town. "I fed her this morning, gave her seven rabbits," Cheever told onlookers. "She is as docile as can be. She's as happy as can be."[98] The Cheever brothers must have been power feeding Ms. Delilah to fatten that lady snake up to four hundred pounds. Seven rabbits for breakfast add up to too many Weight Watchers points.

Multiply those seven rabbits for Delilah's breakfast times any of the estimates of pythons various experts and officials suggest are on the loose in the Everglades: 15,000, 50,000, 150,000. The threat from this nonnative invasive to the local animal population is reminiscent of the invasion of kudzu into the forests of Florida.

CHAPTER TWENTY

Macro Problem, Micro Reality

Snake Hunters Stalk the Wild Florida Pythons

THE BURMESE PYTHON IS LISTED AS A REPTILE OF CONCERN BY THE FLORIDA Fish and Wildlife Commission (FWC). Great title, "Reptile of Concern." It sounds like the lingo police use when they want to talk with someone about a crime, someone not yet named as a suspect: person of interest. Besides Burmese pythons, Reptiles of Concern include Indian pythons, reticulated pythons, African rock pythons, amethystine or scrub pythons, green anacondas, and Nile monitor lizards. In the summer of 2009, with a big splash of publicity, the FWC issued licenses to a handful of snake wranglers, authorizing them to search for and destroy the state's most famous Reptile of Concern on state-managed land. This was to be an old-school hunt. No guns, no traps; just man barehanded against the serpents.

No one expected these hunters to eradicate the huge predators. There were already too many snakes on too much land and in too much water. The hope was to gather data that could be used in attempts to control and contain the Burms' range. Hunters were required to report their kills— where they found the animal, how long and heavy it was, and whether it was gravid, that is, filled with fertile eggs. After fulfilling those requirements, the licensees were free to make use of the snakeskin and eat the meat—if they dared. Burms caught that summer on federal land in Florida proved to contain what the FWC called "extraordinarily" high levels of mercury.[99]

The first official kill of the season took place during a publicity tour. News reporters and photographers roamed an Everglades marsh in Broward County, tagging along with three licensed python hunters. The posse spotted their first victim under the boardwalk at Brown's Camp. Shawn Heflick, a biologist and hunter, literally bagged the snake; he stuffed it in a pillowcase—almost ten feet of constrictor. "We're the predators out here," he announced.[100]

A few days after his successful debut as an official Florida python bagger, he and I talk python plague, Heflick making it clear he does not share Skip Snow's doomsday scenarios. For starters, he thinks the estimates of tens of thousands of pythons on the loose simply do not compute. Government experts concede that they do not know how many pythons roam Florida, but federal and local officials accept tens of thousands as a base number and quote estimates as high as 150,000. The fact that the total population is unknown is an example of how little research supports the work of those charged with controlling the pythons.

With his short brown hair and wraparound dark glasses, his clean-shaven face and hearty hands, Heflick looks like the type who would tromp through swamps grabbing snakes. I ask him for his best guess. "I wouldn't be surprised if across the whole greater Everglades," he says, "there are ten thousand pythons."

"That's still a pretty good number," I venture.

"That is," he acknowledges. He agrees with Snow that the Burmese are a problem because they are a nonnative species. Heflick is a biologist with a long list of professional field experiences. He is associated as a guide with a company called World Eco Adventure Tours. Their publicity describes him as being "far from an 'ivory tower' scientist who will lull you to sleep with dissertations. You will find he is an impassioned professional who captivates you with his knowledge, antics and his empowering presentation. He accompanies all of his tours to give them that award winning touch, bringing with him humor, laughter, his passion for life and nature and a contagious smile!"[101]

Shawn Heflick suggests that Skip Snow and the Everglades crew estimate the wild python population high in an effort to sow fear and hence generate grants for their work. "I'm not under any burden to produce numbers or make this seem like it's a massive problem in monster proportions. I don't have to worry about grant money coming in, about funding for projects. For me it is what it is, and if there's one out there, it's the same as if there's a thousand out there or thirty thousand. It's a problem because they're not supposed to be there." His voice is quick and intense.

Heflick tells me he offered to become one of the handful of state-licensed python hunters because he's a conservation biologist aware of the ecological problems the wild Burmese present; he's also a snake fancier who enjoys prowling the Everglades for specimens. "What's the technique?" I ask him. "With endless square miles of Everglades, how do you find the snake?"

"I've been out in airboats and looked at some of the small islands that are out there that have marsh rabbits and rats on them, which are the prey of these animals. I've also been out driving and walking in wildlands. We've encountered pythons in both instances."

Heflick is not just skeptical when it comes to the number of Burmese pythons gone wild, he also refuses to blame irresponsible pet owners for the infestation.

"I don't believe for a second that all of these pythons stem from pet owners going out and releasing these animals. There has never been one recorded case inside the national park where a person was seen or arrested for releasing these animals." That may be true, but the Everglades National Park is huge and often desolate. Just between the park headquarters and the few miles to Skip Snow's laboratory, I was on a lonely empty road and easily could have dumped a bagful of snakes. At this point it matters little if they were released intentionally or by accident. Either way, they were released from private ownership, and they're roaming the swamps.

Heflick offers another question: Why don't the snakes caught in the Everglades match the rare colors of the prized pets? "Most of the Burmese pythons in captivity are genetic mutations, color morphs. They're albino. They're green. They're green albino. They're all of these weird mutations. If they're being released by pet owners, somebody tell me why not one of these genetic mutations has ever turned up in the wild." The genetic mutations sought after by collectors are recessive, but since the snakes carry the recessive genes, Heflick expects the unusual colorations would show up in some wild offspring.

Not necessarily, says Skip Snow. He thinks the albinos would lose the survival-of-the-fittest competition. "The physical characteristics of abnormal morphs" (Snow is referring to their stark light coloring) "likely reduce the chances of them surviving and reproducing when compared to the normal morphs, which are fairly well camouflaged."

Since Shawn Heflick debunks the discarded pet theory, he is left with the Hurricane Andrew scenario. "Everything points to Hurricane Andrew in 1992. Facilities housing several hundred baby Burmese pythons as well as several dozen adult Burmese pythons were wiped clean, nothing left standing." The pythons took off, over land and in water, he believes, and bred. Although Skip Snow says the storm would not have diffused the snakes throughout the Everglades, Heflick sees no inconsistencies. Over the years, he figures, the snakes migrated. He dismisses Snow's worries about a dearth of literature on the Burmese python's life cycle with a glib "There's a ton now. Even in the wild, this isn't a mystery snake. This isn't something that was just discovered two years ago. I don't want to beat up on Skip, because Skip's a good guy." But in the next breath he again accuses Snow of inflating the python problem to obtain funding for his project. "In the world of science, it's either publish or perish. You need to get that funding, or your livelihood, your means of supporting your family, is gone."

"You think that Skip Snow is motivated by career concerns?" I ask.

"I think every human on this planet is motivated by career concerns. If you can find one that's not, either they're independently wealthy, or they live on the street."

"What about you?"

"Oh, sure," he agrees. But not when it comes to the pythons. "I don't make any money off this. This is a volunteer effort. I'm only motivated about getting the truth out there, which is why I became a scientist to begin with." Although he does not shy from the publicity he's received since becoming one of Florida's official python hunters, he claims it was unwanted. The day he caught the first snake of the hunt, he tells me, he merely wanted to show reporters typical python habitat and hunting techniques. He did not expect to find a snake that day. "And then we catch this freaking snake, and all hell breaks loose. You know, no one could have ever expected that this thing would get this kind of media attention." Maybe he really didn't, but animal stories, especially killer animal stories, always make the paper.

"They've got this message: Don't release your pets," Heflick says about the Florida Fish and Wildlife Commission. "Don't release your pets. Don't release your pets. And along comes this python, and, boy, isn't this the poster child for what we want to educate the people about?"

"Boy, is it," I agree. "It's twenty feet long, it's about two hundred pounds, and it kills little kids. What more can you ask for?"

"Exactly. People hate snakes. The vast majority of people are scared to death of snakes. What better thing to carry your message?" Heflick is riled.

"But you're concerned about nonnative invasives that are destructive to native species," I remind him. "Do you agree that the python is problematic, or do you think it is a sideshow?"

"I think it has potential, but I don't think it is truly the problem everyone is suggesting. You know, we've got another apex predator that's a reptile already in that system."

I've been in Florida long enough to know the reference. "The alligator."

"That's right. It's been in that system for millions of years. There's no shortage. There are approximately 1.5 million alligators in Florida. It has been seen countless times. You know there's video of it. There are still photos of it." The punch line comes next. "Alligators feeding on these pythons."

"And a few pictures of pythons feeding on the alligators," I counter.

"Very few as compared to the reverse," he insists. "I keep hearing that people are saying there are no natural predators of these pythons in the Everglades. There are tons of natural predators in the Everglades that eat these things: alligators, snapping turtles, largemouth bass. When these things are babies, everything can eat them, for God's sake. Raccoons depredate their nests. Fire ants kill tons and tons of alligator nests; they have to be killing python nests as well."

"This is your hypothesis, or you've seen this?"

"It is my hypothesis. But we know they eat all the other indigenous snakes. Why wouldn't they eat pythons?"

Shawn Heflick rejects the abandoned pet theory. He rejects the theory that the Burmese python suffers no predator. I figure he must oppose Senator Bill Nelson's proposed legislation to outlaw the importation of the snake.

"He says there are 100,000 pythons in the Everglades," Heflick says. His voice oozes disgust. "So we're going to stop importation of the pythons to what end? If there are already 100,000 pythons out there, that's a little bit like installing fire extinguishers in a house that just burned to the ground. I honestly think that maybe they haven't thought this all the way through."

Heflick supports the state restrictions on python ownership, the licensing requirements, and the mandates for secure tanks. So why is he so riled up? Is it that he doesn't like others telling him what to do? A common trait among exotic pet owners is that most don't cotton to being told what to do. Owning a snake considered a plague can be an emblem of defying authority.

"Listen, most of us out there are responsible keepers. We don't mind being regulated as long as it's fair."

I offer him a ready comparison from my trip to the Keys. "Look at the sign that's on The Stretch as you head to Key Largo that says so far this year ten people were killed on the highway between Florida City and Key Largo in car crashes. How many people have been killed by pythons?" Of course, while few pythons kill humans, their escape into the Florida swamps is a growing threat to the region's ecosystem.

"Exactly," he agrees and offers his own numbers. "In 2007, 4.7 million people were bitten by dogs in the United States. Over 800,000 of them had to go to the hospital. And of that 800,000, 30,000-plus had to have reconstructive surgery."

Source?

"The Centers for Disease Control." I check with the CDC, and his numbers are correct.[102] But he's got even better examples. "How many people have fallen off chairs in their own home or their beds and died?

How many get killed by bees and wasps? How many get killed by poisoning on purpose or accidentally? Car accidents. Motorcycle accidents. Struck by lightning. Shark bites." Check with the National Safety Council, Heflick demands.

Perhaps the number of fatal car accidents on the road every year isn't enough to outweigh our collective need for fast transport. Nor is the number of dog bites each year enough to scare us away from the emotional and utilitarian benefits of the dogs in our homes. But what value do nonnative pythons provide aside from amusing a relatively few snake fanciers?

"Makes you want to lock yourself up in your house," I say about Heflick's litany of disasters. I've got such stories in my files. "An elderly woman killed by a pack of wild dogs had been out for a walk when she was attacked, and her husband dies trying to fight off the animals when he discovered the bloody scene," is the lead from a late summer 2009 Associated Press story filed in Lexington, Georgia.

"And we've got people who are concerned about pythons in the middle of nowhere?" says Heflick. "This is not a public safety issue." But he concedes that it may be an ecological issue. "I would certainly, not for a second, want these pythons to decimate a population of anything, even if it's a rat that belongs here. But by the same token I am not willing to just automatically say, without any data, that these pythons are out there causing ecological strife and mayhem." He seems freaked out by what he calls overreacting, but then adds, "Nothing ever freaks me out. I'm probably a little too levelheaded and logical sometimes."

Before we say good-bye, Shawn Heflick tells me that on the head of Key Largo there's a private club I passed on my way to see Ron Rozar, a club overrun with feral cats.

"It's a population of around a thousand feral cats. Does that surprise you?"

"Yeah, certainly," I say. "It surprises me that anybody would keep a population of a thousand feral cats. It sounds nuts." I imagine a thousand Schrödingers, and it's a daunting picture.

"Yeah, so tell me why no politician is down there bringing in the news media and talking about a bounty on feral cats, or the fact that they're going to kill all of these feral cats. They shouldn't be here." Heflick's insistent. "They're decimating our population," he says about the wildlife he figures the cats hunt. He wonders if it is feral cats that threaten the Key Largo wood rat. "I mean, come on, let's be honest. You want to talk about an efficient predator?"

"Yeah." I do agree with him. My Bodega Bay neighborhood is plagued with feral cats. A sweet neighbor lady feeds them canned cat food. Another lady in the neighborhood calls animal control periodically to get them rounded up and carted off to oblivion.

"Let's talk about feral cats." Heflick is bombastic.

"Yeah," I say again, egging him on, not necessarily agreeing with him.

"I'm going to answer my own question," says Helflick. "Nobody, no politician in their right mind, is going to touch that with a ten-foot pole."

"That's because Granny likes cats." I feed him the line he seeks.

"That's right," he says, speaking faster. "That's right," he says again. "Nobody's afraid of cats. Hell, we keep them in our houses. We love them, and we feed them, so no politician in their right mind is going to touch that because it would be instant political death. So you tell me, really, where are people's motivations in this python thing? The feral cat population probably is the true reason why that Key Largo wood rat is close to extinction. That's the truth. It might not be something everybody wants to hear, but that's not why I went into science. I don't have all the answers, and neither do they. And I'm not ready to put my neck out there and say things to be facts that aren't. I'm all for getting rid of the python; it doesn't belong here, and something needs to be done. I'm just not all about running around saying the sky is falling, the sky is falling."

⸻

The sky fell for Charles Darnell and his girlfriend, Jaren Hare. It was his pet Burmese python that smothered her two-year-old daughter in the little girl's crib at the house where the three lived in rural Oxford, a crossroads in central Florida. About a month after the child's death, Darnell talked about the ghastly killing, telling *Orlando Sentinel* reporter Anthony Colarossi, "It was an accident. It was a terrible, awful accident." Colarossi listened as Darnell sobbed and shouted his answers to questions. "It's not guilt," he told the reporter about his emotions. "It's remorse and grief. How do you deal with losing a child? You don't deal with it, man. You don't deal with it. You grieve, but you never get over losing a child. When your child dies it takes a piece of you, too." Charles Darnell passed along to the newspaper's readers advice for those considering a big cat, great ape, or long snake as a pet: "Any animal at any time can turn on you for any reason."[103]

Shawn Heflick is sanguine and without much worry about the macro problem of thousands of wild pythons on the loose. Charles Darnell and Jaren Hare are mourning because of the micro reality caused by one loose pet python. Either way, it's difficult for me to consider the value of importing the wild snake from Southeast Asia and promoting it as a pet.

CHAPTER TWENTY-ONE

"I Know It When I See It"

The Old Hippie and the Professor Try to Define a Pet

"BE CAREFUL, THIS IS AN ATTACK-TRAINED ROTTWEILER!" A FELLOW ON THE bench next to me says to a passing family. They smile. I'm sitting in Indian Statue Park in Point Richmond, a town along the San Francisco Bay, enjoying a sunny summer morning as I study my field notes. The fellow on the bench next to me is talking with the regulars, complaining about being hung over, about how long it took him the day before to collect enough money to buy his first beer of the day. On a leash with him is his fluffy little gentle doggie, and he talks to it when he's not calling out to passersby. "What am I going to do with an old dog like you?" he faux-complains with affection. "Let's go bite someone on the toes. I'll bite one toe, and you bite another." The dog does what most dogs do: looks up at him, rubs up against him, and wags its tail. No question they like each other, and no question they need each other, I conclude, after observing the two of them for a few minutes. Companionship and partnership.

That kind of companionship and partnership resulting in a mutually beneficial relationship defines my idealized concept of pet and "owner." It is not the kind of relationship a trophy pet owner can attain with a great ape, big cat, or long snake. How is mutual companionship possible when you need to chain your tiger, secure the vivarium where your Burmese python lives, or lock your chimpanzee—the same animal you've just dressed in clothing designed for a little girl, and fed Jell-O with a spoon at your family dining table—in a cage at night?

The desire to seek such animals, which I can only try to understand because I have no interest in a tiger or even a cute monkey as a pet and certainly not a snake, must be the lure of potential danger combined with at least a latent lust to dominate. Most of us are entranced by the power of apex predators; that's why savvy carmakers choose brand names like

Jaguar and Mustang and Falcon (ironic in the case of the American-made Falcons, those nondescript bottom-of-the-line Fords from the 1960s). Add our acquisitive culture to the mix. Collecting is human nature, as is a desire to talk to the animals. We've all got a little Dr. Doolittle in us. What a thrill to communicate with a great ape or a big cat. (Who would bother trying with a snake?) Who among us hasn't talked to their dog or cat? I often try to make sense of Schrödinger's vocabulary (although he seems to ignore most of what I say to him).

I left the Florida swamplands and connected with Dennis Hill, a life-long animal collector who specializes in big cats. He calls himself an "old hippie" and traces the origin of his tiger collection to his childhood growing up a farm boy. He and his tigers live in the crossroads of Flat Rock, Indiana, between Cincinnati and Indianapolis. Hill is the lead character in the documentary film *The Tiger Next Door,* which producer and director Camilla Calamandrei made in order to call attention to the "near epidemic" problem of wild animal ownership. To prove her point, she follows Hill's activities after the U.S. Department of Agriculture suspended his permit to keep and breed tigers, forcing him to find alternative homes for most of his twenty-four tigers, six leopards, three bears, and cougar. Once he lost his federal license, Indiana law applied, and he needed to prove to state officials that his facilities were adequate to allow him to hold on to a few of his pride. One particularly telling scene from the film follows neighbor after neighbor as they testify at a community meeting about Hill and his animals. There are those in Flat Rock who want to see him out of business, but what I find astounding is the parade of witnesses who express no worries about the tigers next door. Hill says he understands their motives. "It's deeper than me and the tigers. It's about freedom. More and more, everyday, we lose more freedoms."

Stark white hair hangs long around Hill's face, held in place with a headband reminiscent of late '60s styles. His matching white beard and mustache are awesome: The beard literally stretches to his belly, and the mustache completely shrouds his mouth. When he talks, the words come out slowly, formed with care and spoken in a melodic Midwestern drawl. Much of his adult life he's kept wild cats, breeding them and selling them, reaping as much as $15,000, he says, when he makes a sale, and as little as $1,000. But he's not just in it for the money. He loves the cats. "I know what they're thinking, and they know what I'm thinking," he says on camera, patting the paw of one of his tigers. "It's a mutual respect."

He and I talk on the phone as I sit in my office looking at thirteen pounds of Schrödinger co-opting my desk chair.

"I barely can deal with my little house cat," I tell him. "What makes a guy like you want a variation on him that weighs 350 pounds?"

He responds with what sounds almost like a tiger chuff.

"I grew up on the farm. I have a special gift with the animals. I had all wild animals as pets back then."

But wild animals native to Indiana are a far cry from imported tigers and other big cats. Hill says he was smitten the first time he saw a tiger.

"I think tigers are magical, they're spiritual," he says when I ask him again why he keeps the tigers. "They're lords of the earth. People have a lot to gain from the innocence that those cats project and give to us."

Innocence. I find it a strange word to describe these killer cats.

"I believe there is some transplasmatic situation that goes from animals to people," Hill continues to try to help me understand. Great term, *transplasmatic*. "I've seen 'em affected everywhere. I've showed baby tigers to people with major egos, people that wouldn't give you the time of day, people that are stuck on themselves in another world, and tigers just bring 'em right back to earth and make 'em all human again. They're magical."

His tiger work is a calling, he tells me.

"I feel like I'm a middleman or an ambassador between the world that wants to see tigers and a person that is able to keep 'em safely. I feel I have that gift to show the world the truth and innocence that tigers stand for and project."

Dennis Hill agrees that keeping his captive-bred tigers in cages is not the best option.

"Sure, I would love to see every tiger in the world have a hundred square miles each, but that isn't going to happen. I would love to see them roam free. It's not fair," he says about their caged life, a life he perpetuates by breeding more tigers that will live their lives in cages. "I do agree with that," he says about a free-ranging life for wild cats, "but it's not going to happen. It's a good thought. There are a lot of good thoughts about the world."

I ask him what he thinks motivates him to continue to surround himself with tigers.

"I guess you could say it's an obsession. But I feel I was delivered to that obsession."

"Do you consider them your pets?" I ask.

"I call mine 'significant others,'" he says. "I don't own these tigers, they own me." But moments later he champions himself. "My tigers live for me to come out there and talk with them, communicate with them. And you don't always have to say a word to communicate with them."

When he and I talk, his collection is back up to five tigers, four whites and one he calls a golden tabby. These are tigers that will live their lives in captivity. They cannot be introduced into the wild in a native range for tigers because they do not know how to hunt. They would present a danger to themselves and local human populations since they do not necessarily fear people. Most scientists working to preserve wild tigers would not want Hill's tigers in the wilds even were they able to feed themselves because their mongrel genes could pollute native species.

━ ～

At Western Carolina University, psychology professor Harold Herzog studies the relationships we humans create with other species, specifically those of us whose lives are intertwined with nonhuman animals. He's the author of a book on the subject with a great title, *Some We Love, Some We Hate, Some We Eat: Why It's So Hard to Think Straight about Animals*. His love affair with animals, he tells me, started with snakes, when he was a little boy. "There was a draw there that I found really hard to explain. I was struck with their weirdness, their otherness."

Years later and steeped in the question as an academic, his answer as to why people want exotic pets remains much the same: to be different. He tells me the story of a couple that called him in the middle of the night because their two boa constrictors unexpectedly (for the humans) propagated the species. "They woke up, and they had forty-two babies, and they were completely wigged out." He went to their house. "The thing that was so interesting about them was how totally normal they were. It was a suburban house. They were blue-collar types. In the living room they had this huge cage with the boa constrictors. The thing I find remarkable is that oftentimes people whose lives are intertwined with animals are on one level so normal but on another level have these weird quirks."

Other times they might not seem so normal. Dennis Hill with his couple of dozen tigers to support. Fran Ogren conspiring with her daughter to smuggle a monkey from Thailand to Spokane. Sandra Herold at cocktail hour sipping drinks with her chimpanzee. But then what is normal? These "quirky interactions," figures Dr. Herzog, "offer a window into human nature. These animal-related quirks are in some ways simply a manifestation of the same sort of thing that drives people to be insane about their car. It's a manifestation of our humanity in the sense that people get passionate over very, very different things that oftentimes other people don't understand."

We agree that one motivator for such passions—whether for a jaguar with four paws or a Jaguar with four tires—is to escape the mundane.

"Do you have a cat?" Herzog asks me.

I tell him about Schrödinger.

"The thing that amazes me about cats is how much more animal-like they are than dogs. It's like really living with a predator: the fact that my cat can snatch a bug out of the sky, the fact that it can climb up a dogwood tree in five seconds flat, the fact that it can go out and five minutes later bring me a live chipmunk, which it deposits in front of me. Part of the thing I enjoy about living with a cat is that she is a predator, and she is wild."

"So, is your house cat your pet?" I ask him. "What is a pet?"

"It's like pornography; I know it when I see it," he says, quoting Justice Potter Stewart. "I know people who have dogs, yet they really don't fit into their family very well, they don't treat them particularly well. On the other hand, those people who had the boa constrictors, they told me they were like children to them. I'm sure you've heard that before."

Indeed I have, from most of the exotic pet owners I met. I test my hypothesis on the expert. "The lines from wild to tame to feral to domesticated often seem arbitrary and blurry."

"That's so right," he says, and the professor gets excited. "You got it! You and I are on exactly the same page. They're totally blurry."

As if to emphasize his point, that evening at least one raccoon came into the house through Schrödinger's cat door—just a thin plastic partition separating our domesticated home from the wilds of Bodega Bay— ate his food, dirtied up his water, and may have been the culprit who snatched and ate a brownie Sheila left in a grocery bag in the foyer. Or maybe Schrödinger was the brownie thief.

CHAPTER TWENTY-TWO

Getting Marked in Pahrump

Picasso the Tiger Sprays Your Correspondent from Head to Toe

CLIMBING OUT OF LAS VEGAS ON THE BLUE DIAMOND HIGHWAY TOWARD Pahrump, I remember the last news story I covered in the southern Nevada desert community. The town board had enacted what they called the "English Language and Patriot Reaffirmation Ordinance," which required Old Glory be in the supreme position on any Pahrump flagpole and made English Pahrump's official language. The former vice chairman of the board dismissed critics of the ordinance. "I think sometimes people have to stand up and be real men," Ronald Johnson told me. "In this particular case, if people want to take the ordinance on, I guess they just need to jump on their horse and do it." Animal metaphors play a continuing role in the Pahrump Old West mythology, I'm about to learn.

I'm speeding across the desert in my rented gold Mustang convertible, the radio blasting "Take It Easy" by the Eagles. "Don't even try to understand," the band instructs me as I try to keep the mechanical horse under eighty miles per hour. Don't even try to understand seems like it might be good advice as I head out to meet a couple of big cat lovers turned activists—activists working against legislation that restricts exotic pet ownership.

Juniper and piñon pine trees decorate the desert sand with verdant shades, along with a dose of cartoonlike cactus. I love Nevada. The Mustang wants to go fast on the smooth blacktop, past highway signs that warn of bighorn sheep, wild horses, and burros. I slow on the long grade down into Pahrump, past a parade of billboards: EARN FREE CIGARETTES, 10X BINGO, BEST SLOT CLUB, TERRIBLE'S TOWN CASINO, FIREWORKS, FORECLOSURES, TATTOO, and—wearing a leopard skin bikini—a sprawled billboard model advertising the Brothel Museum twenty miles ahead in Crystal.

I follow the directions and turn left off the main highway, calling Slovakian immigrant Zuzana Kukol before I get to the end of the pavement. She'll need to open the perimeter fence on the acreage she shares with Scott Shoemaker, a retired Army intelligence officer, along with Bam-Bam the lion, Picasso the tiger, and a bevy of other big cats.

"I have to tell you something. I hope this won't gross you out," she says in what I learn is her routine voice: rapid fire, enthusiastic, passionate, funny, and with such a pronounced Slovakian accent that I'm forced often to ask her to repeat herself.

"What could gross me out?" I inquire.

She tells me that a local horse wrangler dropped a horse off for the cats to eat, a damaged horse that was to be euthanized. It would end up in the Pahrump dump if she and Shoemaker didn't want it as cat food. They shot it as I was driving to their place and are in the process of hanging it and bleeding it as I arrive. It's a gruesome sight; the blood is already attracting flies. But better the old paint ends its days as pet food than dump fill.

The big cat pets are behind cyclone fencing. Shoemaker is struggling with the carcass; he can't just dump it in the cages. The cats I'm about to meet were raised on store-bought feed: meat already dressed.

"I have to skin it and make sure there's no fur on it," Shoemaker says. He looks as if he could still slip into his Army uniform. He's fit—he needs to be to wrestle with dead horses—with a hint of silver-gray at the temples and steady clear hazel eyes encircled with blue that appear both welcoming and probing.

Kukol joins us as Shoemaker winches the bleeding horse up onto a wooden frame. She looks at the Mustang and says, dropping the article, which highlights her accent, "I told you not to rent Ferrari; it's too low." She had warned me about the unpaved Nevada road to their house. She's wearing aviator shades, a tight camouflage patterned T-shirt, jeans, and black cowboy boots. The desert wind keeps blowing her long blond hair into her face, and it's impossible not to notice the scars on her neck. Was she attacked by one of her pets?

"Some people would be grossed out by this," she says, gesturing to the horse. Kukol moved to Nevada from Washington State after Washington enacted laws restricting private ownership of exotic pets. In Pahrump, the law remains minimally intrusive, but she worries that legislation against her lifestyle may follow her to the desert. I suggest she can always move to Missouri or Ohio or one of the other Midwestern states infamous for their lax attitudes toward what advocates for strict controls against exotic pets call the petification of wild animals.

"Kill me first!" is her response to the idea of such a move. She dismisses the Midwest as "so boring."

Funny, I've stumbled on a prejudice she and the PETA executive director share. When I was at PETA headquarters, I asked Ingrid Newkirk why she thought there are so many Midwestern states where exotic pet trade and ownership are legal.

"I think that the middle of the country is notoriously sort of a refuge from all the things that are happening on the coasts." She smiled and added, "So if you want to do it, you can go there."

Some of my formative years were spent in Madison, Wisconsin. Arrogance and ignorance about our flyover states annoy me, even if I do call California home.

— ⁓

The license plates on Zuzana Kukol's Hummer in the driveway read TIGRLVR. *Lev,* I learn from Kukol, means "lion" in Slovakian. She was born and raised in the city of Levice, which means "lionesses"; the city's herald is a lion with three tails. "Ever since I was a little child, I knew I didn't want to have human kids; I wanted to have my own animals." She likes felines and canines but not apes. "Monkeys are like hairy children," she informs me. "Why bother?"

She and Shoemaker waste no time showing me the pride of their pride: Bam-Bam the lion. He sits on a platform behind two rows of chain-link fence, a regal-looking king of Pahrump. His black and tan and rusty brown mane frames what looks—especially from the security of studying him protected by the fence—like the face of a sweet and gentle animal. "This is brush," she says, gesturing to a stout piece of wood with bristles as we go through the first gate of the double-entry enclosure. "If he is good, he gets brushed with it. It also can be used as a bite stick. If he decides he wants to bite me, I give him this instead." The short-handled brush looks like a poor substitute for a juicy arm or leg. Kukol smiles and displays a can. "And pepper spray, just in case!" Shoemaker and I stay back as she enters Bam-Bam's space. Bam-Bam is good. Bam-Bam gets brushed. Bam-Bam comes over to the chain-link fence and rubs up against it, soliciting a pet from Shoemaker.

The regal lion is almost four and still growing—Shoemaker estimates his weight at over 375 pounds. They don't own a scale he won't break. He was a photo cub, Kukol tells me, and federal government regulations require big cats used as moneymakers for photographers be retired from direct contact with the public when they reach forty pounds or forty-four months. "Photo cubs are socialized," Kukol says, coming back through the gate. "They love humans." Bam-Bam certainly seems happy, nuzzling and rubbing up against her.

Photo cubs, the two of them tell me, often end up in what they call scamtuaries or scumtuaries, self-styled sanctuaries that use the cute cubs to lure donations. They are quick to differentiate their scene from sanctuaries, zoos, roadside attractions, stage shows, and other exotic animal acts. They keep Bam-Bam and the other big cats, they tell me, for the same reason Schrödinger lives in my house: Bam-Bam is their pet and nothing more.

Next to Bam-Bam's quarters are two white tigers, both females. They play with each other, hugging and boxing like kittens—huge kittens. One is white with black stripes, and the other is pure white with crossed eyes. Shoemaker dismisses reports that most white captive-bred tigers are inbred and suffer from birth defects. Crossed eyes are one common result when breeders seek white tigers. "They used to breed white to white, and you had problems with inbreeding. Breeders are now introducing orange tigers into the bloodline," he says with a voice of authority.

Wrong, says tiger scholar Ron Tilson. "They can't be crossing a white tiger or an orange tiger carrying a white gene with an unrelated full orange tiger with no white gene because that will not produce white tigers. They have to come back to the tigers that are carrying the white genes so they get a double recessive when it's mated. So he's full of baloney with what he's saying to you because he doesn't understand genetics."

When I tell Dr. Tilson I met with Zuzana Kukol, he exclaims, "Oh my God, the wild woman! She hates me!" Tilson traces her feelings to his analysis of the psychology behind owning big cats. "Tigers represent everything fine and decent and powerful, everything those people would like to be. It's all an ego trip—big guns, big trucks, and big tigers." He rejects her insistence that it is her constitutional right to be left alone with her cats. "No, lady. You do not understand what a civilized society is about. When what you're doing threatens innocent people, then I say you've crossed the line."

Kukol sees nothing wrong with the captive breeding of tigers. "Animals are property. Once you own property, government shouldn't tell you what to do." Tilson accepts the estimate of about five thousand captive-bred tigers in the United States. A precise figure is impossible to cite because there is no census and not even an informal network connecting owners. The unregulated atmosphere is problematic in his mind for both tiger and human. "Don't think for a moment," he says, "that the private sector is full of responsible people. It is instead full of people who are trafficking in tigers."

"We hate each other," Zuzana Kukol cheerfully says about Ron Tilson. "It comes to money. He doesn't make his own money, he sucks taxpayer's money." In order to keep the research money flowing, she says, he needs controversy. She and Shoemaker, she tells me, are financially independent. "Oh, that is so silly," Tilson says about her charge. "I'm disappointed that's the best she could come up with. If you want to be a successful conservationist, you have to be able to mitigate conflict."

Shoemaker is finishing with the horse, cutting off the head and legs. "I've got to take the guts out," he says. "That's the worst part. That's what takes the longest because I don't want to puncture anything. If you puncture the stomach or the guts, there's a foul smell."

Kukol introduces me to Picasso, an adult tiger suffering from a nasty hotspot. He's wearing a wide collar to prevent him from licking and aggravating the wound with his sandpaperlike tongue. Kukol enters his cage and maneuvers around him to stay away from his rear end. "I better get out; he sprays," she yells out to me, after petting and patting the twelve-year-old retired magic show cat. "He's such a good tiger." He makes a moan that sounds like a cow and chuffs. As we walk past the gate, Picasso turns and shoots a load of spray on us, marking his territory. Kukol calls me lucky. "In zoos you can't get that close," she informs me. I'm wet with his stink from shoulders to knees, hardly what I consider lucky. Shoemaker's interpretation of the event differs. "You're his bitch now," he tells me.

The couple operates a prolific Web site called Rexano, a contraction of Responsible Exotic Animal Ownership. "We support responsible private ownership of exotic animals in any form," they write, "be it noncommercial pet or sanctuary, as well as commercial breeder or exhibitor." Articles with titles like "Extreme Animal Rights Groups: Do They Really Help Animals?" fill the site, along with advice for keeping exotics, the status of pending restrictive legislation, and an array of merchandise, including a poster of Zuzana Kukol in a black (it looks like leather) bikini and black cowboy boots leaning on a motorcycle while holding a leashed Bam-Bam. "Just Say NO! to Exotic Pet Bans," reads the headline. It lists the few casualties exotic pets cause annually and the many other causes of injuries to humans, from lightning to bees to motorcycles.

There are concerned citizens out in the Nevada desert who want more local controls on big cats, much to the disgust of *Pahrump Valley Times* columnist Mark Smith, who writes that "such restrictions ignore the fact that, unless you are incredibly stupid (or you've hired on as Siegfried's partner), the odds of your ever running afoul of a wild cat—tiger, lion, mountain lion, you name it—are virtually nil." Smith worries about the encroaching mundane. "Alas, what some people want is a town that is pasteurized and homogenized out of any real character, to the extent it actually becomes a real-life Stepford town, where even those grubby gunslingers at the Wild West Extravaganza should be expected to smell of Right Guard and Irish Spring, and they all have 2.5 kids and a golden retriever named Dylan and a late-model Volvo sedan named Madison. And their fingernails are clean."[104] I know what Smith means. I keep my old enameled Nevada lapel pin with its legend that cries out, "If you ain't a Nevadan, you ain't shit," as a reminder of the days before leash laws, a time when I lived in Silver City and my dog, Amigo, ran wild chasing rabbits and other dogs.

"If they do some federal ban, it's going to affect us," Kukol says as she launches into a tirade against Tippi Hedren's efforts to end captive breeding and private big cat ownership. "Too bad the birds didn't get her," she cries out. "It's like banning you from driving car because some NASCAR driver got killed." She knows about car wrecks: That's how she got the scars on her neck. Her philosophy regarding pet ownership is simple and straightforward. "I don't think anything should be illegal if you're not endangering anybody. I mean, this is America. They are on my property. They don't bother anybody. You have bleach at home? You drink bleach, and you're dead. People fear the unknown. They know what bleach is, they know what car is. They fear the unknown. They fear predators."

"But the bleach is not going to chase after you," I say. "The tiger or lion might come after you. The bleach is in a bottle."

"Nobody ever got killed in USA by escaped big cat," is her answer. Even the notorious San Francisco Zoo tiger Tatiana, she says, was on zoo property when she jumped out of her enclosure and killed the visitor on the perimeter of her exhibit. Kukol looks catlike herself when she gets excited, and her emotions flare fast when she's talking tigers and lions. Her eyes open wide, enhanced by dark eyeliner, and she peppers her rapid-fire speech with cuss words. "You get attacked by dogs on way to school. Name one case where someone was walking, doing their own stuff, and was attacked by captive-bred cats."

I can't, but Ron Tilson, in his book *Tigers of the World*, does chronicle a few worldwide annual fatalities. "This is a large, dangerous cat that cannot be tamed," he tells me, "cannot be loved to death, and sooner or later can cause havoc or mayhem to just about anyone."

"I don't want you to get attacked," Zuzana Kukol informs me. I'm comforted to hear that, surrounded as we are by a lion, several tigers, a cougar, a bobcat, a serval, and wolves ("three white semi wild mid to high content wolf dogs"), to which Scott Shoemaker is about to feed the horse's head. "But if you do get attacked, you came here; the cat didn't go after you. Same with bleach; you come to the bleach." She's tried to tame the cats, and she's presenting them as creatures she loves, creatures she "owns," but if they hurt me, it's not her fault because I chose to come to her place for a visit. It's at once an attempt to lay claim to powerful animals and a denial of the result of those animals' power if she loses control over them. Nice when you can construct a win–win morality for yourself.

The three of us retire to the front porch, Shoemaker's work clothes bloodied; the horse, minus legs and head, is hanging and bleeding. The big-sky view across the Pahrump Valley to the mountains separating us from Las Vegas offers what my Nevada friend and colleague Chandler Laughlin calls an opportunity to stretch your eyeballs.

What about the animals, I ask them. The enclosures I've seen are big and clean, but the cats are captive.

"Have you ever been to moon?" Zuzana Kukol asks me. Of course, the answer is no. "Can you miss moon if you've never been there? These animals are born in captivity. They don't know what wild is. They can't miss what they don't know."

"But they're built to chase prey, to run free," I protest. "Not to live in an enclosure, even enclosures as big as the ones you've built for them."

She rejects the premise. "The reason they have big territories in the wild is to look for food, not to exercise. Given the choice, cats—especially big cats—sleep, sleep, sleep."

That's certainly Schrödinger's choice at home on our couch.

"If it's okay for domestic cat to be stuck in apartment all its life," she says, "why is it not okay for tigers to be in huge habitats in captivity?" I'm not convinced it is okay for a domestic cat to be stuck in an apartment all its life. When I lived in Berlin, my friend Sigi's cat, Mäuschen (great name for a cat: little mouse!), was sentenced to her second-floor flat for life. At least twice Mäuschen jumped out of the window to test the great outdoors, fleeing from the confines of the flat/cage. Schrödinger comes and goes as he pleases (much to the frustration of our veterinarian, who believes all house cats should live an indoor life for their health and safety).

Zuzana Kukol says when she lets Bam-Bam roam the acreage around their house, he walks about, sprays the property, then comes over to the porch and lies down. "They're fed," she says about the cats, "they're happy. They don't have to hunt."

"How do you know Bam-Bam is happy?" I ask.

"Are we dead?" is Kukol's glib retort. We know our animals, she says, and just as you know when your children are happy, we understand them. "Some idiot from Washington, D.C., who never met my animals cannot tell me my animals are not happy. The same idiot cannot tell you when your children are not happy. That's just some person in an office who's never been close enough to a tiger to get sprayed."

We're looking out at the desert, the tour over, the setting sun casting sagebrush shadows. They've made me feel a welcome guest, I'm comfortable relaxing with them, and it's easy to join first Kukol and then Shoemaker smiling about my big cat baptism. Although I remain ambivalent about keeping tigers fenced in, I'm enjoying our camaraderie. Picasso sits in his enclosure, and I wonder if the smell of his spray will wash out of my sweater and jeans.

Back in Las Vegas, I check into the faded Sahara, where I secure a bargain room. It's at the wrong end of the Strip these days, far from the Disney-like glitz of faux New York and Paris. Black-and-white lobby photo murals of Vegas stars on stage and of a showgirl making an elegant spike-heeled entrance into the hotel from a tanklike 1956 Cadillac recall the hotel's glory days. Big cats follow me here. Magician Rick Thomas is on the Sahara stage this night with his "Magic and Tigers" show; his poster poses are shared with a white-and-black-striped tiger. The TV in my room offers movies. *Hangover* is playing; its drunken stars steal Mike Tyson's pet tiger.

CHAPTER TWENTY-THREE

Good People

Strange Hobby

"WHEN WE TRY TO PICK OUT ANYTHING BY ITSELF," JOHN MUIR WROTE, "we find it hitched to everything else in the Universe."[105] Indeed. Just as was the case when I was investigating the dangerous world of butterflies, as soon as I started searching for stories of big cats, great apes, and long snakes, exotic pets and their keepers seemed omnipresent. It's the nature of focusing; we notice things that barely registered before. I once took a journalists' survival course from a corps of former British Marines, a course designed to help us survive when we work in conflict zones. One of the most valuable techniques I learned from these hard-drinking but hyperalert warriors was how to look past mundane scenes for out-of-the-ordinary, potentially threatening activities. Driving down a city street or taking a stroll in the countryside, we tend to see what we expect to see. But the Marines taught me to look where I would not normally cast my eyes, seek people and things that seem out of place, continually plot escape routes. During the research for this book, I practiced those lessons and found a tiger in the back of a feed store, a colony of chimpanzees in the countryside south of St. Louis, and laundry bags full of pythons in a decommissioned Nike missile base in the Everglades.

As my deadline for this manuscript approached, I remembered another high school classmate with a pet monkey. A girlhood dream came true for Barbara Brower when she convinced her parents to let her rescue a long-tailed macaque from a University of California laboratory at Berkeley. The other lab monkeys ganged up on Isabel, and the university was going to "sacrifice" her. *Sacrifice* is a strange euphemism to add to the list that avoids *kill* but prefers *euthanasia* and *putting to sleep*.

"I was twelve years old," she tells me when we meet in Berkeley to talk apes, "and I always wanted a monkey. Just like you probably wanted a monkey when you were twelve. Doesn't everybody want a monkey?"

No. Everybody does not want a monkey. It never occurred to me to want a monkey.

"'Come on, Mom! I'll take care of her,'" Brower recounts lobbying her mother. "'I'll clean her cage. I'll take her for walks. It'll be great. You won't even know she's in the house.'"

Isabel moved in. She lived in a cage in the kitchen of the family home in the Berkeley hills. Brower, a geography professor at Portland State University who does extensive fieldwork with yaks in the Himalayas, fondly recalls growing up enjoying a siblinglike relationship with a different species.

"She was like our demented little sister. So many things about her were so very human. Her caginess. Her hands. She had these perfect little hands, just like human hands. Her wiles. She was so clearly close to our species." She stopped being a monkey, Brower says about the intimate relationship the two experienced. "It really blurs the species because we learned to be like her, and she learned to deal with us."

The family learned to interact with Isabel on her terms and, years later, at times used macaque devices with each other, insistent hand slapping on a table top to express impatience, for example, or a fierce widening of flashing eyes to threaten.

The monkey and Brower lived together for over twenty years. Isabel followed her to our high school, where she lived in a cage in the science lab when Brower wasn't sneaking her into her dormitory room, and they went off to college together, with Isabel causing relentless trouble.

"She was very vicious. Macaques are terrestrial; they don't escape to the trees. They fight." Isabel's canine teeth were filed to reduce the threat she posed. "One of the horrible things we did to her," Brower says, and her fondness for the monkey is evident as she recounts their time together. "She would bite, and even without her canines, she would leave these bruises that would last for months. She would really rip the hell out of you."

Isabel was clever and used her hands to escape confinement in her cage whenever possible. One memorable escapade occurred when Brower's mother, an editor, was working on a book at home. In those days before word processors, the manuscript was on a table, along with photographs that were to illustrate the book. "Isabel loved paper. She loved to rip it up." She destroyed the manuscript but did not molest the photographs. She engaged the typewriter, and when the mess was discovered, Isabel was tangled in the typewriter ribbon. The book was about primates, and the pictures she left undisturbed were images of other monkeys.

Most of her life, Isabel spent tethered to a leash trolley, giving her the run of the Berkeley backyard.

More than twenty-five years after Isabel's death, it's clear that my classmate loved her monkey and still misses her. Yet when I ask her if others should follow her example and find a monkey for a pet, her reply is immediate.

"Never!" is the emphatic answer. "Never, never ever. Probably nothing should be a pet, but certainly no wild animal should be a pet. It's just not right." But she understands the appeal. "It's interesting to see that this is your cousin not so very far removed. You can see your DNA there. There's family recognition. It's easier to figure out how a monkey's brain is working than a dog's brain. You can guess about a dog, but it's more likely that it's right with a monkey."

But Dr. Brower, who spent her undergraduate years studying primates, draws the line at signing on with philosopher Mark Rowlands and the others who would identify her monkey as a person. "She certainly had her own identity as a worthy being."

"But she was not a person?"

"I don't talk like that. I don't anthropomorphize her. I think she was who she was, phylogenetically really close to us, and an extremely interesting and important creature in her own right who happened to have fallen into our hands, giving us this obligation to make her life as rich as it could be."

"Did she have a sense of self?" I ask, citing one of Dr. Rowland's criteria for personhood.

"I don't know," says Brower with some exasperation.

Her scientific honesty is refreshing.

"I think that is so presumptuous," she says about those who insist they understand the inner workings of a great ape or a big cat. She looks across the table at me, her friend since high school. "I barely know who you are and what you think of yourself."

———

As the work on this book neared completion, a tragedy occurred that caught my attention not just because it involved an exotic pet but also because it seemed to epitomize the ludicrous fantasy that humans can tame wild beasts. Many of us like to think we are the ultimate animal, and that we can tame all the rest of nature, given the chance. My romp through the world of exotic pets introduced me to an engaging cast of characters, many of whom fantasize not just about communing with exotic beasts but also controlling them. Such dreams, even most of these exotic animal lovers eventually admit, can dissolve into nightmares in seconds and without warning.

Meet the Walzes, Kelly Ann and Michael. The late Kelly Ann. For years they shared their rural Pennsylvania property northeast of Allentown with a variety of big cats, along with a black bear they raised from a cub, a bear named—naturally—Teddy. The adorable cub grew into 350 pounds of muscle and claw and instinct. He lived in a fifteen-by-fifteen-foot metal-and-concrete cage, a cage Kelly Ann regularly cleaned. One Sunday night in early October 2009, she followed her usual routine. She opened the cage door, tossed some dog food to one side of the cage to distract Teddy, and started to mop up. Teddy was not interested in the dog food. He attacked Kelly Ann as her horrified children watched. They summoned neighbor Scott Castone. Castone distracted the bear, but it was already too late. Kelly Ann's injuries were fatal, and Teddy started to exit his cage, heading for Castone. The schoolteacher shot and killed the bear. "She's done it 1,000 times," Castone said about the cage cleaning, "and on 1,001, something happened." Another neighbor, Marshall Eldridge, summed up the tragedy, and in doing so, he summed up my experiences with some of the characters I've encountered studying forbidden creatures. "They were good people," he said. "They just had a strange hobby."[106]

I push my rowboat back from the dock and stroke west across Bodega Bay toward the setting sun, past a stand of cormorants drying their wings and lone pelicans surveying the water from their vantage points high on pilings. Sea lions bark from across the bay at Spud Point, and I keep an eye out for my harbor seal friends while I work the oars and consider that statement: Good people with a strange hobby. After a year prowling around in the world of exotic pets, I know the reality is not so simple.

The poachers and smugglers who fuel the illegal exotic pet trade usually are not good people. That underworld is rife with predatory personal opportunists, decimating endangered species for a quick buck—although some of the wildlife suppliers are the desperate poor, ignorant of the environmental damage they cause, struggling to feed themselves and their families.

I think about the mother-and-daughter smugglers Fran Ogren and Gypsy Lawson drugging the monkey they bought for $20 in Thailand and violating international treaties and American laws to satisfy their personal lust for adventure and a cute pet. Those two may not be bad people, but they're certainly misguided. The same goes for Connie Casey out in the Missouri countryside, breeding chimpanzees for private profit. And she brings to mind her most notorious customer, Sandra Herold, owner of the infamous Travis. Does a "good person" continue to keep a dangerous animal in the suburbs for her own pleasure?

From the Kubla Kahn to William Randolph Hearst to David Vanderholm with his tiger, Lilly, locked up in the back of his Idaho feed store, collectors—fetishists, really—seek live exotic animals as one more selfish acquisition. Confining wild animals far from their home range and reducing them to playthings—objectifying them—often is more than just a "strange hobby"; it can be a cruel as well as an unusual pastime. I think of the Lolli Brothers auction in Missouri, where I watched Linda Bilbrey stroking her newborn serval and Teresa Shaffer cooing to her six-month-old monkey. They were happy with their animals, but were the cat and the ape happy? And a few years on from our encounters at the auction house, would any of the four be living happily ever after? The odds are grim for good news.

I know there are no Burmese pythons swimming along next to me as I row across the bay; the water is much too cold. I can't report much concern about the happiness of the thousands of pythons propagating the Everglades. I tend to embrace philosopher Mark Rowlands's dismissive assessment of the snakes when he said that "it's difficult to know if anything is going on there, if the lights are on at all." But the irresponsibility of the pet industry and government to allow the rampant trade of these exotics in a void of knowledge regarding their impact on the fragile Florida ecology is mind numbing.

Throughout human history we've sought other animals as playthings for our own entertainment. Under the best of circumstances, the feelings are mutual, and the animals we keep thrive with us. Perhaps that's the case with some captive-bred exotics. Zuzana Kukol and her lion, Bam-Bam, may be an example; they seem content with each other—and it's hard to imagine a better alternative for him.

We'll always be fascinated by the wild things in our midst. How can there not be a lure when we see ourselves once removed in the eyes and antics of a great ape? Who isn't seduced by the cuteness of the kitten, recognizable even in hundreds of pounds of lion or tiger? Ever since Eve succumbed to the serpent—and there are snake legends in all cultures—we've been entranced by the python and its cousins.

After interacting with exotic pets and their owners, I view our attempts at taming animals as little more than subjugation. That's understandable if our own survival is at stake, or even our comfort. But to subjugate other beings for our amusement diminishes our own self-worth. I watch another seal bob its head up out of the water and check me out as I keep a respectful distance from the sea lions (they're huge and aggressive in their search for easy fish) and row back to my dock. How could I rationalize capturing that wild seal, taking it to a confined pool, and teaching it to balance a beach ball on its nose? I'm lucky enough to live along still-pristine Bodega Bay; the Sonoma County coast is alive with vibrant wildlife. Habitat degradation worldwide threatens species survival throughout the animal kingdom, making the trade in wild exotic pets impossible for me to rationalize—not to mention the potential danger some of them pose to innocent passersby.

If they don't need us as much as we think we need (or want) them, we should leave other animals alone, and they should remain forbidden creatures.

EPILOGUE

We're All at Least a Little Wild

It's well past midnight. I'm on the couch in my Bodega Bay living room, listening to the roar of the surf at the Salmon Creek beach, thinking about exotic pets. Sometimes the surf sounds like freeway traffic. If ever I am forced to live next to a freeway, I hope the traffic sounds like the Salmon Creek surf. Schrödinger is curled up on the ottoman, sleeping, his sweet-looking head resting on his furry paws. He's cute and passive, snoring and the picture of domesticity. I was napping on the couch earlier, and he was asleep next to me, on this couch that he's ruined, sharpening his claws on its corners. I like him, but I'm wary of him, too. He often swats at my bare feet with those sharpened claws. He's licked my feet, and he's hissed at me, unprovoked. He's drawn my blood more than once, scratching for no apparent reason. I like him, but I don't trust him. He's got a wild streak that I recognize; I've got one, too. We can't be tamed. Neither of us would make good pets.

ACKNOWLEDGMENTS

"If the acknowledgments are lengthy," the *Chicago Manual of Style* instructs, "they may be put in a separate section."

I love reading acknowledgments in books. I often find in them what I'm convinced is much more insight into the life of the writer than the lines the "About the Author" biography offer. One of my favorites is the acknowledgments section Anne-Marie Slaughter wrote in *The Idea That Is America: Keeping Faith with Our Values in a Dangerous World*. She and I talked on the *Washington Monthly on the Radio* program I coanchor with my friend and colleague Markos Kounalakis (and a köszönöm szépen for his enthusiasm about this project) about how Slaughter's acknowledgments read like a book within a book, filled with stories such as the one about her Moroccan hairdresser. "I love your history," the stylist told her about America's heritage. "It's so short and cute." "Short" may be from a Moroccan perspective, but not always so cute, as my experience in writing first drafts ascertain—exotic pet stories included.

Somewhat lengthy these acknowledgments are because of all the help I was privileged to receive researching and writing this book. I start with the late Jane Foulds, the Renaissance woman who sent an e-mail message inviting me to visit her butterfly reserve in Nicaragua. That trip seduced me into natural history as a new genre for my journalistic exercises.

My friend dating back to high school, Dana Hayden, gave me the rowboat that I ply across the Bodega Bay communing with wildlife; until now I do not think I've made it clear to him how much pleasure I've derived from what was a casual gift. Another esteemed throwback to high school, my Stammtisch partner Chris Slattery, read early drafts and provided valued critiques. James Fahn, the global director of environmental programs at Internews, sent along detailed background regarding the role of Thailand and Vietnam as source countries for exotic pet traffickers and collectors. From his listening post in Armenia, journalist, author, and friend (not necessarily in that order) Terry Phillips helped fill me in on the antics of tiger owner Ramzan Kadyrov, the Chechen leader. Once he returned to his California headquarters, Phillips, a founding member of the Virtual Newsroom think tank I'm privileged to be a member of, offered detailed editing and feedback on early drafts of *Forbidden Creatures,* as did another of our Virtual Newsroom cabal, close friend, journalist, and author Jeff Kamen (who reminded me that J. Fred Muggs and I both labored for the Peacock Network). The Kamen family graciously opened their beachfront home to me for my South Florida project headquarters. My fine photographer friend Ira Kahn was an important sounding board for the work in progress, as was my novelist friend Michael Hassan.

A tip of the hat to Pam Brown (and to Anne Hill for introducing us); she pointed me to Yi-Fu Tuan's pet studies and the film *Living with Chimpanzees.* Thanks to editor Peter Bloch for the outstanding assignments he sends me off on for *Penthouse* magazine, pets included.

As I look through the manuscript trying to make sure that I miss no one who deserves thanks, I'm reminded that I must express my appreciation to all those who revealed their lives to my prying journalism, especially those with little to gain from such exposure, such as monkey smuggler Fran Ogren and chimpanzee breeder Connie Casey. Their openness to my questions helps us all to understand the intricacies of the exotic pet underworld. Reporter Chris Hayes at the St. Louis television station KTVI shared his chimp files with me. Which brings me to another friend, journalist, and author, Charles Jaco. He and his wife, Melissa, provided needed sustenance and shelter for the Missouri reporting trip, as did my friend and academic colleague Lance Pettitt for the swing over to England. In Washington Alex Roth provided the same critical courtesies, along with needed editorial feedback, despite his arduous schedule on Capitol Hill. More of that needed feedback came from Baghdad, where my brother, George Papagiannis, labors for UNESCO, and in just as weird Austin, from long-time coconspirator Bob Simmons. Fellow Fairfax Heights Improvement Club charter member John Nolan alerted me to the hideous bear attack in Pennsylvania.

Toni and Ralph Jones and their Avatar Community Business Center in Fairfax, California, provided gracious and required back office support, as did Shona Weir at her Business Services Unlimited in Bodega Bay.

Family: It's impossible to imagine a book not edited by my first and harshest critic, my wife, the writer and poet Sheila Swan Laufer, and I thank her again for saving me from myself—often. Moral support, as always, comes from son Talmage, daughter Amber, and their/our Ri-ot. Son Michael exerted support above and beyond the call of duty, joining me on the Missouri trek, experiencing and enduring Chimparty and the Lolli Brothers (tempered by endless games of darts in Hannibal and finally mediated with adequate Black Label at the Jaco St. Louis estate).

And of course there would be no *Forbidden Creatures* without my partners at Lyons Press. My collaborator and editor, Holly Rubino, is brutal and unrelenting. I thank her for her persistence, elegant editing, and friendship. Also thanks to copyeditor Laura Daly, proofreader Ann Seifert, and project editor John Burbidge for their extraordinary work on the manuscript. Here's to Gary Krebs, who introduced me to the house when he was publisher there; we can't seem to share a lunch without coming up with a book project. His successor, Janice Goldklang, continues not only to make me feel at home at Globe Pequot Press, but also provides the type of publisher support too many authors, unfortunately, can only dream of enjoying.

Finally, I want to thank Amigo. No question he introduced me to the happiness an interspecies friendship can bring to a boy and his dog.

NOTES

1. *National Geographic,* "Vietnam Becoming Asia's Illegal Animal 'Supermarket,' Experts Warn," http://news.nationalgeographic.com/news/2006/09/060913-vietnam-wildlife.html.

2. *Scientific American,* "Illegal Pet Trade Devastating Population of Endangered Philippine Forest Turtles," www.scientificamerican.com/blog/60-second-science/post.cfm?id=illegal-pet-trade-devastating-popul-2009-05-19.

3. *Baltimore Sun,* "Illegal Pet Turtles Being Sold on Streets," http://weblogs.baltimoresun.com/features/mutts/blog/2009/06/turtle_rescue.html.

4. Vincent Nijman, *Hanging in the Balance: An Assessment of Trade in Orangutans and Gibbons in Kalimantan, Indonesia* (Petaling Jaya, Selangor, Malaysia: TRAFFIC, 2005), 21.

5. Fox News Web site, www.foxnews.com/story/0,2933,208060,00.html.

6. *People* Web site, www.people.com/people/article/0,20048136,00.html.

7. *Los Angeles Times,* http://latimesblogs.latimes.com/unleashed/2009/06/michael-jackson-animals.html.

8. Sky News Web site, http://news.sky.com/skynews/Home/World-News/Mexico-Drug-Trafficking-Raid-At-Mexico-City-Mansion-Leads-To-Arrests-And-Discovery-Of-Private-Zoo/Article/200810315124416.

9. Reuters Web site, www.reuters.com/article/environmentNews/idUSTRE51503V20090207.

10. Nick Paton Walsh, "Chechen Leader Hones His Image with a Pet Tiger," *Guardian* (UK), January 27, 2006.

11. CBS News Web site, www.cbsnews.com/stories/2004/07/13/national/main629201.shtml.

12. Yi-Fu Tuan, *Dominance and Affection: The Making of Pets* (New Haven, CT: Yale University Press, 1984), 72.

13. A. Cornelius Gellius, *Attic Nights,* Vol. 1 (Cambridge, MA: Harvard University Press, 1927), 427.

14. Tuan, *Dominance and Affection,* 139.

15. Mitch Keller, "The Scandal at the Zoo," *New York Times,* August 6, 2006.

16. CNN Web site, www.cnn.com/US/9711/19/dionne.quints/.

17. Cahal Milmo, "Look at the Humans, Daddy! Zoo Introduces New Species," *The Independent* (UK), August 27, 2005.

18. Tuan, *Dominance and Affection,* 107.

19. Andy Newman and Anahad O'Connor, "Woman Mauled by Chimp Is Still in Critical Condition," *New York Times,* February 17, 2009.

20. Christina Carrega, Perry Chiaramonte, and Jeremy Olshan, "Why Chimp Went Bananas on Gal," *New York Post,* February 18, 2009.

21. *Scientific American,* "Why Would a Chimpanzee Attack a Human?" www.scientificamerican.com/article.cfm?id=why-would-a -chimpanzee-at

22. *Los Angeles Times,* http://articles.latimes.com/2002/mar/15/ local/me-muggs15?pg=1.

23. Friends of Charlie Nash Web site, http://new.friendsofcharlienash .com/.

24. Centers for Disease Control and Prevention, www.cdc.gov/ HomeandRecreationalSafety/Dog-Bites/dogbite-factsheet.html.

25. Fish and Wildlife Service, www.fws.gov/news/NewsReleases/show News.cfm?newsId=18972091-C1CE-5D0A-44AEFA54BC3DA15E.

26. *Inside Edition,* www.insideedition.com/storyprint.aspx?Special ReportID=2922.

27. Oregon Primate Rescue Web site, www.oregonprimaterescue.com/ Monkeys.html.

28. *Inside Edition,* www.insideedition.com/storyprint.aspx?Special ReportID=2922.

29. Reuters Web site, www.reuters.com/article/lifestyleMolt/idUST RE57K0TO20090821.

30. Wild Animal World Web site, www.wildanimalworld.com/gpage7. html.

31. "Monkey That Bit Three Has a History of Being 'Mean,'" *Seattle Times,* March 8, 2008.

32. Bill Morlin, "Three Charged with Smuggling Rhesus Monkey," *Spokesman-Review* (Spokane, WA), March 8, 2008.

33. *Inside Edition,* www.insideedition.com/storyprint.aspx?Special ReportID=2922.

34. Maria T. Galo, "Pet Monkey Attack Puts Its Owner in Hospital: 25-Pound Animal No 'Monster,' Woman Says," *Chicago Tribune,* February 20, 2000.

35. Anne Bowhay, "Monkey Put Down Following Attack," *Daily Southtown* (Chicago), February 23, 2000.

36. Amy Herdy, "Pet Monkey Bites Owner 50 Times," *St. Petersburg Times,* January 14, 1999.

37. "Owner Says Pet Monkey Headed for New Home after Biting Attack," *Tampa Tribune,* January 16, 1999.

38. William Mallen, "It's Pet Monkey Business as Usual as State Curbs Fail," *Chicago Tribune,* May 7, 2001.

39. *National Geographic,* http://animals.nationalgeographic.com/ animals/mammals/kinkajou.html.

40. WTNH Web site, www.wtnh.com/dpp/news/fairfield_cty/news _wtnh_exotic_animal_amnesty_day_a_success_200907251625.

41. *Stamford Advocate,* www.stamfordadvocate.com/ci_12915719 ?source=most_viewed.

42. UPI Web site, www.upi.com/Odd_News/2009/07/25/100-exotic- pets-turned-in-at-Conn-zoo/UPI-91781248575885/.

43. *Federal Register,* http://edocket.access.gpo.gov/cfr_2006/janqtr/ pdf/9cfr3.128.pdf.

44. Born Free USA Web site, www.bornfreeusa.org/b4a2_exotic_ animals_summary.php.

45. CBS News Web site, www.cbsnews.com/stories/2005/03/04/ national/main678061.shtml.

46. Douglas Williamson and Leigh Henry, *Paper Tigers? The Role of the U.S. Captive Tiger Population in the Trade in Tiger Parts* (Washington, DC: TRAFFIC [North America division], 2008), 1.

47. Born Free USA Web site, www.bornfreeusa.org/b4a2_exotic breeding.php.

48. Born Free USA Web site, www.bornfreeusa.org/a3b1_invest.php.

49. U.S. Customs and Border Protection Web site, www.customs.gov/xp/cgov/trade/trade_programs/entry_summary/laws/food_energy/amended_lacey_act/guidance_lacey_act.xml.

50. Iowa Natural Heritage Foundation, www.inhf.org/lacey/overview2.htm.

51. MSNBC Web site, www.msnbc.msn.com/id/8334072.

52. *Animal Finders' Guide,* www.animalfindersguide.com/about.html.

53. Roadside America Web site, www.roadsideamerica.com/set/gator4.html.

54. Snopes Web site, www.snopes.com/critters/lurkers/gator.asp.

55. Agence France Presse dispatch, August 1, 2009.

56. Catherine Shoard, "Tippi Hedren Tells Michael Jackson's Former Pet Tigers of His Death," *Guardian* (UK), July 1, 2009.

57. Mira Tweti, *Of Parrots and People* (New York: Viking, 2008), 188.

58. Alan Green, *Animal Underworld: Inside America's Black Market for Rare and Endangered Species* (New York: Public Affairs, 1999), 99–102.

59. Staples Safari Animal Reserve and Rescue Web site, www.brianstaples.us/celebrities_and_animals.htm.

60. Siegfried and Roy Web site, www.siegfriedandroy.com/conservation/nursery.php.

61. www.salon.com/env/feature/2008/09/08/sarah_palin_wolves/.

62. Mark Rowlands, *The Philosopher and the Wolf: Lessons in Love, Death, and Happiness* (New York: Pegasus Books, 2009), 2.

63. James Serpell, *In the Company of Animals: A Study of Human-Animal Relationships* (Cambridge: Cambridge University Press, 1996), 235–236.

64. *National Geographic,* www.nationalgeographic.com/adventure/news/white-rhino-kruger.html.

65. *Kingman Daily Miner,* http://kingmandailyminer.com/main.asp?Search=1&ArticleID=14733&SectionID=1&SubSectionID=1&S=1.

66. *Practical Fishkeeping* Web site, www.practicalfishkeeping.co.uk/pfk/pages/item.php?news=1034.

67. "Travis the Chimp: He Finally Snapped" [editorial], *New Haven Advocate,* February 19, 2009.

68. Steve Ross, "Chimps Aren't Chumps," op-ed page, *New York Times,* July 21, 2008.

69. Talk Zone Web site, www.talkzone.com/archive.asp?aid=37456.

70. Jane Goodall, "Chimpanzees—Bridging the Gap," in *The Great Ape Project,* ed. Paola Cavalieri and Peter Singer (New York: St. Martin's Griffin, 1993), 10–18.

71. Charles Siebert, *The Wauchula Woods Accord: Toward a New Understanding of Animals* (New York: Scribner, 2009), 16.

72. Howard Thompson, "The Screen: 'Toby Tyler': Disney Film Opens at Neighborhood Houses," *New York Times,* April 20, 1960.

73. Jane Goodall, "Loving Chimps to Death" [editorial], *Los Angeles Times,* February 25, 2009.

74. Marc Bekoff and Jessica Pierce, *Wild Justice: The Moral Lives of Animals* (Chicago: University of Chicago Press, 2009), 1–12.

75. *Inside Edition,* www.insideedition.com/storyprint.aspx?SpecialReportID=2795.

76. *Psychology Today,* https://www.psychologytoday.com/blog/animal-emotions/200907/domesticated-wolf-is-dog.

77. Williamson and Henry, *Paper Tigers?* 3.

78. Missouri Alliance for Animal Legislation, www.maal.org/Large-Carnivore.asp

79. Elizabeth Kolbert, "Flesh of Your Flesh: Should You Eat Meat?" *The New Yorker,* November 9, 2009, 78.

80. African Wildlife Foundation, www.awf.org/content/wildlife/detail/pangolin.

81. *National Geographic,* http://news.nationalgeographic.com/news/2006/09/060913-vietnam-wildlife.html.

82. E-mail exchange with the author, September 14, 2009.

83. Rory Carroll, "Pablo Escobar's Fugitive Hippo Shot Dead," *The Guardian* (UK), July 14, 2009.

84. Marina Belozerskaya, *The Medici Giraffe and Other Tales of Exotic Animals and Power* (New York: Little, Brown, 2006), 343.

85. Julia Morgan Papers, Robert F. Kennedy Library, California Polytechnic State University at San Luis Obispo.

86. Belozerskaya, *The Medici Giraffe,* 345.

87. Jessica Beckett, "Jailed, Man Who Turned Semi into Zoo," *Manchester Evening News,* May, 7, 2009.

88. *Daily Telegraph,* www.telegraph.co.uk/news/newstopics/howaboutthat/5293885/Man-jailed-for-turning-house-into-zoo.html.

89. Anthony Colarossi, "Is Ban on Pythons Next?" *Orlando Sentinel,* August 9, 2009.

90. U.S. Senator Bill Nelson Web site, http://billnelson.senate.gov/news/details.cfm?id=315736&.

91. U.S. Senator Bill Nelson Web site, http://billnelson.senate.gov/news/details.cfm?id=315611&.

92. *Florida Trend,* www.floridatrend.com/article.asp?aID=49389.

93. MTV, www.mtv.com/news/articles/1587800/20080520/ross__rick__rap_.jhtml.

94. Peter Townson, "Spotted: Cheetahs Kept as Pets," *Gulf Times* (Doha, Qatar), July 7, 2009.

95. Marjory Stoneman Douglas, *The Everglades: River of Grass* (Sarasota, FL: Pineapple Press, 2007), 5.

96. Harry W. Greene, *Snakes: The Evolution of Mystery in Nature* (Berkeley: University of California Press, 1997), 292–293.

97. Live Science Web site, www.livescience.com/animals/080305-snakes-fear.html.

98. Anthony Colarossi, "Wildlife Officials Seize 'Monster' 18-Foot Python in Apopka," *Orlando Sentinel,* September 11, 2009.

99. Florida Fish and Wildlife Commission Web site, http://myfwc.com/NEWSROOM/09/statewide/News_09_X_Python4.htm.

100. *Palm Beach Post,* www.palmbeachpost.com/localnews/content/
    local_news/epaper/2009/07/18/python0718
    .html?cxntlid=inform_sr.

101. World Eco Adventure Tours, www.worldecoadventuretours.com/
    guides.htm.

102. Centers for Disease Control and Prevention, www.cdc.gov/Home
    andRecreationalSafety/Dog-Bites/dogbite-factsheet.html.

103. Anthony Colarossi, "Killer Python Owner: 'It Was a Terrible,
    Awful Accident,'" *Orlando Sentinel,* www.orlandosentinel
    .com/news/local/breakingnews/orl-bk-killer-python-owner-
    speaks-073109,0,3498768.story.

104. Mark Smith, "What Pahrump Really Doesn't Need," *Pahrump
    Valley Times,* www.pahrumpvalleytimes.com/2009/Mar-13-
    Fri-2009/opinion/27428358.html.

105. John Muir, *My First Summer in the Sierra* (San Francisco: Sierra
    Club Books, 1988), 110.

106. "Pet Bear Kills Owner in Pennsylvania," Associated Press dispatch,
    October 5, 2009.

INDEX

abuse, animal, 18, 49, 70, 141
Addison, Richard, 138
advertising, animals used for, 84–85,
     131–32, 171
aerial wildlife killings, 60
Alaska laws, 35
Allen (alligator), 31
alligators
     as human threat, 31, 157
     ownership issues, 30
     pythons versus, 193–94, 202
     state ownership laws, 33
     urban legends regarding, 39
     wrestling, 38–39
Amato, George, 77–78
American Boys' Handy Book, The
     (Beard), 191
amnesty days, xii, 30–32, 40–41
Androcles (Roman slave), xvi
Angel (monkey), 26
Animal Finder's Guide, 37–38
Animal Haven Ranch, 34–35
Animal Liberation (Singer), 69, 174
Animal Protection Institute, 35
animal rights activism
     books inspiring, 69, 174
     captive breeding opposition, 109–
          12, 116, 128, 171
     Internet postings for, 47
     organizations for, 51, 52–53, 127–
          28, 171–72, 174–76
     private ownership opposition, 37,
          42, 104–5, 109
Animal Welfare Act, 34
anthropormorphism
     animals as persons theories, 64–66,
          122, 224

family member analogies, 115
     as ownership issue, xvi, 14–15, 82,
          87, 104–5, 137–38
apes. *See also specific species of apes*
     deception behaviors of, 64
     endangerment of, xiv
     human fascination with, 14, 91
     ownership rationale, 90–91, 93
     as persons, 64–65
Apollo (white tiger), 125–26
Apoo/George (monkey), 8–12,
     15–16
Arkansas laws, 35
attacks on humans
     alligators, 30, 31
     bears, 225
     chimpanzees, xvi–xvii, 1–7, 27,
          34–35
     dogs, 6–7, 203, 204
     kinkajous, 28–29
     lions, 37
     monkeys, 26, 223
     as predator behavior, 107, 115
     pythons, xvi, 43, 152, 157, 161,
          203, 205–6
     tigers, xvi, 37, 58
     wild animal play as, 169, 173
auctions, 118–21
automobile analogies, 136, 137, 145,
     157–58, 207–8

Baby (piglet), xv
Baby Luv (kinkajou), xiv
ball pythons, 161
Bam-Bam (lion), 214, 215–16,
     221, 227
Barney (iguana), 147

ownership laws
bans and proposed bans, 21–22,
152, 159, 215
government documentation and
tracking, 55–56
lack of, 33, 45, 46, 215
license and permit requirements,
33, 34, 51, 128, 156, 203
microchipping requirements, 156
opposition to ownership, 37, 42,
47, 52–53, 69, 129, 130, 172,
203, 224
ownership rights arguments, 152–
52, 217–19
state *versus* federal, 21, 33–36
ownership theories and rationale
admiration and beauty, 161,
162–63, 209
animals as property, 217
attention-getting devices, 103–4,
160, 161, 162, 167, 184
captivity conditions and provisions,
127, 147
companionship, 65–66, 104,
137–38, 179
cross-species relationship benefit,
19, 91–92, 93, 95–96, 122
defying authority emblems, 203
escaping mundane as human
nature, 210–11
human superiority and domination,
45, 59, 65–66, 69–70, 114,
142–43, 158–59, 160–61, 162,
167, 176, 207–8
ignorance and illusion, 109
profit, 161
protection of animal, 16, 85
rarity factor and ego building, 136,
145, 157–58, 177, 208, 217
selfish acquisitions, 226–28
sexual projections, 176

unexplainable, 150–51, 210

Pahrump, Nevada, 213
Palin, Sarah, 60
pangolins, 134–35
Papagiannis, George, 153
parasites, 8
Pardito (kinkajou), 28
parrots, 49, 168–69, 174
parts of animals, 110–11, 128,
132–34, 141–42
Patrick (liger), 114–15
Patron, Patricio, xv
Penthouse Pets, xviii, 169
permits, 34
persons, animals as, 64–66, 122, 224
pet, defined, xvii–xviii, 170, 207,
211–12
PETA (People for the Ethical
Treatment of Animals), 51, 52–53,
127–28, 171–72, 174–76
Pet Amnesty Day (Beardsley Zoo),
xii, 30–32
Petey (alligator), 30
Phil (chimpanzee owner), 79–88
photo cubs, 216
Phuong, Tran Quang, 136
Picasso (tiger), 214, 217–18
pigeons, roller, 73–77
pigs, xv
piranhas, xii, 72
Polo, Marco, xv–xvi
property, animals as, 101, 217
pythons, 33, 161. *See also* Burmese
pythons; Florida python plague

Quintland, xviii

raccoons, 29
Rare (hair styling product), 131–32
Rayner, Simon, xviii–xix

ABOUT THE AUTHOR

Peter Laufer, PhD, is the author of more than a dozen books that deal with social and political issues, including *The Dangerous World of Butterflies: The Startling Subculture of Criminals, Collectors, and Conservationists* (Lyons Press); *Mission Rejected: U.S. Soldiers Who Say No to Iraq*; *Wetback Nation: The Case for Opening the Mexican-American Border*; and *Iron Curtain Rising: A Personal Journey through the Changing Landscape of Eastern Europe*. He is the anchor of *The Peter Laufer Show* on radio station KOWS in Sonoma County. He is also the James Wallace Chair in Journalism at the University of Oregon School of Journalism. More about his books, documentary films, and broadcasts, which have won the George Polk, Robert F. Kennedy, Edward R. Murrow, and other awards, can be found at peterlaufer.com. He lives in Bodega Bay, California.